Narrative in Performance

Narrative in Performance

Edited by Barbara Sellers-Young and
Jade Rosina McCutcheon

methuen | drama
LONDON • NEW YORK • OXFORD • NEW DELHI • SYDNEY

METHUEN DRAMA
Bloomsbury Publishing Plc
50 Bedford Square, London, WC1B 3DP, UK
1385 Broadway, New York, NY 10018, USA
29 Earlsfort Terrace, Dublin 2, Ireland

BLOOMSBURY, METHUEN DRAMA and the Methuen Drama logo
are trademarks of Bloomsbury Publishing Plc

First published 2019 by RED GLOBE PRESS

Reprinted by Methuen Drama

Copyright © Barbara Sellers-Young and Jade Rosina McCutcheon,
under exclusive license to Springer Nature Limited 2019

Barbara Sellers-Young and Jade Rosina McCutcheon have asserted their rights under the Copyright,
Designs and Patents Act, 1988, to be identified as the authors of this work.

For legal purposes the Acknowledgements on p. ix constitute
an extension of this copyright page

All rights reserved. No part of this publication may be reproduced or
transmitted in any form or by any means, electronic or mechanical,
including photocopying, recording, or any information storage or retrieval
system, without prior permission in writing from the publishers.

Bloomsbury Publishing Plc does not have any control over, or responsibility for,
any third-party websites referred to or in this book. All internet addresses given
in this book were correct at the time of going to press. The author and publisher
regret any inconvenience caused if addresses have changed or sites have
ceased to exist, but can accept no responsibility for any such changes.

A catalogue record for this book is available from the British Library.

A catalog record for this book is available from the Library of Congress.

ISBN: PB: 978-1-3520-0416-8
ePDF: 978-1-3520-0417-5
ePub: 978-1-3503-1660-7

To find out more about our authors and books visit
www.bloomsbury.com and sign up for our newsletters.

Contents

List of Tables and Figures	vii
Acknowledgements	ix
Contributors	xi

1 **Introduction**   1
   Barbara Sellers-Young, York University, Canada; Jade Rosina McCutcheon, University of Melbourne, Australia

Part I   Performing Narrative Identity in Culture   19

2 **The *Zar*: Enactment of Social Drama in the Southern Sudan**   21
   Barbara Sellers-Young, York University, Canada

3 **Maranga Mai**   37
   Janinka Greenwood, University of Canterbury, New Zealand

4 **Her-stories in Indonesian Dance Drama**   53
   Kathy Foley, University of California, United States

5 **Decolonizing Techno-Art**   73
   Praba Pilar, Performance Artist, United States/Canada

Part II   Popularizing Performance   89

6 **Steps in Time: The Evolving Role of Dance in the Broadway Musical**   91
   Mary Jo Lodge, Lafayette College, United States

Contents

7 The Multiple Narratives of Cirque du Soleil — 111
Katie Lavers, Edith Cowan University, Australia; Louis Patrick Leroux, Concordia University, Canada

8 Personal Agency and Community Empowerment: Moth Style Engagement — 133
Judith Halebsky, Dominican University, United States

9 Narrating and Negotiating Identity in World of Warcraft — 149
Jonathan Osborn, York University, Canada

Part III Rocking the Boat: Revolutionary Integrations — 165

10 Ellen Lauren: The Art of Extreme Acting — 167
Scott T. Cummings, Boston College, United States

11 People Like Us: Revolutions in Australian Theatre — 187
Julie-Anne Long, Macquarie University, Australia

12 Jacques Lecoq and This Theatre Called My Body — 205
Nikole Pascetta, Professional Actor, Canada

13 Pina Bausch: Narrative, Gender, Reception — 225
Jade Rosina McCutcheon, University of Melbourne, Australia

14 Narrative Pivots: Text and Movement in Crystal Pite's Dance-Theatre — 241
Peter Dickinson, Simon Fraser University, Canada

15 Future Narratives: Community, Technology and Globalization — 283
Barbara Sellers-Young, York University, Canada; Jade Rosina McCutcheon, University of Melbourne, Australia

Index — 295

List of Tables and Figures

Table

Table 9.1   Popular culture origin of character dances   157

Figures

Cover image: Meryl Tankard in *Kontakthof* (1984) surrounded by male dancers of the Pina Bausch Company including Dominique Mercy, Jean Laurent Sasportes, Arthur Rosenfeld, Hans Po and Francis Viet. Stockholm, Sweden. Photographer: Regis Lansac

Figure 2.1	Saida surrounded by other women during the ritual of sacrifice	27
Figure 5.1	Performance still of *Dirty Cochinas of the AMERICAS*. Left, Praba Pilar, right, Luna. At Urban Shaman Contemporary Aboriginal Arts Gallery, Winnipeg	80
Figure 5.2	Enigma Symbiotica Decoding Machine	84
Figure 6.1	David Costa in costume for the Pas de Demons from *The Black Crook* (1867)	93
Figure 6.2	Scene from the stage production *Shuffle Along* (1921)	97
Figure 10.1	Ellen Lauren as Clytemnestra in the SCOT Company production of *Electra* directed by Tadashi Suzuki	175
Figure 10.2	Ellen Lauren as She and Will Bond as He in the SITI Company production of *Chess Match No. 5* directed by Anne Bogart	184
Figure 11.1	*Nothing to Lose* by Kate Champion, produced by Force Majeur	197
Figure 12.1	The *Croquis* ensemble, Théâtre de la Jacquerie	209
Figure 13.1	Meryl Tankard in *Kontakthof* (1984) surrounded by male dancers of the Pina Bausch Company including Dominique Mercy, Jean Laurent Sasportes, Arthur Rosenfeld and Hans Po. Stockholm, Sweden	232
Figure 14.1	Eric Beauchesne (on floor) as Prospero and company in *The Tempest Replica* (2011)	263
Figure 14.2	Tiffany Tregarthen and Jonathon Young in *Betroffenheit* (2015)	274

Acknowledgements

The editors and publisher wish to thank the following for the use of copyright text material in the book:

Anne Bogart, for her comments on the work of Ellen Lauren used as an epigraph at the start of Chapter 10.

Garry Lester, for extracts from 'Kai Tai Chan: A Different Path' (2000, unpublished doctoral dissertation, School of Contemporary Arts, Deakin University, Melbourne, Australia) in Chapter 11.

Tadashi Suzuki, for his comments on the work of Ellen Lauren used as an epigraph at the start of Chapter 10.

Contributors

Scott T. Cummings is Professor of Playwriting and Dramatic Literature in the Theatre Department of Boston College, where he served as Chair from 2010 to 2014. He is the author of *Charles Mee, Anne Bogart and the SITI Company* (Cambridge University Press, 2006) and *Maria Irene Fornes* (Routledge, 2013) and the co-editor (with Erica Stevens Abbitt) of *The Theatre of Naomi Wallace: Embodied Dialogues* (Palgrave Macmillan, 2014). His scholarship has been supported by fellowships from the Howard Foundation, the Whiting Foundation and the Rockefeller Foundation's Bellagio Center. His directing work for Boston College includes four different programmes of fully produced one-acts by BC student playwrights, an original devised work called *Ashley's Purpose*, and plays by Shakespeare, Marivaux, Beckett, Fornes and Mee.

Peter Dickinson is Professor of English at Simon Fraser University, where he also teaches in the School for the Contemporary Arts and is an associate member of the Department of Gender, Sexuality, and Women's Studies. He has published widely on theatre, dance and performance studies. His most recent book is *World Stages, Local Audiences: Essays on Performance, Place and Politics* (Manchester University Press, 2010), which includes a discussion of Crystal Pite's *Lost Action*. The current chapter is part of a larger project on 'The Theatre of Dance-Theatre: History, Politics, Feeling'.

Kathy Foley is a Professor of Theatre at the University of California, Santa Cruz. She teaches in the Theatre Arts Department and has also taught at the University of Malaya, the University of Hawaii, Yonsei University and Chulalongkorn University. She is author of the SE Asia section of *The Cambridge Guide to World Theatre* and editor of *Asian Theatre Journal*. Her articles have appeared in *TDR*, *Modern Drama*, *Asian Theatre Journal*, *Puppetry International* and other journals and various books. She trained in mask and puppetry in the Sudanese region of Indonesia.

Janinka Greenwood is a professor at the University of Canterbury where she teaches drama education and research methodologies. She is the author of journal articles and books which consider the intersection of global and local knowledge. They include an edited volume with J. Shu, P. Chan, P. L. A. McCammmon and A. Owens (Eds) *Planting Trees of Drama With Global Vision in Local Knowledge: IDEA 2007 Dialogues* (2010) and *History of a Bicultural Theatre: Mapping the Terrain* (2002).

Judith Halebsky is Associate Professor of English at Dominican University of California. She holds a PhD in Performance Studies from the University of California, Davis. She trained in storytelling with San Francisco's Porchlight group and has performed in the Naked Truth storytelling series in Mill Valley, California. Willamette University staged her play *The Weaver and the Dress* in 2016. Her articles on performance and cultural translation have been published in the *Asian Theatre Journal* and *Theatre Research* in Canada. Her honours include a Graves Award for Outstanding Teaching in the Humanities, a MacDowell Colony Fellowship and the New Issues Prize for her collection of poems, *Sky=Empty*.

Katie Lavers has a doctorate in circus studies from Edith Cowan University. Her writing on circus has been published in numerous scholarly journals, and she is co-editor with Peta Tait of *The Routledge Circus Studies Reader* (2016). She is currently writing a book on contemporary circus for Routledge, which is due for publication in 2019. Katie also writes as a circus and dance reviewer for ArtsHub, Australia. As a director and producer of intermedia circus and as a co-founder of the Australian circus company, Skadada, her works combining circus, dance, interactive video, text, electronic sound and live music have toured throughout Australia and Asia to critical and public acclaim.

Louis Patrick Leroux is a professor at Concordia University and the Founding Director of the Montreal Working Group on Circus Research. He is also a playwright and a director. He has published extensively and given many international talks on contemporary circus, and has worked closely with the Québec circus scene as a researcher, collaborator and teacher. He is an ongoing Associate Researcher and guest teacher at the National Circus School of Montreal. He has been a Visiting Scholar at Duke University, Charles University (Prague) and at France's Centre national des arts du cirque. He is currently involved in simultaneous research projects, all-team based, including a Québec-funded project exploring circus dramaturgy; a Canadian-funded project studying physical literacy, creativity and resilience; and a Canadian-funded historical synthesis and socio-aesthetic analysis of Québec theatre. Recent scholarly collections include *Cirque Global: Québec's Expanding Circus Boundaries*, co-edited with Charles Batson (McGill-Queen's UP, 2016), 'North-South Circus Circulations' edited issue of *Québec Studies* (2014), 'Le Québec à Las Vegas' edited issue of *L'Annuaire théâtral* (2010), and *Le jeu des positions. Discours du théâtre québécois*, co-edited with Hervé Guay (Nota Bene, 2014).

Mary Jo Lodge is Associate Professor of Theatre and English at Lafayette College in Pennsylvania, and a performer, director and choreographer. She previously taught at Central Michigan University and founded their B.F.A. musical theatre programme. She holds a PhD from Bowling Green and an MA from Villanova, both in Theatre, and a BM in Musical Theatre from Catholic University. She has published numerous articles and book chapters on the musical and has directed and choreographed a wide range of professional, college and summer stock productions. In 2013–14, she was the recipient of a Fulbright award to London where she conducted research and taught at the University of Roehampton. Her research has been published in the edited volumes *Gestures of Musical Theater*, *Women in American Musical Theater*, *Heroes of Film, Comics and American Culture* and in such journals as *Studies in Musical Theatre* and *Theatre Journal*.

Julie-Anne Long is Lecturer in Dance and Performance at Macquarie University, Sydney, Australia, and an award-winning independent dance artist in Sydney. She has performed and choreographed on a wide range of projects, with companies such as Human Veins, One Extra, Open City, Theatre of Image, Legs on the Wall, Flying Fruit Fly Circus, Bell Shakespeare Company and Dance Works. From 1991 to 1996 Long was Associate Artistic Director of One Extra Company with Artistic Director Graeme Watson. She has worked in a variety of dance contexts as mentor, dramaturge, curator and producer including Acting Director of the dance research organisation Critical Path (2006/2007) and Dance Curator at Campbelltown Arts Centre (2009/2010). She has a Master of Arts (Honours) from the University of Western Sydney, and a PhD from the University of New South Wales. Long was awarded an Australia Council Dance Fellowship in 2007, which encompassed research, development and the realization of a body of work entitled 'The Invisibility Project'.

Jade Rosina McCutcheon is a graduate from the Director's course at the National Institute of Dramatic Art in Sydney receiving a Master of Creative Arts from the University of Wollongong, and a Doctor of Creative Arts from U.T.S. Sydney. She is currently a PhD candidate in Film Studies at the University of Melbourne. She is the author of *Awakening the Performing Body* and co-editor of *Embodied Consciousness: Performance Technologies*. She has taught at Charles Sturt University, Oregon State University, University of California/Davis, Colorado College and the University of Melbourne. As a member of the Holland-based performance group KISS she visited Pina Bausch's company in 1981–2.

Jonathan Osborn (MA in Dance Studies, BA in English Literature) is a PhD candidate in Dance Studies at York University and a graduate member of Sensorium: Centre for Digital Arts and Technology. His current SSHRC-funded dissertation examines the staging of animal bodies and the simulation of habitat at zoological institutions and within video games. An accomplished artist and choreographer, Jonathan has received support from the Toronto and Ontario Arts Councils and maintains a movement practice invested in the solo form, speculative fiction and inhuman bodies.

Nikole Pascetta is a graduate of the Jacques Lecoq Theatre School in Paris, France (1990–2). Her PhD and MA (York University, Toronto) were informed and shaped by her physically based performance training. Her research examines the foundations of meaning-making (corporeal consciousness) in the construction of knowledge (epistemology). An artist educator and CAEA/ACTRA professional actor, she was a core member of the France-based repertory company Théâtre de la Jacquerie. Other notable international credits include: Gaulier (France), Strasberg (New York), Gina Kapetanaki (Greece), Commedia dell'Arte with Donato Sartori (Abano Terme, Italy), Fabio Mangolini (Ferrara, Italy) and Antonio Fava (Reggio Emilia, Italy). Her work has been presented at the Canadian Society for the Study of Education, the University of Windsor, Brock University, the University of British Columbia Okanagan (UBCO) campus, the University of Regina and the 14th Annual World Festival of Children's Theatre on 'Play!' (Stratford, Canada).

Praba Pilar is a mestiza/muisca Colombian artist keen on disrupting the overwhelmingly passive participation in the contemporary 'cult of the techno-logic' through counternarrative performances, street theatre, interactive installations, digital artworks, video, writing and websites. Her wildly diverse work has been presented nationally and internationally at museums, galleries, universities, performance festivals, conferences, public streets and radio airwaves. Pilar has received numerous awards, and has been written about in numerous books, most recently *The Multispecies Salon*, edited by Eben Kirksey (2014); *Latin American Identity in Online Cultural Production*, by Claire Taylor and Thea Pitman (2013); and *Body As Evidence: Mediating Race, Globalizing Gender*, by Janell Hobson (2013). Her most recent writing has been featured in *Scholar & Feminist Online*, the *Lateral Journal of the Cultural Studies Association*, *Dance Current*, and *Women's Eco Artist Dialogue*. Pilar has a PhD in Performance Studies, with designated emphases in Studies in Performance Practice as Research and in Feminist Theory and Research from the University of California, Davis.

Barbara Sellers-Young is a senior scholar and Professor Emerita in the Dance Department at York University. She is former dean of the School of Arts, Media, Performance and Design at York as well as past president of the Congress on Research in Dance and has taught at institutions in the United States, Australia, China and England. Her books include three single authored books and four co-edited volumes including *The Oxford Handbook of Dance and Ethnicity*.

1

Introduction

Barbara Sellers-Young and Jade Rosina McCutcheon

Theresa de Lauretis, in her book *Alice Doesn't* (1984), argues that 'narrativity because of its inscription of the movement and positionality of desire, is what mediates the relationship of image and desire' (1984: 79). Here the term 'desire' arrives as a blueprint threaded throughout image; desire is the driver behind the way we receive images and the narrative embedded within. According to de Lauretis, the spectator's movement is the movement of the narrative, 'the very work of narrativity is the engagement of the subject in certain positionalities of meaning and desire' (106). From birth, we are inundated with stories of family, community and nation that are fundamental to our identity. Poet and playwright Jo Carson describes these stories as a hunger for narratives that explain our lives:

> The hunger for stories is not a body hunger, but it is a huge and fierce hunger, and it is as necessary for human well-being as food is for the body. We have to make stories or our brains don't work right, and when we consume stories, we are consuming life. Stories carry energy, they make patterns in the way we think and behave, and we have to have them to live in a social order.
>
> (2014: 7)

These stories take the form of 'narratives' that exists across culture, from literature to film, theatre, dance, opera, song, circus, musicals, rituals and online games (Goffman, 1978). For the purpose of this volume, narrative is defined as the following: a narrative is made up of all the events that we see and hear, plus all those that we infer or assume to have occurred, arranged in their presumed causal relations, duration, frequency and spatial locations. Within the framework of theatre and dance performance, a narrative is achieved by an integration of text and movement as presented through the body of a performer at a venue and observed by an audience. The structural organization of a narrative is a culmination of influences which includes the community where the performance is produced, genre of performance, the function of the narrative within the community, the artistic vision of the director and/or choreographer, the thematic material of the narrative and the images associated with it. Each of the latter influences the style of text and movement of the performers, the kind of performance space and the makeup of the audience. The goals of this manuscript are to create an informed and critical dialogue regarding the role of narrative in dance, theatre and performance, to provide a method of exploring the context of a particular form or artist, and to increase an ability to critically reflect on performance.

Narrative and History

Narratives have been fundamental to the mythic and religious histories of communities and nations, thus, the basis for national and religious rituals. Approaches to narrative in performance have been documented in such early manuscripts as Aristotle's *Poetics* (Aristotle, [355 BCE] 2013), Bharata Muni's *Natya Shastra* (500 BCE–500 CE; Rangacharya, 2014), the secret texts of Japanese artist Zeami (Zeami, 2013), the poetic scripts of classical China (Lovrick and Wang-Ngai, 2014) and in ongoing oral traditions throughout the globe. Increasingly contemporary narratives are constantly made and remade through the media: newspapers, magazines, television news, websites, books (fiction and non-fiction), blogs, Facebook, Twitter and online games. As Asma advocates in *The Evolution of the Imagination* (2017), the images from these sites integrate with our daily experience and fuel our imagination.

Dance and theatre artists interrogate these images by creating performances in which the performer's body acts as an imagistic space for the narrative of a written or movement text that is articulated through characterization, choreographed movement, costume, props, digital images, set and light design. Whether communicated in written, physical or oral forms, the goal of performance is to combine written or physical text that uses vocal and physical techniques to convey a point of view about history including the mythological past, the contemporary moment or what we might anticipate in the future (Nellhaus, 2016). As audience members, we construct a secondary narrative interpretation from this collection of symbols that is infused with our own identity construction and history. As such, our interpretation is a living 'weaving of meaning' created between the performance and our personal point of view (Taylor, 2003).

Historically, oral performance narratives were 'in the moment' events for a community that could never be repeated. The audiences for these performances sometimes sat quietly, participated in a call and response relationship between performer and audience, or in the case of Japanese Kabuki appreciatively shouted out the names of the performers. At our current point in history, theatre and dance performances are still live but there are also digital performances on screens at the local cinema as well as on television, computer, iPad and iPhone—in some cases, on the screen next to your subway stop (Art in Transit, 2016). The construction of narrative in traditional forms of theatre and dance has moved from a linear idea, for example, the three-act structure or balance, disturbance, protagonist, plan, crisis, resolution, to more open-ended structures allowing for a more complex viewing of interaction (Nellhaus, 2016; George-Graves, 2017).

Regardless of structure, in dance and theatre, the medium for the narrative has been the body of the performer, even if this body is represented through a puppet representation of the body or, in the case of current digital technology, an avatar. Throughout history, the training of the performer's body has been an extension of the role of the performance within the context of the community. The bodily techniques of performance may be based on special initiation rites as in the shamanic practices of indigenous communities or the families associated with specific masks of African dance/theatre. As African scholar Praise Zenenga states, 'African total theatre is essentially a self-perpetuating and integrative artistic concept in which hybrid blending of dance, theatre and music is very much a defining feature' (2015: 238). Performance knowledge may be passed on directly from one generation to the next via a mimetic imitation of the body of performer as is the case of guru traditions of Asia (Zarrilli, 2008). Dramatic performance styles have also historically been transferred through community groups as in the medieval guilds of Europe. In the last 200 years, specialized schools of theatre and dance have evolved around the world to train the bodies of the performers in a specific style of performance. These have included schools of dance with a focus on ballet, modern, jazz and urban dance styles. Theatre training for the stage has concentrated on the theories of Konstantin Stanislavski (2004) with an inclusion of Michael Chekhov (1993), Vsevolod Meyerhold (Pitches, 2003), Bertolt Brecht and Marc Silberman (2013), Augusto Boal (Babbage, 2004) and more recently Anne Bogart (2003, 2007) and Tadashi Suzuki (2015). Throughout the twentieth century a training overlap evolved between theatre and dance in the area of somatic studies and the methodological approaches of Frederick Matthias Alexander (2001), Moshe Feldenkrais (2009) and other somatic practitioners.

Intercultural Exchange

A dramatic exchange of narratives, ideas, images and movement vocabulary has been an ongoing part of the globe's social cultural history. Sometimes these exchanges have taken place on a regional level such as Japan's adoption of musical (Gugaku), movement styles (Bugaku) from China and Korea in the seventh century (Brazell, 1999) and other times on a global level as demonstrated by Montreal's Cirque du Soleil inclusion of Chinese acrobats (Leroux, 2014). Transformations of modes of communication and transportation from the fifteenth to the twenty-first century have, however, speeded up the processes of exchange and development of local versions of ballet; a representation of the aesthetic ideal of the Italian and French courts in the fifteenth and seventeenth centuries. In terms of ballet, this process was aided when France's Louis XIV founded the first professional ballet company, the Académie Royale de Musique, from which emerged the first professional theatrical ballet company, the Paris Opera Ballet. The ballet was by the nineteenth century an independent art form with those trained in the school beginning to spread it across Europe (Lee, 2002). The forces of colonialism in the nineteenth and twentieth centuries then spread ballet to new colonies that European powers set up throughout the globe bringing with it specific narrative structures that, via a form of osmosis, informed the cultures of those colonies (Gainor, 1995).

Correspondingly, the evolution of theatre companies in Renaissance Europe, the rediscovery of the classical Greek texts and the innovation of the printing press increased the development of text-based dramas that could be written, printed and distributed. Although many plays were printed and distributed, those of William Shakespeare have had the greatest global impact and his plot narratives and characters have become the basis for performances that unite language and movement imagery across the world, such as the work of Singaporean-based artist Ong Keng Seng and Japanese director Tadashi Suzuki. With the opening of a reconstruction of Shakespeare's Globe Theatre in 1997, the company began a series of programmes that brought artists from around the world to share their versions of Shakespeare (Purcell, 2017).

Shakespeare's texts are not the only examples of artistic exchange between distinctly different cultural communities. Creative performance narratives followed the trade routes initially over the oceans by boat but beginning in the nineteenth and twentieth centuries by rail and plane and ultimately through popular social media. John Heilpern documents in *Conference of the Birds* (1999) the journey English director Peter Brook took with a group of actors across the unfamiliar terrain of the Sahara in Northwest Africa in an attempt to develop a form of theatre that was not reliant on cultural assumptions. Japanese dancer Tatsumi Hijikata borrowed the expressive style of German dancer Mary Wigman in the evolution of Butoh (Barber, 2010). Konstantin Stanislavski incorporated Indian yoga techniques in the training of actors at his Russian studio (Tcherkasski, 2016). Pioneer of dance in the United States, Ruth St. Denis, portrayed her interpretation of the spirit of Egypt, India and elsewhere (1939). Singapore director Ong Keng Seng initiated an intercultural and collaborative 1997 narrative version of *King Lear* with performers from Japan, Thailand, China and Indonesia that toured across Asia and Europe. Individuals from around the globe integrate text and movement in individual YouTube performances, some of which go viral. Yet, artists and performers also resisted the forces of globalization and created new pieces that reaffirmed their identity or confirmed a modernist version of it. Such is the case of the Bangarra Dance Theatre of Australia (2016), referred to as an indigenous incubator archive, library, memory bank and engine room by its current artistic director Stephen Page, who is known for creating dance theatre by and about contemporary Aboriginal people, tracing their bloodlines, re-connecting with their traditional heritage and living modern Aboriginal lives in a challenging urban society.

Director and performance theorist, Rustom Bharucha, points out the demands that intercultural exchange incorporating culturally different performance training make on a performer's body:

> At the best of times, interculturalism is an enormously taxing practice in the demands it makes on the body. It is not only a matter of learning other disciplines and techniques – martial arts, Yoga, Kathakali – where one is compelled to 'break' one's existing reflexes and rhythms, balance and co-ordination; the demands on the body in intercultural work are so infinitesimal that they are invisible in their subtle pressures, as one takes in different physical and sensory stimuli from an alien space. These stimuli interact with the memories and sensations that have already been internalized in the body from another space and time – a space and time so intimate that one tends to describe it as 'home.' Contrary to the euphoria that generally accompanies descriptions of intercultural workshops, there is an incredible conflict that takes place within the body, as its psycho-physical assumptions are dislocated.
>
> (Bharucha, 2000: 153)

Bharucha suggests that 'conflict' within a performer's body when learning movements, speech or ideas from another culture is a consequence of unfamiliar metaphors holding specific cultural meanings dislocating the 'different' body. In the *Philosophy in the Flesh* (1999), Mark Johnson and George Lakoff argue that consciousness and the related processes of cognition are inherently embodied and that abstract concepts are expressed through metaphors which are evolved primarily unconsciously through the intersections of a body/mind's interaction with an environment. These metaphors' integral connections are spread via contemporary media to create a circumstance in which 'the most remote phenomena could be seen as intimately related to one another' (de Lauretis, 1984: 117). The metaphors shape our imagination and the way we communicate both on and offstage.

Rituals engage these deeply held metaphors through the cultural narratives associated with them. Playwrights, directors, choreographers, performers and designers integrate the ritual past with the present by bringing these metaphors to the stage in words, physical actions and visual imagery. They create definitive characters unique to each cultural milieu to portray, and sometimes challenge, aspects of identity, gender, class, nationality and ethnicity. Within the narrative structure of theatre and narrative-based dances this is inscribed in the personality and physical actions of a character's response to the plot. For example, Shakespeare's *Romeo and Juliet* engages the imagistic metaphor of young love. In non-narrative dance pieces, it is conveyed within the expressive gestural language created by the choreographer: for example, Pina Bausch's *Café Müller* (1978), in which dancers continually collapse against each other, reflects the complexity of gender relations in an urban environment.

Our personal metaphors evolved within our families and communities often inform our approach to training regimes. Some metaphors become part of mainstream culture, such as 'no pain no gain'. Our gender as masculine or feminine is often defined by the visual metaphors of the media. As audience members, we respond to theatre or dance performance by engaging our experiential imagination with related personal metaphors to create meaning of the why of a character's actions or the visual language of a dance. Increasingly the imagistic metaphors of dance and theatre share the same stage. One such example is Toronto's Canadian Stage's 2018–19 season in which the productions of Akram Khan, Sandra Laronde and Hofesh Shechter share the stage with the plays of Molière, Shakespeare and Duncan Macmillan.

Organization of this Text

An examination of the history of theatre and dance reveals three performance genres that function within several conceptual realms simultaneously. There are: performances that focus on performing the narratives of culture identity; popularizing performances that interact across stages including street performances; popular music and social dances; and finally, directors and choreographers who 'rock the boat' to create revolutionary integrations to revise previous narratives, both in content and in form, through new integrations of movement and written texts. The chapters by fourteen authors consider the role of dance and theatre across these genres of performance to reveal the significance of cultural identity, the role of popular culture, the social impact of revolutionary ideas that provide an activist voice for marginalized communities and the new conceptualizations of self related to new technologies. The sections provide a variety of narrative representations including the role of the female character in Asian dance drama (Foley), trance possession ritual as narrative metaphor that engages dramatic forms of theatre (Sellers-Young), performance as a means to embody a social/cultural image (Pascetta), intercultural performance (Cummings), social power (Greenwood), staged performances of identity on the stage and in online video games (Halebsky, Osborn), interpretation and contestation of meaning (McCutcheon, Long, Pilar), the dialogue within popular culture genres (Lodge, Leroux and Lavers), and finally, the blurring of body and technology in the creative process (Dickinson).

As noted in pivotal texts (Luckhurst, 2006; Hansen and Callison, 2015), an addition to the artistic teams of theatre and dance performances is the dramaturg. The dramaturg is someone familiar with the aesthetic, social, cultural and political context of a performance. The dramaturg combines research and related discussion to help the director or choreographer develop the narrative structure and the metaphorical expression of the performance. If the dramaturg is associated with a specific theatre or dance company, they may be involved in auditions, the rehearsal process, providing pre-performance lectures and guiding post-performance discussions. The dramaturg thus acts as an integrating force for the production.

This text takes a dramaturgical approach and asks you, the reader, to use the material in the chapters and related reference material to ask questions regarding the development of dance and theatre narratives in performance across five areas of performance – text, body, stage, technology, and audience. Some questions to consider are: What is the narrative? What is the form discussed – theatre or dance – or some combination? Who are the performers? How are they trained? Where is the form performed – on the street, in a theatre, in a home, on the internet? How does the form convey the narrative? Is the movement style associated with the form associated with a particular group within a community? Are there specific value systems related to gender, ethnic identity or nation that are inscribed by the written narrative or the presentation of the body? What are the themes and related metaphorical content of the performance? Is the body of the performer transformed or enhanced by extensions to the body or by an engagement with digital technology? Who is the audience? Does the audience experience it live or via a digital platform? What is the interaction between the performer and the audience? Is the relationship between performer and audience formal or informal? How does the audience react during or following the performance?

Following is an outline of each of the three parts. Each chapter is accompanied by a set of discussion questions.

Part I: Performing Narrative Identity in Culture

Among some scholars, ethnicity and its associated identity is viewed as a political choice individuals and groups make for social, economic and material advantage. For example, Anthony Shay in *Choreographing Politics* (2002) describes how twentieth-century nation states created staged narratives of ritual and folk forms to project a unified identity that influenced internal and external politics. These values presented onstage represented deeply held aspects of daily life. In fact, for many groups these rituals, celebrations and staged performances were the embodiment of the community narrative symbolically expressed in performance.

Performance theorist Langellier suggests that the narrative of a nation state is built from the relationship between the personal and the social political, 'Personal narrative performance gives shape to social relations, but because such relations are multiple, polysemic, complexly interconnected, and contradictory ... a story of the body told through the body makes the cultural conflict concrete' (Langellier, 1999: 208). The chapters in this section examine the complex contextual references of performance that as Langellier notes, has multiple influences in the formation, maintenance and evolution of identity across a range of performance venues from trance rituals to activist performance, gender performances of Southeast Asia and addressing the issues of colonization and identity through performance art. Barbara Sellers-Young discusses the connection between social drama and trance ritual (Turner, 1982; Schechner, 2010) in the Southern Sudan with a specific reference to the relationship between the Azande and Arab communities. Janinka Greenwood provides an example of the role of the integration of ritual modes of communication with activist theatre to impact the public narrative position of Māori identity in New Zealand (Potiki, 1991). Kathy Foley provides an opportunity to reflect on the position of gender in the narrative structures of the dance dramas of Southeast Asia. Praba Pilar shares a narrative of migration and how a location in a new community caused her to re-examine her personal narrative and ultimately her performance art as someone of an indigenous ancestry.

The chapters in Part I invite the following questions: 1. What are the narrative structures of the representation of identity in dance, theatre and performance including location of performance, relationships between the performers, between the performers and the audience, the movement vocabulary, the musical accompaniment and the clothing and/or costumes? 2. What are the ideological forces that influence any of the latter? 3. What is the difference between an outsider's assumptions about identity from signifiers they may misinterpret versus one's understanding/expression of their own representation? 4. How are the narrative structures of rituals staged within different styles of performance? 5. Do narrative structures change over time within a community or do they remain the same?

Introduction   11

Part II: Popularizing Performance

Popular culture is often synonymous with entertainment, whether it is sports, music, television or film, and the significant personalities that become the feature stories on celebrity-based CBS's *Entertainment Tonight* or in *People* magazine. The popular narratives portrayed on the stage by these celebrities are an extension of the stories of everyday lives of love and conflict that take place in families and communities. Thus, these popular performances reflect the ongoing cultural changes through music, text and dance of the social values of our society. One of which is the intersection between technology and performance.

In his seminal 1999 manuscript *Liveness*, Philp Auslander addresses the issue of the mediated performance to consider the distinct experience of the audience member between the live and mediated image. His conclusion was that live and mediated performances were two separate experiences. There has been since 1999 an ever-expanding popular culture engagement with technology in which images are live streamed on a variety of mobile devices, games include online environments, and virtual reality brings people into the worlds of dinosaurs or outer space.

The chapters in Part II provide examples of different forms of narrative in popular culture including those made possible by digital technology. There is the ongoing transformation of musical theatre as it responds to the increased influence of rap and hip-hop and its impact on cultural discourse through MTV and YouTube. Mary Jo Lodge traces the impact of popular dance styles on the narrative style of musical theatre including the musical *Hamilton*. Leroux and Lavers share the increased concern with the life of animals on the planet which has influenced the transformation of an animal-based circus into a human-body-based circus such as Cirque du Soleil. These human circuses combine imagistic popular narratives, the acrobatic ability of the human body and a highly designed technology that frames and enhances a performer's athleticism. As such, the circus has been contemporized to fit the new narratives of an urban environment.

The concept of the character's quest that is the foundation of Cirque du Soleil is also a pivotal component of Judy Halebsky's and Jonathan

Osborn's chapters on personally organized narratives and the creation of identity at the intersection of the stage, web-based venues and the ever-expanding context of social media. Halebsky describes the improvised storytelling community called 'The Moth' and the integration of voice, body and movement to provide a narrative conception of self on local stages and online via YouTube. Beginning with his personal engagement with World of Warcraft, Osborn explores the dances built into the game environment of World of Warcraft that imitate the movement vocabulary of popular music stars. The game-based dance scenarios of World of Warcraft become the basis for personalized staged versions of characters' national game conventions. The two chapters provide an opportunity to examine the relationship between stage, aesthetics, identity, technology, the body and, ultimately, the biopolitics of narrative.

These chapters on popular culture ask you to consider a series of questions: 1. What is the role of the performance narrative in popular culture? 2. What is the role of celebrity in creating a popular culture form? 3. How do popular staged performances integrate dance and text to create a narrative? 4. What is the relationship between the popular culture form and changes in society? 5. How are a character's narrative identities formed through dialogue, music and movement? 6. How is technology changing our consumption of popular culture?

Part III: Rocking the Boat: Revolutionary Integrations

Directors and choreographers have challenged our cultural conceptions of the body, identity, community and contemporary politics throughout the last two centuries. At the beginning of the twentieth century Isadora Duncan (1877–1927) challenged the image of the female body represented by the traditional vocabulary of ballet. Ruth St. Denis (1879–1968), Martha Graham (1894–1991), Doris Humphrey (1895–1958), Merce Cunningham (1919–2009) and numerous other dancer/choreographers continued to stage challenges to cultural narratives of gender, sexuality, race, environment and more. Their performances have existed alongside the discourses of realism, naturalism, symbolism, absurdism, existentialism and such directors and playwrights as Konstantin Stanislavski, Michael Chekhov, Lugné-Poe, Peter Brook and Edward Albee.

The dialogue between choreographers and directors in the twentieth and twenty-first centuries has been encouraged by the forces of communication, transportation and technology. This has expanded the volume and the scope of exchange across the boundaries of culture and aesthetics. Directors and choreographers across the globe have borrowed from each other's classic and mythic texts as well as training techniques to evolve new narratives and theatrical images. The performances of these companies are incorporated into international festivals around the globe that include such major urban sites as Edinburgh, Hong Kong, Singapore, Sydney, Cape Town, Athens, Zurich, Shanghai and more.

The chapters in Part III provide a context for this dialogue. Scott Cummings interviews Ellen Lauren for her insight into her negotiation of the intercultural artistic aesthetics of two of the twentieth century's most noted directors, Anne Bogart and Tadashi Suzuki (Suzuki, 1986; Bogart, 2003, 2007; Cummings, 2006). Australia's 1980s performance scene is brought to life by Julie-Anne Long's chapter with a focus on the choreographic legacy of two pivotal participants, Kate Champion and Kat Tai Chan. Nikole Pascetta takes us inside the Jacques Lecoq School of Paris and the implications of his theatre theories to create a narrative that moves across cultural borders. Jade Rosina McCutcheon examines two of Pina Bausch's seminal choreographies from the 1970s, *Kontakthof* and *Café Müller*, to consider Bausch's approach to gender during the second wave of the feminist movement with a specific reference to the audience's reception of her projects. Each of the artists discussed used the body and text in performance to challenge and ultimately transform our aesthetic conception of how narratives are staged. Their approaches individually and collectively are incorporated into dance and theatre training programmes around the world.

The final chapter of Part III is an extensive chapter by Peter Dickinson. Using the concept of the pivot as a metaphor for choreographer Crystal Pite's artistry, he examines the intertwined histories of post-dramatic theatre and postmodern dance that proceed her. In his discussion, he references postmodernism's discomfort with previous narrative structures, the search for new narrative modes and comparative experience of the audience through the framework of performances engaging the sensuality of textscapes, a complex intersection of words and movement. Dickinson illustrates his argument with a thick description of two of Pite's works, *Dark Matters* and *The Tempest Replica*; and, ultimately, articulates an argument for the narrative integration of theatre and dance – text and movement – as the performance style of the twenty-first century.

Potential questions are: 1. What were the global narratives that became important sites for critical analysis by these performance innovators? 2. Were there specific performance histories on which their performances were developed? 3. What methods did they use to integrate the narrative with the body? 4. Were there intercultural aspects to their methods? 5. What were the implications of their narrative style of performance for training the actor or the dancer?

Future Narratives: Community, Technology and Globalization

The final chapter of the book engages the organizing structures of narrative, text, body, technology, stage and audience to consider what directions performance, dance and theatre might take in the twenty-first century. As part of its speculative analysis the chapter incorporates material from the previous chapters with current trends in globalization, technology and community, with specific focus on how the evolution of social media is influencing the expectations of an audience.

Works Cited and Resource Material

Alexander, F. M. (2001) *The Use of the Self* (New York: Orion Press).
Aristotle ([355 BCE] 2013) *Poetics* (Oxford: Oxford University Press).
Art in Transit (2015) http://artintransit.ca/index.php/exhibitions-2/, accessed 23 May 2016.
Asma, S. T. (2017) *The Evolution of the Imagination* (Chicago: University of Chicago Press).

Auslander, P. (1999) *Liveness: Performance in a Mediatized Culture* (London: Routledge).
Babbage, F. (2004) *Augusto Boal* (New York: Routledge).
Bangarra Dance Theatre (2016) http://bangarra.com.au/, accessed 19 June 2016.
Barber, S. (2010) *Hijikata: Revolt of the Body* (New York: Solar East).
Barton, R. and A. MacGregor (2015) *Theatre in Your Life* (London: Wadsworth).
Bharucha, R. (2000) *The Politics of Cultural Practice: Thinking through Theatre in the Age of Globalization* (Middletown, CT: Wesleyan University Press).
Bogart, A. (2003) *A Director Prepares: Seven Essays on Art and Theatr*e (London: Routledge).
———. (2007) *And Then, You Act: Making Art in an Unpredictable World* (London: Routledge).
Brandon, J. R. and I. Takeda (1982) *Chūshingura: Studies in Kabuki and the Puppet Theater* (Hawaii: University of Hawaii Press).
Brazell, K. (1999) *Traditional Japanese Theatre* (Cambridge: Cambridge University Press).
Brecht, B. and M. Silberman (2013) *Brecht on Performance: Messingkauf and Modelbooks* (New York: Bloomsbury Methuen Drama).
Carson, J. (2014) in *Anne Bogart What's the Story* (New York: Routledge) p. 7.
Chekhov, M. (1993) *On the Technique of Acting* (New York: Harper Books).
Climenhaga, R. (2008) *Pina Bausch* (London: Routledge).
———. (2012) *The Pina Bausch Sourcebook: The Making of Tanztheater* (London: Routledge).
Cummings, S. T. (2006) *Remaking American Theater: Charles Mee, Anne Bogart and the SITI Company* (Cambridge: Cambridge University Press).
De Lauretis, T. (1984) *Alice Doesn't* (Bloomington, IN: Indiana University Press).
Dickinson, P. (2014) Textual Matters: Making Narrative and Kinesthetic Sense of Crystal Pite's Dance-Theater, *Dance Research Journal*, 46(1), pp. 61–83.
Doughty, S., K. Francksen, M. Huxley and M. Leach (2008) Technological Enhancements in the Teaching and Learning of Reflective and Creative Practice in Dance, *Research in Dance Education*, 9(2), pp. 129–46.
Feldenkrais, M. (2009) *Awareness Through Movement: Easy-to-Do Health Exercises to Improve Your Posture, Vision, Imagination, and Personal Awareness*, reprint (New York: Harper).
Gainor, J. E. (Ed.) (1995) *Imperialism and Theatre: Essays on World Theatre, Drama and Performance* (London: Routledge).

George-Graves, N. (Ed.) (2017) *Oxford Handbook of Dance and Theatre* (Oxford: Oxford University Press).
Goffman, E. (1978) *The Presentation of Self in Everyday Life* (New York: Harmondsworth).
Hansen, P. and D. Callison (Eds) (2015) *Dance Dramaturgy: Modes of Agency, Awareness and Engagement* (London: Springer).
Harris-Warrick, R. (2005) *Musical Theatre at the Court of Louis XIV: Le Mariage de la Grosse Cathos* (Cambridge: Cambridge University Press).
Heilpern, J. (1999) *Conference of the Birds: The Story of Peter Brook in Africa* (London: Routledge).
Johnson, M. and G. Lakoff (1999) *Philosophy in the Flesh: The Embodied Mind and Its Challenge to Western Thought* (New York: Basic Books).
Kominz, L. (1995) *Avatars of Vengeance: Japanese Drama and the Soga Literary Tradition* (Ann Arbor: University of Michigan Press).
Langellier, K. M. (1999) Personal Narrative, Performance, Performativity: Two or Three Things I Know for Sure, *Text and Performance Quarterly*, 19(2), pp. 125–44.
Lear (1997) http://globalshakespeares.mit.edu/lear-ong-keng-sen-1997/, accessed 5 September 2016.
Lee, C. (2002) *Ballet in Western Culture: A History of Its Origins and Evolution* (New York: Routledge).
Lepecki, A. (2006) *Exhausting Dance: Performance and the Politics of Movement* (London: Routledge).
Leroux, L. P. (2014) Contemporary Circus Research in Quebec: Building and Negotiating and Emerging Interdisciplinary Field, *Theatre Research in Canada/Recherches Théâtrales au Canada*, 35(2), pp. 28–32.
Lotman, J. M. (1979) The Origin of Plot in the Light of Typology, *Poetics Today*, Vol. 1, No. ½ Special Issue: Literature, Interpretation, Communication (Durham, NC: Duke University Press) pp. 164–84.
Lovrick, P. and S. Wang-Ngai (2014) *Chinese Opera: The Actor's Craft* (Hong Kong: Hong Kong University Press).
Luckhurst, M. (2006) *Dramaturgy: A Revolution in Theatre* (Cambridge: Cambridge University Press).
Magowan, F. (2000) Dancing with a Difference: Reconfiguring the Poetic Politics of Aboriginal Ritual as National Spectacle, *The Australian Journal of Anthropology*, 11(3), p. 308.
Mulrooney, D. (2002) *Orientalism, Orientation, and the Nomadic Work of Pina Bausch* (New York: P. Lang).

Murray, S. and J. Keefe (2007) *Physical Theatres: A Critical Introduction* (London: Routledge).
Nellhaus, T. (Ed.) (2016) *Theatre Histories: An Introduction* (New York: Routledge).
Park, C., P. H. Chou and Y. Sun (2006) A Wearable Wireless Sensor Platform for Interactive Dance Performances. March. PerCom 2006. Fourth Annual IEEE International Conference on Pervasive Computing and Communications.
Pitches, J. (2003) *Vsevolod Meyerhold* (New York: Routledge) pp. 6–20.
Potiki, R. (1991) A Maori Point of View: The Journey from Anxiety to Confidence, *Australasian Drama Studies*, 18, p. 57.
Purcell, S. (2017) *Shakespeare in the Theatre: Mark Rylance at the Globe* (London: Bloomsbury Arden Shakespeare).
Rangacharya, A. (2014) *The Natyashastra: English Translation with Critical Notes* (New Delhi: Munshiram).
Schechner, R. (2010) *Between Theater and Anthropology* (Philadelphia, PA: University of Pennsylvania Press).
Shay, A. (2002) *Choreographic Politics: State Folk Dance Companies, Representation and Power* (Middletown, CT: Wesleyan University Press).
Sparacino, F., G. Davenport and A. Pentland (2000) Media in Performance: Interactive Spaces for Dance, Theater, Circus, and Museum Exhibits, *IBM Systems Journal*, 39(3/4), pp. 479–510.
Sparacino, F., C. Wren, G. Davenport and A. Pentland (1999) Augmented Performance in Dance and Theater, *International Dance and Technology*, 99, pp. 25–8.
Stanislavski, K. (2004) *An Actor's Handbook: An Alphabetical Arrangement of Concise Statements on Aspects of Acting* (New York: Routledge).
St. Denis, R. (1939) *An Unfinished Life: An Autobiography* (New York: Harpers).
Taylor, D. (2003) *The Archive and the Repertoire: Performing Cultural Memory in the Americas* (Durham, NC: Duke University Press).
Suzuki, T. (1986) *The Way of Acting: The Theatre Writings of Tadashi Suzuki* (New York: Theatre Communications Group).
Suzuki, T. (1993) *The Way of Acting: The Theatre Writings of Tadashi Suzuki*. Trans. T. Rimmer (New York: Theatre Communications Group).
———. (2015) *Culture is the Body: The Theatre Writings of Tadashi Suzuki*. Trans. K. Steele (New York: Theatre Communications Group).
Tcherkasski, S. (2016) *Stanislavsky and Yoga* (New York: Routledge).
Thelen, L. (2002) *The Show Makers: Great Directors of the American Musical Theatre* (London: Routledge).
Turner, V. (1982) *From Ritual to Theatre: The Human Seriousness of Play* (New York: Paj Publications).

Ulyate, R. and D. Bianciardi (2002) The Interactive Dance Club: Avoiding Chaos in a Multi-participant Environment, *Computer Music Journal*, 26(3), pp. 40–9.

Zarrilli, P. (2008) *Psychophysical Acting: An Intercultural Approach after Stanislavski* (New York: Routledge).

Zeami (2013) *The Spirit of Noh: A New Translation of the Classic Noh Treatise the Fushikaden*. Trans. W. W. Wilson (New York: Shambala Press).

Zenenga, P. (2015) The Total Theater Aesthetic Paradigm in African Theater, in N. George-Graves (Ed.) *Oxford Handbook of Dance and Theater* (Oxford: Oxford University Press) p. 2.

Part I

Performing Narrative Identity in Culture

2

The *Zar*
Enactment of Social Drama in the Southern Sudan

Barbara Sellers-Young

Researchers in the social sciences have, over the last thirty years, attempted to bridge the gap between their disciplines and those of the arts and humanities by comparing the world of ordinary reality and everyday social relations to the world of extraordinary reality – the theatrical stage and its intensified images of social relations. This includes the research and writings of sociologist Erving Goffman (1974), historian Kenneth Burke (1969) and anthropologist Victor Turner (1982). These scholars consider theatre as a root metaphor (Goffman and Burke) and a process (Turner) that societies use to portray social experience.

Performance scholar, Richard Schechner, contends that theatre and ritual extend along a continuum with elements of each existing in the other. He suggests the primary difference between the two is the sacred nature of ritual as opposed to the secular nature of modern Western drama (Schechner, 2010). Victor Turner takes a more nuanced view and argues that society operates as a series of smaller and larger 'social dramas' that are the result of 'public episodes of tensional irruption' (1974: 33). He also refers to them as 'units of aharmonic or disharmonic process, arising in conflict situations' (1974: 37).

According to Turner, community social dramas are played out in a series of four stages: breach, crisis, redress and reintegration. A breach occurs when norm-governed social relations are not easily addressed by daily social processes. This breach evolves into a crisis for the family or the community and ultimately requires a public reordering of the situation. The redressive action required to resolve the breach can be an informal process or involve more formal legal avenues and, in some cases, lead to a ritual performance. The goal of any redressive action is to reintegrate the individual or group into the community (Turner, 1985). Turner and Schechner jointly conclude that a community social drama is often the basis for written and oral narratives, associated myths and ultimately sacred or secular staged performance.

This chapter examines the relationship between the personal social drama of Saida in Yambio, Southern Sudan, and the *zar*, a ritual that Natvig describes as a form of spirit possession:

> found in Ethiopia, Eritrea, Djibouti, Somalia, Arabia, south and south-west Iran, Egypt, and the Sudan. It is not a uniform phenomenon throughout this vast region, where it occurs among Christians, Muslims, Falashas, and among adherents of tribal religions. There are ceremonial and cosmological differences, and the socio-sexual catchment areas as well as the consequences of participating in the cult vary from place to place. The aim of the cult, however, is the same: the curing of illnesses or misfortunes caused by possession by a species of spirit called zar.
>
> (1987: 669)

It is believed the *zar* ritual spread from northern to southern Sudan via Arab traders.

I consider the *zar's* position within a particular society of women in Yambio, Sudan, as a ritual of exorcism that engages dramatic means of theatre and dance to embody the complex dynamics of life in Yambio. The observations are informed by the research of Kenyon (1995, 2007, 2012), Eltahir (2003), El Guindy and Schmais (1994), Natvig (1987), Boddy (1989), Fakhouri (1968), Constantinides (1991), Lewis (2003), Kennedy (1967) and Zenkovsky (1950). Boddy and Constantinides reporting on the northern Sudan and Lewis in Somaliland have made a clear case for the relationship between *zar* possession and the status of women brought about by social pressures that are part of the life of women in a male-dominated society that places the highest value on woman's fertility, especially her ability to produce sons.

Yambio, South Sudan

Yambio is the capital city of Gbudue State, one of the twenty-eight states that constitute the Republic of South Sudan.[1] The population has grown from over 5 million in 1983 to approximately 12.23 million in 2018. The community is primarily Christian with a small Muslim population. It is the home of the Azande, an ethnic group that also lives in the Central African Republic and the Democratic Republic of the Congo. The Azande have a history as a warrior tribe that conquered others as they moved eastward from the savannahs of the Central African Republic into the Southern Sudan. Today, there are 85,000 in the Central African Republic (2017 estimate), 730,000 in the Democratic Republic of the Congo and 350,000 in South Sudan (1982 estimate), amounting to a total population of just above 1 million.[2] The Azande are primarily small-scale farmers, historically supplying much of the grain for the region.[3]

There has been a long history of conflict in the Sudan between the north and the south and between tribal groups in the South Sudan. The clashes between northern and southern Sudan are in part based on the practice of Arab slavers removing people from their villages and sending them north as slaves. This problematic relationship has also been influenced by different religious beliefs of the Islamic north and the Christian south, and in particular the unequal situation created by Anglo-Egyptian rule which provided more opportunity for modernization in the north. The internal tribal clashes in the South Sudan have been related to the difference in lifestyle between settled farmers and nomadic cattle herders. Since Sudan's independence in 1956 and the subsequent independence of South Sudan in 2011, there have only been brief periods when there has been peace. One of these was 1972 to 1983. During this period, there was increased trade between north and south and a number of Arab traders and their families made Yambio their home.

The Scenario of Saida

Saida, a woman born and raised in Khartoum, is married to a wealthy Arab trader based in Yambio. After three years of marriage, she has failed to become pregnant. Her husband is concerned when she becomes lethargic and refuses to eat. Finally, he sends her with female friends to consult Amelia, the local female cure or *shaikha*. Amelia diagnoses Saida as being possessed by a *zar*. Her husband is then prevailed on to finance an expensive four-day *zar* ritual costing approximately 300 Sudanese pounds, the equivalent to 300 US dollars.

An examination of the scenario reveals that the first three stages of Turner's social dramatic framework have been played out in Saida's personal drama. The initial breach is the separation from her natal family in Khartoum. This is followed by a crisis-created illness which is the result of anxiety over her failure to become pregnant and the assumption that this is caused by being possessed by a *zar* spirit. The attempt to redress the situation begins with the visit to the curer and continues when a *zar* ritual is recommended by Amelia the ritual healer. The *zar* ritual is then performed to insure Saida's self-esteem and status with the social group is restored.

The Yambio *Zar*

No public *zar* rituals occur in Yambio as they do in some areas of northern Sudan and Egypt. The *zar* ritual for Saida took place in the private compound of Amelia, a member of Balanda tribal group.[4] Amelia became a curer after she 'died' three times within her life, the third time as a young woman. During her third death, she was visited by the spirit of a white man named Johnny. He told her that unless she used his help to heal people she would die permanently. Johnny and the Old Woman are the two helpers Amelia claims to use in healing people. Women may become possessed temporarily with other *zar* spirits but the majority of the songs or 'threads' are to Johnny and the Old Woman.

The four-day ritual lasts each day from noon or late afternoon until late at night. The beginning of each day is much like a theatrical performance.

A set of backstage preparations take place within Amelia's house which only adepts (those who frequently work with Amelia) are allowed to attend. The rest of the participants, a combination of women from the Arab and Azande communities, sit in a semi-circle around the edge of the ritual performance space. This includes the area from the front of Amelia's toucal to an altar made of branches in the centre of the compound. The space is considered sacred before and after the *zar* and people entering or leaving the compound must remove their shoes while walking across it. The entire *zar* ritual takes place in front of the altar, or in the area between the altar and Amelia's front door, or within Amelia's house.

Amelia begins the public portion of the ritual with three hard beats on a *gaza* or large elephant ear drum. She then starts a song in praise to Johnny which is repeated by everyone. The combined Arab/Azande audience continues to sing along as various women and young girls, including Amelia, take turns playing the drum.

Although the adepts in Yambio wear the dress of specific characters during certain portions of the ritual, their mimetic dances do not seem to be as illustrative of the characters as those described by Boddy or Constantinides in northern Sudan, Kennedy in Nubia or Saunders in Egypt. The southern Sudanese movements are instead minimal outlines of a character. A rocking step back and forth from front leg to back leg is the total movement of the Holy Man; a step hop is supposed to represent the Arab population; a swaying side to side, the Ethiopian; shuffle steps, the old woman; and a simple walking step forward and back represents Johnny, the white man.

Once the repetitive drumming and singing begin, the women present dance in character sometimes as solo and other times in groups of two to four. At some point, a dancer goes into a trance and is overcome by the spirit of the *zar* and falls on her knees with a set of convulsive isolations of the torso and head, until she lies down exhausted. At this point, one of the adepts comes and turns the dancer so her feet are facing the same direction as the shrine, almost due east, then the adept straightens out the hands and legs of the dancer, finally grabbing her hands and pulling her upright. The adept twists the woman's head from side to side, tilting it first one way then the other, blowing in each ear. Still holding the dancer in place, the adept walks her hands up and down the person's spine, finally placing her hands on the dancer's shoulders so that the person does not tilt either left or right nor fall backwards. When the adept is certain that the dancer is stable she straightens out each of the feet and all of the toes. This finished, the adept repeats the same gestures with the hands and fingers. Turning to the shrine the adept throws her hands as if she is throwing something away. She then reaches down and grabs the hands of the dancer and pulls her to a standing position and together they both shake their hands at the shrine. The adept and the dancer walk away from the area where the dancer had fallen; the dancer to sit on the side and sing or to start dancing again and the adept to care for another fallen dancer.

Midway through the evening of the first day of the *zar* Amelia called the adepts into her house. Sitting outside, I could hear the repetitive chants to Johnny and smell the incense burning. After about twenty minutes a long line of people came out of Amelia's house with Saida, the woman whom the *zar* was for, in the lead and Amelia at her side. Saida is dressed in a long white dress that resembles a *jelabiya*, her head and face is covered with a white cloth while her hands and feet are decorated with henna. Singing, the women walk in procession around the shrine in a counterclockwise direction. Included in the group are two women with huge trays piled high with special food and clothes that Saida brought to use during the *zar*. A third woman carries a small porcelain bowl containing two candles. They circle the shrine seven times and bring Saida to a sitting position in front of it, placing her feet straight forward on a large grass mat. The two trays are placed on small rectangular tables with the candles in the centre. Saida sits on the mat as women surrounding her start to chant. Finally, she gets up and starts a shuffle step in place on the mat. None of the other dancers or Amelia pay much attention to her. After a time, Saida is taken back into Amelia's house and the group of Arab and Azande women return to their homes.

The second day is the day of sacrifice. People begin arriving about 11.30 a.m. with the Arab and Azande women sitting in separate areas drinking orange squash while waiting for the sacrifice to start. Once again, the adepts both Arab and Azande are called into Amelia's house to prepare for the ritual. The smell of burning incense and the sound of chanting fills the compound. Periodically, one or two of the adepts come outside the hut to get something and then re-enter by backing through the door of the house. After approximately forty-five minutes, Amelia and Saida come out leading a counterclockwise procession around the shrine. The adepts are dressed in either green or white dresses or shirt and pants. As they circle the shrine a goat is untied and brought forward so it can be put between Saida's legs, as if she were riding it. It is an imitation of a woman's bridal journey. The goat in place, they continue to circle the shrine seven times, stopping periodically to adjust the position of the goat under Saida's legs. Since Saida is totally veiled it is a very slow process that requires continual adjustment of her garments, which tend to slip. Saida's demeanour throughout is quiet and subdued. The women are quiet without any of the vocal ululations that usually accompany other community gatherings and ceremonies (see Figure 2.1).

Stopping in front of the shrine, they place a mat down for Saida to sit with her legs stretched out in front of her. A pan of water is brought and the goat is washed and covered with a white cloth. Amelia and one of the helpers lifts the goat into the air with a cry seven times. The final lift of the goat is over Saida's body and then it is placed over her legs. Amelia's nominal husband comes to do the actual killing of the goat as well as

Figure 2.1 Saida surrounded by other women during the ritual of sacrifice
Photographer: Barbara Sellers-Young

the three chickens. At this point, the participants are arranged in rows in front of the shrine: Amelia and Saida, the adepts and the chorus of young girls. When it is time to slaughter the goat, everyone but Amelia and Saida turn their back until after Saida has drunk the blood of the animal. Amelia brings some of the blood in a bowl and anoints the forehead, chin and upper chest of the women present. Saida is then allowed to stand and is offered a glass of whisky. The entire group, standing in a semi-circle around the shrine, begins to sing and dance again to Amelia's special spirit, Johnny. Saida returns to Amelia's house and the day ends as the rest of the group returns to their homes.

On the third day, Saida is brought out of the hut dressed in the bloodstained clothes of the previous evening. She sits on the same mat in front of the shrine. Three bowls with the cooked internal organs of the chickens and goat are brought and set in front of her and she is required to eat from each. She then returns to Amelia's house while a table is set up in the centre of the performance space surrounded by palm arches and covered with a variety of food. Shortly, a group of female adepts comes out of the house dressed in clothes that represent either the Old Woman or Johnny. The Old Woman's representatives wear white dresses with white scarves on their heads. Those who represent Johnny are dressed in either long pants or shorts and white shirts with some kind of hat. Amelia and her primary adept Mary are dressed exactly alike in striped long pants, full blouse tops, raccoon skin bibs, tennis shoes and straw hats. All carry some form of a walking stick commonly referred to as a British swagger stick. The group of adepts walks around the table, but not around the shrine and then performs a short group dance consisting primarily of forward and back steps, much like a 'tea for two' number while they swing the swagger sticks.

After the performance, the adepts and Saida gather around the table and eat while the rest of the gathering of women sit in the background, sing and drink beer that Amelia brings to them. A special plate of food as well as cigarettes and a bottle of whisky are placed on a table next to the shrine for Johnny. Following the feast, Amelia once again returns to Amelia's house and the others return home.

On the fourth and final day Saida is ritually washed in a local stream and returns to her home in central Yambio. She will remain in a separate room at her house for seven days and not come out even to cook. At the end of this time, the *zar* spirit who possessed her is believed to be tamed and Saida can be reincorporated into the community.

Although much research about the *zar* has referred to its dramatic potential and Leiris (1958) in his monograph on the Ethiopian *zar* discusses its theatrical elements, the *zar* as an act of expressive culture has not been considered as fitting into a larger Islamic aesthetic and creating a stage in which women from a community of both Muslims and non-Muslims can meet to share common concerns through the medium of trance performance. An analysis of the Yambio *zar* notes two primary theatrical devices that help to separate the experience of the *zar* from ordinary reality. First, there is a specified stage on which the action takes place. Second, the women assume characterizations expressed in the movement and costume that are representative of the British social history of the community. For example, in the case of Amelia's spirits, there is Johnny as a representative of the British and the Old Woman as a representative of women tribal elders. Other technical elements of performance that find similar components in the *zar* are the curer as director and an audience of women, as well as producer-relatives who agree to finance the cost. And of course, there are those elements of imagery present in the *zar* that are common to performance and ritual, such as music and dance. There are also elements of the *zar* that are more common to ritual than performance, such as sacrifice, cleansing and shared food. Finally, there is the element of trance that is not always present at rituals or performances, although there are those who maintain that actors inhabiting a role are in a form of possession (Bates, 1987).

Distinctive Qualities of Yambio *Zar*

The *zar* in Yambio does not seem to contain many of the characters that Boddy and Constantinides describe as part of the *zar* in northern Sudan. In the north, the dramatic stereotypes range from Darawish or holy men to include Ethiopians, both males and females, Muslim nomads, Khawajat or Westerners, Pashas, Sygrian gypsies, West African Muslims on pilgrimage to Mecca, black slaves or servants from the southern Sudan and, the most dangerous of all, the cannibal witches, who are considered to be the dreaded Nyam-Nyam or Azande. Nor does the Yambio *zar* appear to contain the dramatic enactments described by either Boddy or Kennedy. Participants in the Yambio *zar* may dance the holy man or Ethiopian during the first two days of the ritual, but they do not wear the costumes associated with them nor do they represent them in movement on the third or feast day of the *zar*. From a performance standpoint, the Yambio *zar* is a minimalist performance, in which only the bare outlines of the characters are developed.

Thus, the northern and southern Sudanese *zars*, although they contain a similar plot structure, differ in the development of characterization; a difference that I believe is the result of differing social/cultural environments. The Arab communities in the northern Sudan are by culture and religion a relatively homogeneous social group. Yambio, as a centre of government for Gbudue State, contains a diversified population dominated by the Azande. The Arab population within this area in 1982–3 were either traders or administrators for the northern-dominated government and generally perceived as outsiders and distrusted. They live in obvious comfort in enclosed brick homes within the confines of the Yambio market district. Their dress, one of the primary signs of wealth, separates them from many of the natives in style and quality. Men generally wear white *jelabiyas* and women a wrapped garment called a *thobe*, and their garments, especially those of the women, are made of expensive fabrics. The general social life of these two groups of women, Arab and Azande, are quite separate. Arab women live in town in enclosed households while Azande women for the most part live in the surrounding countryside in open compounds. At social functions that I attended in the Arab or Azande communities in Yambio or the surrounding area, both groups were never present except for the functions held at the local schools or political gatherings. Even at these official functions, the interaction between the two groups of women was minimal.

Yet, these women, despite their differences, do share common life experiences. First, there is the concern that their husbands may add additional wives to the household. Despite the presence of Christian influences both Catholic and Protestant in the south, the tradition of more than one wife among men who can afford it has been maintained from the pre-colonial period. Second, although the birth of sons is apparently not as important among Azande families as among Arab, fertility and the ability to give birth to children is a primary goal of Azande women—a goal that is often not achieved especially among Azande due to the high rate of tropical disease. A third area of common experience is best represented by the story of Jane, one of Amelia's primary adepts, a Zande woman married to a local government supervisor. She is a well-educated woman who has lived with her husband in both Egypt and Khartoum. She found it difficult to adapt to living with the political tensions that existed between the northerners and the southerners in the area and within her husband's government position. Many Arab women as a minority in the area would potentially share her anxiety.

The *zar* ritual, directed by a traditional curer, is a performance event in which women from different ethnic groups reduce the anxiety of their lives through participation in an event that overtly, through danced characters, expresses the common history they share (old women and white men) and covertly displays unity of women who demonstrate their own power by convincing husbands to periodically prove their continuing concern for a wife by financing a four-day ritual. It is then not surprising that the Yambio *zar* emphasizes those *zar* spirits or dramatic stereotypes of old woman and white man that communicate common symbolic significance to both Arab and Azande women. It is a ritual theatre and dance performance in which all participate as opposed to secular performance on a stage in which the conventional audience's only participation is in watching; it allows the women to experience a commonality of bodily physical expression that Turner refers to as 'communitas'. This is the feeling of 'at oneness' with those who share a ritual experience.

As an act of expressive culture, however, the *zar* displays several Islamic aesthetic concepts (Al Faruqi, 1978). These concepts seem to have been adopted by the Azande women unconsciously as they involve themselves in the *zar*. First of all, there is an emphasis within the performance of the dancing as a serial structure or succession of incidents, each leading to a mini-climax or *dafqah*. Each thread calls forth a spirit which takes its turn upon the stage much as the line of an arabesque design flows from one dramatic motif into another. Second, the performances for the most part are abstract and non-narrative. They present the symbolic elements but do not necessarily enact in narrative fashion the story of any one character. Finally, all the performances are unrehearsed and rely on the improvisation of the individual spirit as transformed within the personality of the possessed woman.

The Yambio *zar* is a personal social drama resulting in community ritual containing elements that are reflective of the community within which it exists but are also contained within the totality of Islamic aesthetics. The *zar's* presence in the southern Sudan among the Azande is an indication of their partial acceptance of Islamic aesthetics. Within the ritual, the personal social drama and the community drama overlap. The overt drama of personal illness feeds into the social process or diagnosis of possession to create the performance of the community drama. The performance includes elements that are symbolic to the community but exists within an aesthetic that includes Islamic communities in general.

This use of possession among women as a binding force is not unique to the southern Sudan. The trance state, as D'Aguili et al. (1979) have pointed out, creates a physical experience of wholeness of unity due to an overload in both brain hemispheres. Anita Spring in her work among the Luvale of Zambia also found women breaking down traditional barriers during possession rituals:

> Women cooperate with each other during curing rituals, sharing their expertise or simply their participation in the dancing and singing ... As a result of this cooperative policy of ritual participation, unrelated women build up ties with each other. Women in close residential proximity, who are often affinally related, may participate together in rituals. Hence, women are linked in groups wider than their matrilineage and for purposes other than domestic. They help the entire society attain more cohesion through this cooperative mechanism.
>
> (Spring, 1978: 187)

It is possible to argue that, in addition to providing a semblance of power for individual women, one of the primary functions of the *zar* is to provide women, as a group, the opportunity to share common concerns and social history through the enactment of a ritual.

Discussion Questions

1. Are there social narratives in your family or community that would fit Victor Turner's concept of social drama? How does the community resolve these narratives? Are there rituals associated with the resolution?
2. Are there situations in your communities in which individuals become possessed by a spirit? How is this spirit possession resolved? Is dance or acting out a character involved in the organization of the resolution?
3. Are there plays or choreographies that include trance or possession as part of the narrative action? Which characters become possessed? What causes the possession? By which spirits are they possessed? What is the physical manifestation of their possession? Is there a ritual included in the production that resolves their possession?

Images and Videos on the Internet

There are numerous videos and images on the web for South Sudan, Yambio and Azande.
There are also numerous video and images for the *zar* in other areas of North Africa.
Here are some I would recommend:
Understanding Sudan: http://www.understandingsudan.org/
General style of Azande music. The tall drum is used during the *zar*: https://www.youtube.com/watch?v=uOlQshItUhQ
Two versions of *zar* in Northern Sudan by Norwegian Anthropologist Gerasimos Makris:
https://www.youtube.com/watch?v=VNMDc3H2LbM

Notes

1. South Sudan became an independent country under the name Republic of South Sudan on 9 July 2011.
2. Lewis, M. Paul (Ed.) (2009) *Zande. Ethnologue: Languages of the World*, sixteenth edition (Dallas: SIL International).

3. The research for this chapter took place from August 1982 to July 1983.
4. Balanda are an ethnic group living in the South Sudanese state of Western Equatoria and Western Bahr el Ghazal states. They number about 243,000.

Works Cited and Resource Material

Al Faruqi, L. I. (1978) Dance as an Expression of Islamic Culture, *Dance Research Journal*, 10(02), pp. 6–13.
Bates, R. H. (1987) *Essays on the Political Economy of Rural Africa* (Vol. 38) (Berkeley, Los Angeles and London: University of California Press).
Boddy, J. (1989) *Wombs and Alien Spirits: Women, Men, and the Zar Cult in Northern Sudan* (Madison, WI: University of Wisconsin Press).
Burke, K. (1969) *A Grammar of Motives* (Vol. 177) (Berkeley, CA: University of California Press).
Coldiron, M. (2004) *Trance and Transformation of the Actor in Japanese Noh and Balinese Masked Dance-drama* (New York: Edwin Mellen Press).
Constantinides, P. (1991) The History of Zar in the Sudan: Theories of Origin, Recorded Observation and Oral Tradition, in I. M. Lewis, A. Al-Safi and S. Hurreiz (Eds) *Women's Medicine: The Zar-bori Cult in Africa and Beyond* (Edinburgh: Edinburgh University Press for the International African Institute) pp. 35–50.
D'Aguili E., M. Manus and C. Laughlin (1979) *The Spectrum of Ritual* (New York: Columbia University Press).
El Guindy, H. and C. Schmais (1994) The Zar: An Ancient Dance of Healing, *American Journal of Dance Therapy*, 16(2), pp. 107–20.
Eltahir, E. G. (2003) *Comparing the Incomparable: Religion, Chanting, and Healing in the Sudan, the Case of Zār and Zikr* (Madison, WI: University of Wisconsin Press).
Fakhouri, H. (1968) The Zar Cult in an Egyptian Village, *Anthropological Quarterly*, 41(2), pp. 49–56.
Goffman, E. (1974) *Frame Analysis: An Essay on the Organization of Experience* (Cambridge, MA: Harvard University Press).
Hurreiz, S. (1991) Zar as Ritual Psychodrama: From Cult to Club, in I. M. Lewis, A. Al-Safi and S. Hurreiz (Eds) *Women's Medicine: The Zar-bori Cult in Africa and Beyond* (Edinburgh: Edinburgh University Press) pp. 2–25.
Kennedy, J. (1967) Nubian Zar Ceremonies as Psychotherapy, *Human Organization*, 26(4), pp. 185–94.

Kenyon, S. M. (1995) Zar as Modernization in Contemporary Sudan, *Anthropological Quarterly*, pp. 107–20.

_____. (2007) Movable Feast of Signs: Gender in Zar in Central Sudan, *Material Religion*, 3(1), pp. 62–75.

_____. (2012) *Spirits and Slaves in Central Sudan: The Red Wind of Sennar* (Basingstoke: Palgrave Macmillan).

Leiris, M. (1958) *Race and Culture* (New York: UNESCO).

Lewis, I. M. (2003) *Ecstatic Religion: A Study of Shamanism and Spirit Possession* (New York: Psychology Press).

Lewis, M. P. (Ed.) (2009) *Zande. Ethnologue: Languages of the World*, sixteenth edition (Dallas: SIL International).

Makris, G. P. (1996) Slavery, Possession and History: The Construction of the Self among Slave Descendants in the Sudan, *Africa*, 66(02), pp. 159–82.

Natvig, R. (1987) Oromos, Slaves, and the Zar Spirits: A Contribution to the History of the Zar Cult, *The International Journal of African Historical Studies*, 20(4), pp. 669–89.

_____. (1988) Liminal Rites and Female Symbolism in the Egyptian Zar Possession Cult, *Numen*, 35(Fasc. 1), pp. 57–68.

Njaradi, D. (2012) Trance in Western Theatrical Dance: Transformation, Repetition and Skill Learning, *Journal of Dance & Somatic Practices*, 4(1), pp. 23–41.

O'Fahey, R. S. (2006) Does Darfur Have a Future in the Sudan, *The Fletcher Forum of World Affairs*, 30, p. 27.

Schechner, R. (2010) *Between Theater and Anthropology* (Philadelphia, PA: University of Pennsylvania Press).

Spring, A. (1978) The Epidemiology of Spirit Possession among the Luvale of Zambia, in J. Hock-Smith and A. Spring (Eds) *Women in Ritual and Symbol* (New York: Plenum Press).

Turner, V. (1974) *Dramas, Fields, and Metaphors: Symbolic Action in Human Society* (Ithaca, NY/London: Cornell University Press).

_____. (1982) *From Ritual to Theatre: The Human Seriousness of Play* (New York: PAJ Publications).

_____. (1985) *On the Edge of the Bush: Anthropology as Experience* (Tucson, AZ: University of Arizona Press).

Zenkovsky, S. (1950) Zar and Tambura as Practised by the Women of Omdurman, *Sudan Notes and Records*, 31(1), pp. 65–81.

3

Maranga Mai

Janinka Greenwood

Maranga Mai was a theatre performance that grew out of the ferment of protest about Māori rights, the loss of Māori land and racial inequality in 1970s New Zealand. It toured schools, it was performed outside school walls, on *marae*, in other public places and, controversially, in the executive wing of the parliament building in 1980. Its raw simplicity captured much of the assertive and angry energy of the movements of political and cultural realization and contestation of the period. At the time of its performance it roused heated opposition and antagonism as well as eager affirming acclaim. In its content, its form and its ethos it crystallized a moment in history of both the awareness of the country and of the evolving shape of theatre. Now traces of the work exist in archival snippets of news and commentary, in short descriptions of New Zealand history (Walker, 1990), brief mentions in accounts of cross-cultural theatre in New Zealand (Greenwood, 2002) and perhaps in privately held videos of a performance. This chapter returns to the work and investigates it as a slice of theatre archaeology (Greenwood, 2010), an artefact embedded in the soil of its period. It examines it as a narrative artefact and as means of understanding the issues and values of its period as well as its place in the evolution of New Zealand theatre.

The Time and Place

Maunder (2010) reports that *Maranga Mai* first appeared as a fifteen-minute skit created by members of the Otara[1] Waitangi Action Committee. Brian and Roma Potiki, Huhana Oneroa, Ana Meihana, Hori and Henare

Hapimana, Jackie Davidson, Cyril Cahpaman, Liz Marsden and Bouffy Pihema further developed the initial skit to an hour-long performance and added the music of Hori Chapman (Locke, 2012). Maunder further reports that a Māori youth worker in Otara invited the group, also using the name *Maranga Mai*, to perform in schools to raise the consciousness of school students. The first school performance thus took place at Mangere College. The performance was followed by outrage from viewers, and later public media comment, about the attack it posed to the image of apparently harmonious race relations in New Zealand and so the Minster of Education intervened and stopped it being performed in schools. The group then performed it outside school fences. Consequently, the media controversies grew more heated.

The publicity drew the attention of emerging Māori leaders, Pita Sharples and John Tamihere, who invited a performance of *Maranga Mai* at an event on a West Auckland *marae*.[2] There the work was seen as a new but comfortable addition to the making of speeches and the performance of *kapa haka*: a new form of storytelling with songs and movement elements with an embedded invitation to debate. The play then began to tour, using Māori networks, especially those associated with the current protest movements, as hosts.

In 1980 a Māori Member of Parliament, Whetū Tirikātene-Sullivan, invited the group to perform in the parliamentary theatre. More controversy followed. At the end of the performance, in an unscripted moment, a beer bottle was smashed against a wall. There was a tussle between a National Party Member of Parliament, Norman Jones, and supporters of the performing group. Norman Jones announced his intention to complain to the Race Relations Conciliator. Whetū Tirikātene-Sullivan, on the other hand, asserted that the play was 'a totally valid art form for the moment' (Schrader, 2014). Debate followed in Parliament. Norman Jones asked the Minster of Internal Affairs to explain the criteria whereby the Council for Māori and South Pacific Arts can justify funding $1,000 to *Maranga Mai* to enable it to tour a play ridiculing the courts and the police. On behalf of the Minister, the Under-Secretary to the Minster of Internal Affairs replied that the grant was made under a special arts project scheme that covered a 'broad range of cultural activities which are the sources of innovation, experimentation and progress in the arts. To which Jones shot back: 'Does the culture mentioned in the Minister's answer include abuse of the Police and the courts' (Hansard, 1981: 4998)? The argument continued for several further exchanges with Norman Jones calling the performance 'guerrilla theatre' and the Under-Secretary stating that the Minister certainly did not condone anything that might ridicule the police or indicate antisocial behaviour, but that the funding decision had been made by an independent body (Hansard, 1981: 4998). Ranginui Walker (1990), the renowned Māori critical historian, later described *Maranga Mai* as guerrilla theatre that was 'a direct threat to Pākehā[3] definitions of reality' (226).

The Narration

Maranga Mai tells a story of protest. The play begins with a call, a *karanga*, which invites the audience into its space, calls on the ancestors to witness and support the performance, and lays down the *kaupapa*, the issue that is to be addressed by the performance. Then in a collage of songs, narratives, vignettes, placards and oratory, it highlights important moments in the struggle for Māori rights: the Land March of 1975, the protest against the building of the Raglan golf course, the occupation of Bastion Point, the confrontation of He Taua with drunken engineering students, and the repeated *hikoi* to Waitangi protesting broken Treaty promises. It interweaves this history with the story of Māori youth drawn from their rural communities into the city where they face unemployment, addiction, policy brutality and imprisonment. It proclaims the assertion of *Ka whawhai tonu matou, ake ake* (we will fight on forever and forever). The play ends with the suicide of a youth who has been imprisoned and a *tangi*, a ritual of lament and commemoration, for his death.

As well as telling a story about protest, the play was an active voice within the orchestration of protest that was accumulating throughout New Zealand. As such the play is a scene within a larger narrative that was performed in the public space of politics and direct action throughout New Zealand and crystallized in specific dramatic events where Māori activists challenged not only the government and local corporations but also the public assumption that New Zealand was a land of equality and racial harmony—what Walker called the *Pākehā* definitions of reality (Walker, 1990). The incident and subsequent debate in parliament, described above, are an example of the intense dramas that were being played out in the public arena. These events, as well as the continuing story of confrontation in which they are placed, can be considered in terms of what Schechner (1993), emphasizing that he does not use the term metaphorically, calls 'direct theatre' (Walker, 1990), whereby 'large public spaces are transformed into theatre where collective reflexivity is performed' (83).

The roots of Māori protest reach back to the act of colonization itself, with repeated submissions to both the British Crown and to the New Zealand parliament as well as acts of resistance to the illegal acquisition of land (Walker, 1990; Orange, 1987). However, in ways that have correspondences throughout the world, mainstream New Zealand consciousness had erased uncomfortable aspects of its history and so was more than a little complacent in the 1970s about its identity as a unified and fairly just society.

In 1975 Whina Cooper, a matriarch of the Far North and a woman who had been an active Māori leader at local and national levels, led a march to Parliament to protest the continuing alienation of Māori land. Fifty marchers left Te Hapua, the northernmost part of New Zealand, and began a thousand kilometre walk down the length of the island to Wellington. The renowned poet, Hone Tuwhare, later wrote about the aching process of walking down the land: 'We are stroking, caressing the spine of the land. We are massaging the ricked back of the land with our sore but ever-loving feet' (Tuwhare, 1994). About 5,000 marchers arrived at Parliament presenting a memorial of rights and a petition signed by 60,000 people. A tent Māori embassy was set up in parliament grounds. The eyes of national media were spectators of the march, and its films and newspapers reconstructed and replayed the drama in new performances of opinion and debate. The figure of the old woman, one hand on her walking stick and the other holding the hand of her grandchild, has become part of the semiotic heritage of New Zealand.

Marangi Mai's narrative moves from the Land March to the occupation of the Raglan golf course. The land, which held sacred burial grounds, had originally been seized from the Tainui people by the government during

World War I to build an airbase and bunker. Some years after the end of the war the government justified keeping the land through the Public Works Act of 1928. In 1976 the government sold the land to the Raglan golf course without consultation with the local Māori people. The golf course demolished homes and graves. Eva Rickard and the Tainui people made unsuccessful petitions to the local Council, the golf course and the government, and led protests and occupations.

Although an Act of Parliament set up the Waitangi Tribunal in 1975, creating a mechanism for land claims from any future Crown actions, it did not provide for retrospective claims. In 1978 the local Māori people occupied the golf course and elders carried out *karakia*, traditional religious rituals, to acknowledge the burial grounds and to affirm the work of the protestors. The police came, they were met with a *haka* or dance of challenge by the protestors, and arrests began. Eve Rickard was dragged away by the police at the ninth hole. The arrest was televised and variously recreated in the media. With the intertextuality of direct theatre, a leading Māori activist responded by playing a televised round of golf in the front of parliament grounds.

The occupation of Bastion Point was played out in the full blaze of media attention. Bastion Point was a block of prime land in the urban area of Auckland. At the time the original Treaty was signed, Ngati Whatua of Orakei were major landowners in what became the Auckland area. Over the next hundred years as the city of Auckland grew they became practically landless. Over the first half of the twentieth century the tribe initiated continuous complaints and legal actions against unjust land sales, and failed. In 1976 a plan was announced to develop high-cost housing on the land at Bastion Point which the Crown held, disputedly, as a reserve. In response, the Orakei Māori Action Committee occupied the point and held it for 506 days. It was a peaceful protest on ancestral land. Makeshift houses were built. In 1978 a massive convoy of army trucks brought 500 police to the occupied site. They were met by the 200 or so protesters standing by their meeting house, singing, performing *karakia* and chanting a *haka* of defiance. The protestors were forcibly evicted. This time newspapers and television media were not the only ones recording and playing back the events. The Māori film-maker, Merata Mita, and her colleagues captured images of army trucks coming through the city streets, a helicopter circling overhead, the ranks of dark coated policemen in white helmets surrounding the protesters, a matriarch holding fiercely onto a pole in front of the meeting house, and protesters dragged off the grounds (Mita et al., 1980).

Maranga Mai also tells the story of a group of Māori activists, He Taua, who in 1979 confronted engineering students preparing to perform a mock *haka*. The engineering students' mock *haka* had become a regular feature during the Auckland University capping parade. The students, most of whom were cheerfully drunk and some with genitals and swear words painted on their chests, wore grass skirts and lampooned the *haka*. Petitions to stop the parody through official channels had been ineffective. The activists demonstrated that a *haka* is a challenge that can be responded to accordingly. Arrests were made and protestors were charged with causing a riot. 'Misinformation and sensationalism' (Harris, 2004) flourished in the media. In many ways, the heavy caricature that is evident in *Maranga Mai*'s portrayal of the court scenes and the police action was also manifested in the media's performed commentaries on the trial and its implication for New Zealand society.

In 1979 the Waitangi protests were resumed with denunciations of the Treaty of Waitangi,[4] which guaranteed Māori ownership of their lands and their *rangatiratanga*,[5] as a fraud. The banners held in the hands of the actors of *Maranga Mai* read: *Treaty is a Broken Contract; Ka Whawhai Tonu Matoy Ake Ake Ake; Wiatangi: Day Off or Rip Off; Boycott Waitangi; The Treaty is a Fraud*. They paralleled those carried in the 1979 and subsequent marches. *Maranga Mai* was itself performed during several *hikoi*.

Alongside the narrative of major national protests, *Maranga Mai* tells the story of young Māori people who have come to the big urban centres like Auckland. The transition from rural community to the loneliness of the city is alienating. Locke (2012) reports how vulnerable Māori youth with little education and no paid work were going to the city and getting into trouble with drugs and prostitution and meeting with police violence, court, borstal or imprisonment. The play portrays the lack of options experienced by young Māori who have fallen out with the law: it ends with a song commemorating the actual recent prison suicide of two brothers which had at that time impacted strongly on young, and older, Māori, and a *tangi* lamenting their death.

Reviewing the play nearly forty years later,[6] it is noteworthy how *Maranga Mai* was both participant in and commentator on major events in the history of Māori protest against the denial of Māori rights and in the claim to be heard as Māori in the determination of the future of New Zealand. The narration in the play on the one hand turns a spotlight onto the events that took place and the angry passion with which many young activists understood them, and on the other hand it re-inscribes those events into a collective yet personal statement about injustice and how it should be addressed.

The Body

Narration in theatre, as is repeatedly emphasized in this book, is carried out through the body, through its movements and sounds and the words and semiotics that come from the body in performance. This section examines how the body was performed in *Maranga Mai* from three perspectives: the body of the performer, the body of work, and the body of the *marae* that is invoked by the work.

The actors of the *Maranga Mai* group were not trained professionals. The body they brought into their performance was that of their daily way of being in the world. It came with a number of developed skills. Most of the group were activists and were accustomed to standing their ground and asserting their views: that gave them a body that was balanced through its core and a voice that flowed freely with the outgoing breath. They were at home on *marae* and in other Māori contexts and were accustomed to stand to *wiaita*, to work as a team to swing *poi* or to perform the *haka*: that gave their body flexibility and an embodied sense of how to be part of a collective movement. It also enabled them to move with ease from skit to Māori performative styles, and these easy transitions were what gave the power to a work that might otherwise have been a purely political rant. Nevertheless, the overall impact of their physical presence onstage was that of normal people speaking out to the audience on issues that were of passionate importance.

The performance at Mangere College, as reported by Harris (2004: 99) 'was often described as crude, offensive and extremely militant'. Harris also reports that 'many audiences found the performance harrowing, made endurable only by clever and artistic uses of music and protest lyrics' (99). I have showed video of a performance to successive groups of drama students as part of the history of New Zealand theatre and I saw that many of them were shocked by the anger of the expression and felt they were being assaulted for injuries that they did not believe they were historically a part of. No doubt many of the actors' contemporary audiences felt a similarly defensive reaction. The body of actors, unseparated from audience by lights or stage, provokes a correspondingly strong reaction in those viewing.

While the angry body, the placards and the vehemence of spoken language confronted audiences, even sometimes those who agreed with the message, a potential bridge to the audience was created by the compelling rhythm of the protest lyrics and the way the music captured grief, love and passionate allegiance to a Māori way of being. I was one of those who at the time were riveted by the sheer intensity of the commentary made by the performance on the social and political realities that we were then living through, and perhaps choosing to be agentic in changing.

Maranga Mai fits easily into the mould of agit prop. Perhaps one of the best known, and arguably most polished, examples of agit prop theatre is John McGrath's (1973) *The Cheviot, the Stag and the Black Black Oil*. Agit prop theatre is overtly political. It combines stereotypic characterization, parody, declamation and rousing song. It is usually performed in an open space, with minimal props and costuming. It is often hastily and collectively devised, and rough in its form. As is the case of John McGrath's work, it can sometimes have the potential to wrench emotions, to provoke critical thought and to awaken social responsibility. *Maranga Mai* was collectively made and speedily evolved. It is a collage of rousing, sometimes moving, song and satiric skit. It is declamatory and overtly political. It has rough edges. It aligns with the body of agit prop. However, it can, and has, also be seen in terms of an entirely new form, that of *marae* theatre. Balme (1990: 151), for instance, heralded McGrath's play as the first of the new Māori plays, a form of theatre that is somehow Māori in its form rather than in alignment with the conventional expectations of Western theatre.

It is useful, therefore, to consider the body of *Maranga Mai* in terms of the elusive form that is called *marae theatre*. The *marae* foreground, the *marea atea*, is an open space where parties from different sides meet. On the one side are the *tangata whenua*, the home people, on the other are the *manuhiri*, those who have arrived for some purpose. There will be a ritual of encounter in which both parties will identify themselves and their relationships with the place. It will begin with charged energies and the potential of confrontation. It will end with the sharing of breath and the merging into a joint community, at least for the time of the encounter. In the formal proceedings, there will be an exchange of speeches, each followed by a carefully linked *waiata* or song. When the formalities are over and the business of the encounter is being attended to, there will be more speech-making around the house, some of it humorous and some of it openly didactic. There will be the cut and thrust of debate, and many of the contributions may be laced with a song. A very provocative contribution might be followed by a *haka*. At stages of the proceedings there will be breaks for meals and entertainment, perhaps by the local *kapa haka* group.

Maranga Mai was most frequently performed in open spaces. The absence of elaborate props, scenery, lights and other stage paraphernalia means that there is no separation of actors from audience. The relationship between actor and audience is somewhat like the relationship of parties across the *marae atea*. The everyday body of the actors also contributes to such a relationship. The flow of speech-making, interlaced with *haka* and song, is also resonant with the style of debate on the *marae*. The skits bring a new dimension into the normal performativeness of *marae* debate, but they are consistent with the humour that is often inserted as leaven to serious comments.

Confrontation is an accepted strategy in *marae* debate, but it is accompanied by expectation of response and of the continued flow of dialogue until there is some kind of shared, and, perhaps partial and temporary, resolution. The confrontational style in *Maranga Mai* can thus be seen as part of the *marae* tradition. However, what makes it different is that when the performance took place in public places other than on *marae*, the audience had different expectations.

One of the complexities of *Maranga Mai* is that it was played to two very different kinds of audiences. It was probably first written to speak to other Māori about the issues of the time. Some of those audiences were expected to be equally passionately activist about the issues discussed, and others may have been more moderate in the way they wanted to deal with the issues but also very aware of their existence and the need to address them. Both kinds of audiences would have readily understood the semiotics of the form and appreciated how this theatre was a contribution to ongoing debate.

The other kind of audiences were not Māori. Some were openly shocked or affronted. They would have read the play as finished theatre, not as an invitation to further dialogic exploration. And probably the cast did not expect productive dialogue from those audiences. Other non-Māori audiences responded to the play with enthusiasm, recognizing in it a dramatic platform that resonated with and made visible their own understandings of the land issues and racial tensions. Many of these audience members relished the opportunity to see these issues discussed in a dramatic form that was distinctively Māori, and that spoke so directly of the *marae* experiences that some of them had had. Those who were theatre-goers were sometimes inclined, like Balme (1990), to greet it as a new form of theatre, and to respond to it for its theatricality as well as its message.

It was suggested above that the term '*marae theatre*' is an elusive one. It is elusive because, while it carries strong connotations of form and place, no such specific genre of theatre has developed. The *marae* has always been a home for Māori performative traditions. In the 1970s Māori (for instance, Hapipi,[7] 1976; Tuwhare,[8] 1977; Stewart,[9] 1979) were writing theatre that addressed loss of land and the inequalities of the justice system in forms that pushed past the boundaries of conventional Western theatre by the use of Māori language and Māori performative elements such as *haka* and in some cases by the layering of Māori and Western concepts of reality through introducing ancestral figures as dramatic agents. Since then, especially in the 1980s and 1990s, a number of Māori companies, and some non-Māori companies, have performed in theatres and in public spaces incorporating aspects of Māori protocol such as welcoming the audience (in some cases being welcomed by the audience) and opening the space after performance for discussion. However, in the last three decades a considerable body of Māori theatre (such as Grace-Smith, 1997; Kauka, 1996; Ihimaera, 2000) has been written and performed that draws extensively on Māori language, Māori epistemologies and Māori performative styles but places them within the overall vehicle of Western form, which is itself rapidly changing and adapting to different cultural voices and ways of being in the body. While *marae theatre* may not have turned out to be the new form of Māori theatre that Balme (1990) predicted, the influence of the *marae* and of its *wharenui*, or ancestral meeting house, is not to be underestimated. The meeting house and its surrounding *marae* is the third aspect of body I will discuss in relation to *Maranga Mai*.

The meeting house is seen as the body of the ancestor that embraces the people. The ridgepole is the spine and the carved entrance is its enfolding arms. Each carved post within the house and each weaving is an embodiment of ancestry and connection to the land. Moreover, it is often said that the words spoken in the house remain on its walls and so the walls carry the spiritual legacy of histories and debates. Hone Tuwhare's *In the Wilderness* (1977) shows how the meeting house is a live entity. The play begins with a group of young people refurbishing a long-neglected meeting house and failing to discover the identity of some of the carved figures. At a point in the play when an apparently irreconcilable dispute has broken out in the house, the carved figures step forward, very much alive, and chasten their descendants. The moment is more than a theatrical metaphor; it is a performance of the life force of the meeting house and of its histories. By invoking the rituals of the *marae*, the performance of *Maranga Mai* also invokes the spiritual force of ancestry and of spiritual as well as legal claims to land and to a society that is nurturing to Māori young people. The concept of body in these performance is thus something that is multi-layered: the actors' performative bodies, the art form of the play and the invisible body of ancestral values and claims are each present and interrelated in the performance.

The Legacy

As the above summary of the play's history shows, *Maranga Mai* made a strong impact on the audiences of its time. It was applauded, censured and feared. Above all it was debated. In this way it contributed to the nationwide performance of that time of outrage and action about the loss of land, the alienation of young people and the broader betrayals of promises made by the Treaty of Waitangi. It was fed by the energy of protest and in turn it fed that energy.

The protest movements created change: both in awareness and in practice. Some years later the Waitangi Tribunal was given the power to address historic grievances. The lands at Raglan and at Orakei were eventually returned. Parodies of the *haka* or of other cultural artefacts are widely not tolerated. The right to lands and waterways and other resources are still issues of contestation, as is the right of Māori to control their own well-being. Protest takes new forms, but, as is the case with history, the contribution of the activists of the 1970s has forced mainstream New Zealanders to re-think issues of race and of the implications of the Treaty and it has nurtured ongoing assertions of Māori rights.

The events described here were not of course the only forces that challenged awareness and compelled change at that time. Other examples of the active energies of the time include the following. There were hundreds of non-Māori who were themselves activists who joined Māori on the *hikoi* to Waitangi and other protests movements. The Human Rights Commission collated submissions and published *Race Against Time* (Tauroa, 1982) influencing government policy to pay attention to race. Māori groups and agencies and a growing number of *Pākehā* worked to raise public consciousness. There was a major campaign to address the monocultural bias of the education system and to introduce teaching of Māori language (Hill, 2009). HART collaborated with Māori activists to mount a nationwide and successful campaign to interrupt the all-white South African rugby tour (Minto, 2006). Nga Tamatoa launched a petition for the inclusion of Māori language in schools, which gathered 30,000 signatures and was presented to Parliament in 1972 (Harris, 2004). Arnold Wilson developed a programme that took students, their teachers and education administrators to live together on their school's local *marae* to directly experience Māori values and to create artworks from local histories through negotiation with elders (Greenwood and Wilson, 2006). One of the legacies of *Maranga Mai* is to point to a time of strong activism throughout New Zealand.

The play also provided a springboard for other Polynesian groups to create their own approach to telling their story. Maunder (2010) reports that a group of Samoan students, including Samson Samasoni and Ete Etuati, were inspired by seeing the performance in Wellington to form their own group, Le Matou. As well as the experimentation with the forms of theatre, what was important to both groups was the exploration and development of sightlines that were Māori or Samoan respectively. Gilbert (1998) develops the concept of sightlines as a way of exploring how race, gender and nation are expressed in the materiality of theatre contexts as well as in the ideas and values that form the story of theatre. An important legacy of the strong public presence of the play *Maranga Mai* is that it offered an alternative sightline of the ways both society and theatre could be seen.

Conclusion

When an archaeological site reveals an artefact, it opens up an opportunity to examine the artefact as an object in its own right. It also invites examination of how the object speaks of the period in which it was made. *Maranga Mai* was born out of the grievances and protest action of the 1970s. It forged its form from the performative movements of its time: the slogans and rhetoric of political rallies, the *hakas* and *waiata* of defiance and grief, the traditions of oratory and debate on the *marae*, and the hard-edged satire and parody of agit prop theatre. Its body is a collage of song, placard, skit and oratory in both English and Māori. It aimed to communicate with audiences that, for the most part, had little interest in theatre or little exposure to Western theatrical traditions and no affinity with its conventions. It drew instead on the traditions of the *marae*: the flow of debate in *whaikorero*, the punctuation of key moments with song and *haka*, the weaving together of humorous anecdote and serious issues. As an artefact, it is an object that has its own distinctive and interesting form. However, it is an artefact that carries narratives, both those it explicitly performs and those it echoes through its performance. It narrates some of the landmark protests and issues of its period, and by doing so it now draws our attention back through history to a recent time when the public, complacent monocultural face of New Zealand cracked in the full glare of national and international media. It speaks of a time when politics of race were expressed in forthright and often angry assertion as well as in passionate dedication, a time when emotions were sometimes scraped raw and senses of reality were often severely fractured. *Maranga Mai* speaks of a time of significant and important changes. As an artefact, it embodies multi-layered narratives of who we, as New Zealanders, were, and so of who we are and who we are becoming.

Discussion Questions

1. What were the major issues that *Maranga Mai* addressed?
2. What was the relationship between Māori activist performance and traditional narrative styles of communication and expression? How did *Maranga Mai* integrate twentieth-century performance styles into a traditional mode of expression?
3. Did *Maranga Mai* have an impact on the issues of concern to the Māori?
4. Can we discern a particular Māori narrative identity from the review of the history of *Maranga Mai*?

Websites for Māori Dance and Theatre

Auckland, New Zealand home of Māori Theatre: https://tepoutheatre.nz/
Kahurangi Māori Dance Theatre: https://www.kahurangi.com/
Taki Rua: http://www.takirua.co.nz/

Notes

1. Otara is a low-economic area of Auckland with many Māori, Polynesian and now a new range of poorer immigrant groups. It is often stigmatized in the media, now as well as then, as the site for crime and social unrest.
2. Māori communal space.
3. *Pākehā* has become the comprehensive term for referring to New Zealanders of non-Māori origin.

4. Readers who would like to know more about the Treaty of Waitangi are referred to Orange, 1987.
5. In the Māori version of the Treaty, which was the one signed by the chiefs, only governorship was passed to the British Crown; chiefly authority, or *rangatiratanga*, was guaranteed to Māori.
6. Readers who are interested in the further history of Māori protest are referred to Harris, 2004.
7. *Death of the Land* was performed by amateur casts and made into a film in the 1970s. Published in 1991.
8. *In the Wilderness* had readings and amateur performances, but was not performed in professional theatres until Don Selwyn's 1984 production.
9. *Broken Arse* was initially a short story given a dramatic reading at the PEN/Victoria University Conference in 1979. It was later rewritten as a play script, which was performed in Wellington in 1990, televised and published by Victoria University Press in 1991.

Works Cited and Resource Material

Balme, C. (1990) New Māori Theatre in New Zealand, *Australasian Drama Studies*, 15/16, pp. 149–65.

Gilbert, H. (1998) *Sightlines: Race, Gender, and Nation in Contemporary Australian Theatre* (Ann Arbor: University of Michigan Press).

Grace-Smith, B. (1997) *Purapurawhetu* (Wellington: Huia Publishers).

Greenwood, J. (2002) *History of a Bicultural Theatre: Mapping the Terrain* (Christchurch: Christchurch College of Education).

____. (2010) A Slice of Theatre Archaeology: Mulgan's For love of Appin and other plays, *New Zealand Journal of Research in Performing Arts and Education: Nga Mahi a Rehia*, 2, https://www.drama.org.nz/publications/new-zealand-journal-of-research-in-performing-arts-and-education-2010/, accessed 10 July 2018.

Greenwood, J. and A. Wilson (2006) *Te Mauri Pakeaka: A Journey in to the Third Space* (Auckland: Auckland University Press).

Hansard (1981) *Parliamentary Debates*. House of Representatives. Vol. 435. Comprising the period 6–27 Nov 1980.

Hapipi, R. (1976) Death of the Land, in S. Garret (Ed.) (1991) *He Reo Hou: 5 Plays by Māori Playwrights* (Wellington: Playmarket).

Harris, A. (2004) *Hikoi: Forty Years of Māori Protest* (Wellington: Huia Publishers).

Hill, R. (2009) *Māori and the State: Crown-Māori Relations in New Zealand/ Aotearoa, 1950–2000* (Wellington: Victoria University Press).
Ihimaera, W. (2000) *Woman far Walking* (Wellington: Huia Publishers).
Kauka, H. (1996) *Waiora* (Wellington: Huia Publishers).
Locke, C. (2012) *Workers in the Margins: Union Radicals in Post-war New Zealand* (Wellington: Bridget Williams Books).
Maunder, P. (2010) The Rebellious Mirror, Before and After 1984: Community-based Theatre in Aotearoa. Thesis, University of Canterbury.
McGrath, J. (1973) *The Cheviot, the Stag and the Black Black Oil.* Touring production of the 7:84 Theatre Company.
Minto, J. (2006) 1981 Springbok Tour, https://nzhistory.govt.nz/media/video/john-minto-1981-springbok-tour (Ministry for Culture and Heritage), accessed 7 September 2017.
Mita, M., L. Narbey and G. Pohlmann (Directors and Producers) (1980) *Bastion Point: Day 507* (New Zealand: Film).
Orange, C. (1987) *The Treaty of Waitangi* (Wellington: Allen & Unwin).
Potiki, R. (1991) A Māori Point of View: The Journey from Anxiety to Confidence, *Australasian Drama Studies*, 18, pp. 57–63.
Schechner, R. (1993) *The Future of Ritual* (London and New York: Routledge).
Schrader, B. (2014) Arts and Social Engagement – Criticising Society, in *Te Ara – The Encyclopedia of New Zealand*, http://www.TeAra.govt.nz/en/photograph/45285/maranga-mai-theatre-group-performing-at-the-beehive-1980, accessed 4 September 2017.
Stewart, B. (1979) Broken Arse, in S. Garret (Ed.) (1991) *He reo hou: 5 Plays by Māori Playwrights* (Wellington: Playmarket).
Tauroa, H. (1982) *Race against Time* (New York: Human Rights Commission).
Tuwhare, H. (1977) In the Wilderness, in S. Garret (Ed.) (1991) *He reo hou: 5 Plays by Māori Playwrights* (Wellington: Playmarket).
_____. (1994) Pāpāptuānuku, in *Deep River Talking: Collected Poems* (Honolulu: University of Hawaii Press).
Walker, R. (1990) *Ka whawhai tonu matou: Struggle Without End* (Auckland: Penguin).

4

Her-stories in Indonesian Dance Drama

Kathy Foley

This chapter will focus on the female depiction in Southeast Asian traditional dance drama narratives, drawing its examples from primarily Indonesian forms, but arguing they are related to wider patterns in the classical dance dramas of the region.

Gender and Genre

Classical dance drama genres in Southeast Asia prior to the twentieth century included two major variants: all-male groups and female troupes (with one or two male clowns sometimes added). Forms that were all male include *wayang wong* ('human' puppet-style theatre) in Java and Sunda (West Java); *gambuh* (a court genre telling stories of a prince of East Java); *wayang wong* (*Ramayana* masked performance); *calonargan* (exorcistic story of a powerful witch) in Bali; *lakhon nok* (drama 'outside' [the palace]) and *khon* (aristocratic mask) dance theatre in Thailand; the corresponding *lakhon khol* (mask) genre in Cambodia. These were traditionally all-male genres presenting the most important stories (local versions of the *Ramayana*, *Mahabharata*, or selected local tales), and were, with the possible exception of *gambuh* and *calonarang*, related to and/or derived from the puppet genres in story, movement and music.[1] Male styles since at least the twentieth century have been performed by mixed-gender casts (both male and female), but the trace of their male roots may still remain. Stories tend to include greater focus on battle sequences (with men fighting over kidnapped wives, mystical power, or magic weapons), deaths of kings, and these forms, when associated with court ritual, were thought to enhance the power of the elite, especially since performers themselves were often of noble blood or close retainers of the lords. What is more, such performance was often associated with festivals that honoured the ruler.[2]

Performances by female troupes included palace/aristocratic genres,[3] including forms like Javanese *bedhaya* and *srimpi*, which were traditionally performed by the consorts or female relatives of the ruler; the *legong* of Bali, performed by young girls who were likely to be married to the members of the elite after pubescence and who danced in a style derived from the *sanghyang dedari* (holy goddesses, young girls chosen to channel the divine in trance dances). *Lakon nai* (drama 'inside' the palace) was the dance of Thai palace ladies, while *lakhon krabhac boran* was the Khmer court equivalent. In Malaysia the major classical female dance drama was *mak yong* of Kelantan. These female genres ranged from shorter dance choreographies, which told no particular story but still had elements of character type (for example, refined princes and princesses), to dances with either an abstract or clear story. An example of an abstract story in the iconic 'Legong Kerton' (Palace Female Dance) of Bali, references an episode from the Panji tales in which the King of Lasem bids his wife farewell, sees a bird of ill omen, and is defeated in battle (Ediana Putra, 2017). In other performances, full dance narratives would be mounted; for example, Javanese *langendriyan*, a sung dance drama which tells tales of Damar Wulan, a local hero who rises from stable boy to monarch, and which was developed by the Solonese Prince Mangkunegoro IV (1853–81) for an all-female troupe (though the clown's attendants were male). Another full narrative in the Thai *lakon nai* repertoire featured stories from the Rama story (*Ramakien*) with the most important version in the refined *klon* verse written by Thailand's King Rama II (r. 1809–24). The same ruler also wrote his version of the Javanese Panji cycle (called *Inao* in Thailand, Tonnum53, 2011).[4] Scenes, like the *Mani Mekala* episode in Cambodia (where a heavenly woman beats out the demonic god of thunder for the diamond ball of lightning and brings rain (Cherries01, 2011) to full dance dramas on *Reamker* (Ramayana) themes, were part of the Khmer palace repertory.

Episodes dramatized by the women might either deal with the same narrative as that of the men (for example, the *Ramayana/Ramakien/Reamker* is an important theme in Thailand/Cambodia for both male and female forms), but the choice of episodes might differ – kidnapped Sita/Sida languishing in the garden of the asoka tree rather than tales of monkeys in all-out war with demons. Ladies, unhappily married to a king (Menak Jingga) who would be played by a woman accompanied by the male clown Dayun (see Jogja Budaya TV, 2016), might be helping out a handsome hero like Damar Wulan (also played by a woman) who saved the women from their ogre-like husband.

Panji, Damar Wulan and other themes were popular tropes for 'female' forms in Java/Bali. Since the twentieth century, as women have moved into the 'male' genres to play female and sometimes the refined male roles, we may see some attention to these romantic stories of young lovers wandering in search of each other. Still, these tales have generally not been considered the 'important' repertory, which, as I noted above, is more linked to male trauma. I suggest narratives favoured in the female dance repertory display a female sensibility: the forms often featured delicate singing, ornate poetry (sometimes composed by the ruler or his surrogate), or scenes of seduction in which female desire is as often at work as the male gaze.

In sum, male genres give more space to rivalries (often highlighting disenfranchisement of noble rulers, killing ferocious demons/opponents, and dance battles) in which local martial arts movement traditions, for example, *pencak silat* in the Indo-Malay world (Tholib, 2016), might be refigured into aesthetic dance. Female genres, by contrast, bend toward love and pathos, wherein heroines like Sita the wife of Rama may be warding off the unwanted advances of the demon King Rawana or defending herself against false accusations of infidelity and being pregnant by this kidnapper.

While battles are part of the female genres, love affairs – between beautiful young people whose path to true love never does run smooth – are uniformly featured. Pure queens may be falsely accused (for example, Sita). The 'hussy' tempts the husband (for example, Sarpakanaka the sister of Rawana). The lady's newborn son does not meet his king-father's expectation (for example, *Sang Thong* in Thailand, where the queen gives birth to a snail and mother and child are banished even though hidden beneath that hard shell is a noble prince who is every mother's dream).

The ideal male in these female dance dramas is a refined hero such as Rama (*Ramayana*) or Arjuna (*Mahabharata*). In both puppet and human versions, these refined heroes must have slight bodies and speak in modulated tones. Such characters are easily presented with an all-female ensemble. Meanwhile beautiful ladies in these productions, cross-dressed as men, were/are enticing to viewers – both male and female. Though some see the 'metrosexual' as a trope of modernity, in classical theatre and literature of Southeast Asia the androgynous s/he had been dancing for hundreds of years:[5] threatening imperial kings and ogre-fathers abound, but they merely form the 'obstacles' that the lovers must and will overcome. The centre of the story is the suffering heroine and a love-sick hero, aided by their spritely go-betweens – often clowns who were sometimes females but perhaps more often one or two males who could also have ritual functions in palace ceremonies as in Central Java (Stutterheim, 1956). In the performance, such clowns make off-colour jokes but, male or female, they know their real task is to make sure lovers make the match.

These court genres, male or female, were generally created for an ideologically male audience, although elite women were both performers and viewers. Additionally, more senior aristocratic females, including consorts, were traditionally trainers and troupe leaders. Since Indonesian independence many of these training functions have shifted from aristocrats to government arts academies, but, until the 1970s, elite ladies might still be trainers. Thus, the ideal viewer or the author of the sung text might traditionally be a male aristocrat/ruler, but the themes, as previously noted, were often sympathetic to female trials, frustrations and dreams – topics not essentially removed from contemporary romantic comedy tropes in a contemporary 'date night' film.

I have linked male forms to themes of political wrangling at the court level. When this male genre is moved back toward more local, village concerns, it can be linked to dealing with negative spirits and death rituals. For example, in Indonesia the *wayang* puppetry a *dalang* (puppet master) were normally invited to do the *besih desa* (cleansing the village) to dissipate bad spirits/energy and honour ancestors. This male performance genre was likewise associated with *ruwatan* (exorcistic performances) for those potentially threatened by negative forces (Foley, 1982a). By contrast, village level female arts, which include dance, poetry and comic banter between the sexes, are correlated with rice, fertility, rain making and good luck. In Indonesia, for example, *pantun* verses, which accrue to the female singer/dancer, have formal characteristics that are found in the light-hearted rhyming of traditional courting games between young males and females during village rice pounding and are linked to rice harvesting – they are games of life, love and the pursuit of prosperity (Foley, 1989). Hence, there is a sexual division of performance labour at a village level: men get death and exorcism and women get ceremonies of life and birth.

Thus, male genres with their traditionally all-male cast are linked to puppet genres which themselves have historical links to rituals of safeguarding the community from negative forces of the spirit world. Arguably, from such plebeian roots, mighty court arts grew and at the same time, theatre efforts, of themselves, could pragmatically help the monarch rule successfully: the male community was kept productively engaged in lauding the ideal prince-leader (a new Rama/Arjuna), as the local ruler was seen as a living expression of this heaven-sent hero. Such theatre activities kept male relatives/retainers of the ruler (in large families where an aristocrat might have many wives and, hence, dozens of potentially rival offspring) busy. Putting on a show together is a community-building activity and diminishes time available for court intrigues, given demands for long practice in refining dance technique and a year or more of rehearsal for an individual performance (Kam, 1987). Clifford Geertz in his 1980 book *Negara* on Bali coined the concept of 'theatre state', where performance ceremonies (including but not confined to actual theatre displays) were a political strategy whereby a ruler's cultural capital was both displayed and built. Geertz's idea regarding Bali has resonance with other areas of Southeast Asia. The factual hierarchy might be at work with the highest status aristocrats playing the central roles. Putting on a good show in this area was important for a ruler and his family.

Three Female Types and Sample Stories

While there are differences in the tone of the story (tragic/heroic male genres and romantic/pathetic female ones), the dancers traditionally were not defined by their biological sex but by their body type, movement, costume and vocal contours in performance. Slight males/females were needed for most female roles as well as refined heroes. The character's gender was performed, not biologically determined by the body of the dancer. I will note the major female character types in Sunda (West Java), which I see as refined and semi-refined, and add a discussion of the demonic female from Bali, as examples of major roles, but I argue implications extend to other Southeast Asian areas. For each type, sample stories will clarify how roles intertwined with character and frame female possibilities. Classical Southeast Asian dance drama forms generally have three female role types (refined, semi-refined and ogress) in terms of movement and vocal parameters.

Refined Female

The refined (*lenyepan*) female in Sundanese dance drama is associated with the slowest walk, the deepest *plié*, the most elaborate rotations of the wrists (*ukel*) and swivels of the head (*godeg*). Her diction is measured and her voice low and melodious. Her energy is largely re-circulated within her own kinesphere. Her eyes focus on the floor about one and a half body lengths in front of her. This character gives the impression of calm power and energy that is circling back into its self. She will not attack. Nothing – kidnapping, threats of violence, darkness of humanity – will cause her to move from graciousness that is her core (for example Sita with attendants, Giri Komara, 2015). This female character, of course, has a male equivalent – the refined hero.

The sample characters that I relate to this *lenyapan* type are Sita and Sumbadra (also Subadra). Sita is the wife of Rama who fearlessly follows him into the forest when Rama is unjustly exiled by his father. Coveted and kidnapped by demonic King Rawana, Sita is ever pure and true. Her virtue is proven by a test of fire, but gossip persists; banished and alone (for supposed adultery), she raises Rama's exemplary sons, Kusa and Lawa. For much of India and Southeast Asia, Sita is the ideal wife/mother/woman. In Indonesia, she is usually associated with Dewi Sri, the rice goddess.

A corresponding refined character in the *Mahabharata* is Sumbadra, the first wife of the iconic hero Arjuna. She is the sister of Kresna [Krishna] (an incarnation of the preserver god Wisnu [Vishnu]). Her second brother Baladewa wants her to marry into the powerful Kurawa clan (100 siblings known for their greed and injustice), but Sumbadra knows good when she sees it; she chooses Arjuna, the hero of the Pandawa (the five noble brothers who will win the 'great' war [*bharata yudha*] against their evil Kurawa cousins). Sumbadra is a perfect wife and mother to her son Abhimanyu. Distraught after her son's death at the hands of his vicious Kurawa uncles, Sumbadra languishes. She, like Sita, is the perfect wife-mother.

The character – Sita or Sumbadra – is danced with ultimate refinement. Whether the dancer is male or female, the body must be small and the energy relaxed and internal. Whatever the world throws at these women, they will never be thrown off balance and never raise their voices. While some of the *lakon* (plays) feature their weddings, the most performed episodes show them suffering (Sita while kidnapped by Rawana or Sumbadra kidnapped and – temporarily – murdered by the Kurawa henchman Burisrawa or mourning her dead child). This *lenyapan* type demands a technically perfect and subtle dancer, modulated voice and ideal deportment. A true *lenyapan* lady can do no wrong.

Semi-refined Female

Semi-refined (*ladak*) women by contrast – while also svelte, beautiful and smart – act up, act out and sometimes make mistakes; Srikandi, a second wife of the hero Arjuna, and Mustakaweni her female opponent are examples (Kuman, 2016). They move faster in *keupat* (a walk with a faster beat). They hold their head higher, looking straight ahead, and speak quickly on a higher note than the refined type (though as with *lenyapan* refined characters, the *ladak* figure can be male or female).

Indeed, some gender confusion adheres to this role. In dance gestures, *ladak* women spend more time performing the stylized movements that represent combing hair, adjusting earrings, putting on lipstick – showing their attachment to things of this world. They are flirtatious, daring and, unlike the refined female who is always inherently good, these women may be judged ambivalently. For example, Banowati remains in love with Arjuna, the Pandawa hero, while still married to Duryodhana, leader of the Kurawa.

Sarpakanaka, the demon princess in the Ramayana who tries to win Rama away from Sita and later persuades her brother Rawana that kidnapping Sita is a good idea, is another *ladak*-related example. While Sapakanaka may sometimes be portrayed in her demonic body with an ugly face (in which case she might be played by a male), she will more often be seen in dance dramas as using her magic powers to transform into a *ladak* female character when she tries to convince Rama and subsequently his brother Laksmana to marry her. Of course, not all *ladak* characters are suspect like Banowati and Sarpakanaka. Srikandi and figures from the *Panji* cycle are positive, but they are still more implicated in creating the story action (often getting themselves in trouble) than *leyanpan* ladies who generally have things done to them. *Ladak* women do.

Srikandi in Indian versions of the *Mahabharata* is a woman who turns into a man. By contrast, in Java she is a woman with male bravado and fighting skills. She learns archery from Arjuna and then becomes a co-wife with Sumbadra. At the time of the great war with the Kurawa, none of the Pandawa heroes are strong enough to defend against the Kurawa general Bisma. Srikandi – a reincarnation of Amba, a woman Bisma wronged – takes to the battlefield and eliminates him. In more everyday stories, Srikandi may complain Arjuna has been gone from their Princedom of Mandukara for too long. So, she talks Sumbadra into dressing as a man to search for him. Sumbadra naturally makes a girlish man, but Srikandi always puts up a good fight: even Arjuna in stories has trouble figuring out who s/he is and will battle her until his mentor Kresna launches his magic *cakra* (discus) and hits Srikandi, revealing her female identity.

In the *Panji* stories, women also portray this *ladak* character type, and, interestingly, the pattern of refined ladies transformed into men is repeated. When temporarily jilted by a betrothed, seeking a missing sibling, or averting an unwanted marriage proposal, women in the *Panji* stories may disguise themselves as men. Alternatively, the god Narada will affect an actual – if temporary – sex-change; females become males (as males like Gunung Sari [Candra Kirana's brother] sometimes become female). The standard couples (most importantly, Prince Panji and his betrothed, Princess Candra Kirana; but also Panji's sister [Ragil Kuning] and Candra Kirana's brother [Gunung Sari]) tend to fall in love with their missing partners – but sometimes while the women are temporarily males. This has everyone confused and, therefore, makes for exciting theatre. Scholars and artist-activists have pointed out the gender-bending nature of this repertory (Emigh and Hunt quoted in Diamond, 2012: 109). The loose frame of beautiful young people in love, wandering the world in search of their beloveds, but failing to recognize them when they meet, parallels gender confusion in the *Orlando Furioso* or Shakespearean plays.

In mask dance of Java, which is often associated with these *Panji* stories, some of this gender confusion goes deep. The Pamindo (second) character in the Cirebon *topeng* (mask dance) is usually thought of as a female, but the mask itself is often named Samba (a son of Kresna [Krishna]) and may also be analogous to Gunung Sari (the brother of Princess Candra Kirana, a female-ish male) (Supodo, 2016). The interest of many of these stories and the character type is its gender slippage – both male and female seem present.

With the demise of all-female troupes in the twentieth century, the need for and perhaps the appeal of *Panji* stories in Southeast Asia has faded. However, the *ladak* characters, male-ish females or female-ish males, remain. Indonesian women choreographers of the 1970–80s often featured *ladak* women. In West Java, Irawati Durban Arjo's troupe performed and widely taught 'Kandegan' choreographed by her teacher Ceceh Somantri in 1957 (Indrawan Nur Cahyono, 2012). *Jayeng Renggana* (Brave Elaborations), one of Irawati's own choreographies, extended her guru's innovations and showed strong female-warriors, tossing the long dance scarves (a feature of warrior dances) over their head with the thrust of an arm or the kick of the foot as they grasp the cloth with their toes. This repertoire of strong women dances, however, has been, since the 1990s, somewhat in retreat, as the Islamic revival has promoted veiling in Muslim West Java and more feminized female representations advance. Nonetheless, in Bali, *Panji Semirang* (Princess Candra Kirana transformed into Prince Semirang, Lord of Bali) is still going strong: it represents Candra Kirana at war with her beloved Panji (Artho, 2013). And women in West Java can still dance the strong characters, when they don the mask of a strong male.

Demonic Female

The final female role type is the ogress: Sarpakanaka the demoness of the *Ramayana* in her demonic form participates in this category, as does Permoni (Durga) who appears in various *Mahabharata* episodes, including the *ruwatan* ('making safe') performances. In Bali, of course, this character is seen most explosively presented in the *calonarang* dance drama. There she wears the sacred mask of Rangda (Widow-Witch) and represents the angry mother of the beautiful Ratna Menggali, a girl whose hand in marriage is scorned; what man wants a widow-witch for his mother-in-law?

In terms of movement the demonic female characters walk in the same rhythm (*kepat*) as *ladak* characters. The voice has more screeches and scale glides but is still related to the fast and high-pitched tone of the *ladak* character. While the puppet iconography has pendulous breasts, a protruding nose and crisscrossed eyes (which connote meditation/sacred power), no female in West Java normally appears in such an outfit. In the *Ramayana*, Sapakanaka usually appears in her *ladak* disguise – the beautiful version but not the demon – and seduces in a relatively circumspect way, to be rejected by Rama and his brother Laksmana before the latter raises his *kris* (knife) to slice her nose. She raises her scarf (*soder*) to cover her face, letting us know the cut has happened, and vanishes.

By contrast, *calonarang* in Bali presents the full female demonic (Bateson and Mead, 1951). But here widow-witch Rangda/Calonarang/Durga – dressed as an old woman and later the monster – is played by a man. Only a male is considered powerful enough to portray her.

Infuriated that her daughter is being passed over by suitors, Rangda sends her students (who since the mid-twentieth century have been played by young girls, dancing in female semi-refined style) to wreak havoc. They leave the stage and are replaced by the *leyak* (witches) with fangs, shaggy hair, long claws, dancing. They represent females but are played by males in strong male style. The forces of evil steal a doll representing a stillborn child and may try to grab children from the audience. Laughter and screams fill the air. One of the *leyaks*, Celuluk, is a nymphomaniac and creeps up on sleeping village men who may fondle her until their eyes open and they realize she is a *leyak*.

Minister Bhardah arrives to defeat the widow-witch and Rangda, with pendulous breasts, her magic mask, long nails, scarf with magic imagery and billowing hair, will face off against Barong (the leonine incarnation of protective powers/Wisnu [Vishnu] and Bharadah's analogue). Groups of young men (*kris* dancers), hypnotized by the witch Rangda, go into trance and start stabbing themselves. The village priest will weave in and out of this chaotic playing space set by the village death temple, bringing the *kris* dancers or other participants out of trance. Holy water is blessed when the beard of the 'male' Barong is dipped into the water. Positive male power trumps and contains (but does not end) the negative/ambivalent female power of the female gone wild.

Men onstage playing a female demon of course can be scary and salacious, making the scenes funny, fun and dangerous. An actual woman yelling and 'coming on' to a man has shock value but scares rather than empowers male viewers. The body of this demonic female Rangda is larger than a normal human's, her breasts bigger, her spiritual power devouring. Though post-menopausal women potentially have some of the characteristics of the character (drooping breasts and greater leeway to address sexual issues), they still lack the musculature and, people say, the spiritual power, to wear the mask of Rangda (heavy both in physical weight and magic potential). To show the inner nature and sexual power of the demonic female, who has both comic and terrifying dimensions, a male performer is preferred. In the same way that female impersonators in the West often cultivate clothing, words, actions that out-female any females, this 'she' has little to do with an actual woman. She is a male imaginary.

Gender, Tradition and Contemporary Styles

Dancers in trance forms are often chosen for appropriate body type. Small bodies – females or slight, adolescent males – will be guided toward refined and floating trance manifestations as in Java's *sintren* (a girl's trance game) or *lais* (a male version of the same), in which the trance dancer releases her/himself from bonds and puts on a costume of a 'heavenly goddess' while trapped under a small cage, then dances with floating and somnambulant movements. This goddess dances in a style that reminds one of the refined *lenyapan* dancer.

Sintren forms traditionally have another interlude where the trance dancer goes back in the cage and redresses as the opposite gender: this section partakes of more spritely movement (*On the Spot – Misteri Tarian Magis Sintren*, 2016). The trance dancer might actually dance with an audience member of the same or opposite sex. The behaviour might remind us of *ladak* figures. At the end of the performance, the dancer returns to her/his normative gender. These trance forms are currently games that are associated with bringing rain, luck and foretelling marriage partners.

By contrast, larger male bodies will normally appear in heavier duty and more exciting trance forms with jumps and screams. For example, in Balinese *sanghyang jaran* (holy horse dance) and *kuda kepang* (woven bamboo horse dance, also called *jatilan*), of the Javanese and other groups, males go into trance while riding hobby horses and become possessed 'horses' who perform all kinds of antics including opening coconuts with teeth, eating glass or walking on fiery coals. The *calonarang* performance via both its witch figures and *kris* dancers has traits of this more aggressive model. These male trance dances tend to have a protective function – safeguarding against black magic, freeing the community from evil spirits, and responding to threats. For example, after the Bali bomb set off by Islamic fundamentalists in 2002, exorcisms via *calonarang* performances were widespread in the hopes that tourism, so vital to the economy, might return. Such village trance forms may have set the stage for the much more refined and elaborated palace genres, creating three significant types.

High palace women if beautiful, young, refined, will be the correct body (or puppet) for the ideal *lenyapan*. They dance, mother, suffer and do not talk back. They are important in life and fiction, but rarely take control of the story. They know tears, endure and gain respect. Melodrama is their story.

Women who were spritely, forthright and skilled in improvisation might slide into the second role type and might allow a kind of drama therapy. Perhaps one cannot choose one's own marriage partner or firmly hold a spouse who is expected to marry other co-wives. One will probably not lead an army in real life: but on the stage, all these things are/were possible. Stories such as *Panji* and *Damar Wulan* like contemporary romantic comedy have some travail, but the heroines take some action and laugh their way through, then revert to the good wife at the end. Comedy is their story.

Demon roles were too powerful and in opposition to the fertility and good luck functions that women appropriately controlled. Men in masks could put on the hanging breasts, fangs and the perceived spiritual power of such figures. The social liability of playing this character would slide off a male back – it allowed him to show spiritual potency by taking on the negative female role. Women often would not take this risk.

And yet a kind of irony inheres. His story tends to be the 'important stuff' of tragedy – politics, war, death and destruction. Her story may be the *leyapan*'s melodrama or the *ladak*'s cross-dressed comedy. She gets life, luck and children. But when the stakes get high (as with Rangda) the woman disappears. Her stories are, by a sexual division of labour, 'lightweight'. When a woman rises to tragic dimensions she has become a man.[6]

Contemporary Rethinking

We live in a time when male and female Southeast Asian artists question traditional narratives.[7] I will choose two examples from Bali where the *calonarang* narrative has been addressed in new narratives. One I will call surrogacy, since the role of the Rangda has been danced not by a local but a foreigner. The other form I will call re-envisioning, where the character has been borrowed from the tradition but the interpretation has changed. In the first instance, a troupe under Luh Nyi

Desak Nyoman Suwarti, a noted artist, created a version of *calonarang* in the early 2000s. To avoid problems that might be inherent in the full normative trance dance version where *kris* dancers stab themselves and often attack Rangda, measures were taken. Long-time Balinese resident and American dancer-scholar Rucina Ballinger (who married into a princely family in Peliatan, Bali) danced the Rangda role with a mostly Balinese cast. Western women are of course already considered masculine in their behaviours and given latitude by locals beyond Balinese women. This *calongang* was a step, but, perhaps a larger Western woman dancing Rangda, in the eyes of the Balinese audience, is not quite the same as an Indonesian woman attempting the role. A foreigner is already half a man.

Writer-theatre artist Cok Sawitri and choreographer Bulantrisna Djelantik moved the goal posts further. Cok Sawitri in her novel (2007) and solo women performances (Diamond, 2012: 108–11) envisioned Calonarang as a powerful witch, but one who is performing white, not traditional black, magic. Rangda's kingdom, in Cok Sawitri's version, is a Shangri La where liberty, equality and justice are universal. The patriarchy that surrounds her therefore demands the destruction of this powerful woman who poses a threat to the 'male' Darwinian world. Cok Sawitri performed this as a set of one-woman modern drama performance poetry pieces *Pembelaan Dirah* (In Defence of Dirah [Rangda's kingdom], 1990), *Namaku Dirah* (My name is Dirah, 1992), *Kawean* (Clearly Seen, 1999) and *Badan Bahagia* (Joyful Body, 2004) and she has inspired others to create multiperson performances that reinterpret the Rangda legend. Cok Sawitri's pieces simultaneously critiqued the political situation of the late Suharto era and the government's suppression of Megawati Sukarnoputri's party. Megawati would eventually become the first woman president of the country. Cok Sawitri's status as a Balinese woman of noble blood means she has the status and power to take on this potent character in readings and performance art. Her treatment removed the piece from its normal context. The performance was not at a death temple or in the graveyard. There is no consecrated mask endowed with *taksu* (divine energy/power) which is usually a hallmark of a Rangda mask. No one went into trance. The performance is in the safe confines of a contemporary secular theatre and the event not a reaction to a current local problem. Instead the interpretation is a contemporary writer-performer calling out the sexism she sees in the story and resultant impacts on female identity. Inspired by Cok Sawitri's interpretations, Bulantrisna Djelantik, another member of the Balinese royalty, created a dance drama in the Indonesian capital in 2014; the dancers were young urban Indonesians of Balinese and mixed Indonesian ethnicity, presenting a concert. Rangda, in this dance interpretation, *Alkisah: Satua Calon Arang* (IndonesiaKaya, 2017), was not the entranced male, jumping jerkily or threatening. There was none of the flailing and young males trying to stab themselves with knives. However, there was a new character dancing: an older woman versed in Siva-based tantric thought. In the experiments of Cok Sawitri and Bulantrisna Jelantik and the younger artists they inspire, we see an attempt to push out the parameters of the female character and enlarge her story.

Discussion Questions

1. What is the movement style of female characters?
2. How does this style reflect the narrative of gender of women in Indonesia?
3. What is the role of improvisation in the creation of the narrative? How can it influence the structure of gender performances?
4. Are there new performances that are creating a different narrative? How does this influence the physical gestures of the character?

Websites

The story of the Ramayana:
   https://www.maxwell.syr.edu/moynihan/sac/The_Ramayana_A_Telling_Of_the_Ancient_Indian_Epic/
There are many examples of the refined female dancing on YouTube. Here is one of a Legong at Ubud Water Palace:
   https://video.search.yahoo.com/search/video?fr=mcafee&p=legong+dance#id=6&vid=68e5a3f74a2ce4e62caba1220e8d5f94&action=click
The trance dance is a portion of the Rangda and Barong performance. The evil witch Rangda destroys the followers of the good Barong but they are revived

by Barong and in a trance turn the knives on themselves to ward off any evil left by Rangda: https://video.search.yahoo.com/search/video?fr=mcafee&p=rangda+and+barong#id=1&vid=b6f175fdc4536fdcccdb51604ad19fe2&action=click

Notes

1. See Soedarsono 1990, p. 1ff., Dhaninivat (1975), Sumandhi (1979). Puppetry and masking are linked arts in the region. Due to lack of space, I will not in this chapter delve in detail into Laos, Burma, which may have analogous forms, nor Vietnam or the Philippines, which have different trajectories, or the many archipelagic societies, which without such developed hierarchies lacked court theatre forms. My comments work best for countries where Indian culture had some impact on indigenous patterns, creating highly stratified societies where cults of the monarch as a sacred ruler developed.
2. See Holt's descriptions of dance drama in the central Javanese courts in the period leading us to World War II (1967: 155–66) as well as Soedarsono (1990: 90–108). See Rutnin (1993) and Bandem and deBoer (1981: 29–49) on *gambuh* court form telling *Panji* stories; 65–75 on *wayang wong* mask genre telling Ramayana; and 131–43 on *calonarang*, which tells of a widow-witch of East Java, which is discussed later in the Bandem and deBoer (1981) article.
3. Due to space limitations, this discussion will focus on these court forms – for some discussion of courtesan traditions (*ronggeng* in the Indo-Malay region) see Foley (2015).
4. See Robson (1996: 40) who traces borrowing to the Malay region of Southern Thailand (Patani) and notes the *Dalang* (an earlier version of the Panji story) is credited to Kuntol and Mongkut, two daughters of King Bokomakos (1732–58) who reportedly heard the tale from their Malay maids (p. 44).
5. Piayura (2013) notes the male hero in Thai classical literature has characteristics that anticipate the modern metrosexual ideal.
6. I acknowledge that there are roles such as beautiful ladies – Panji's mother, for example, orders Panji's commoner wife Angraeni killed; Sapakanaka of course pursues Rama and Laksmana; and Malay and Thai stories often have ogresses who conceive a love for the hero and may disguise themselves as the truly refined that disguise themselves as queens. My point is such scenes/characters are de-emphasized or often played by males.

7. For Thai examples see Diamond (2012: 37–40) who discusses some reinterpretation of traditional characters by contemporary Thai choreographers, such as Pornrat Damrhung and Pinchet Kluncheun's *Overcoming Fire* (Lui Fai, 2000).

Works Cited and Resource Materials

Artho, S. (2013) Amazing Balinese Dance – Tari Panji Semirang, https://www.youtube.com/watch?v=FEKlHny7cu4, accessed 6 February 2018.
Bandem, I. M. and F. deBoer (1981) *Kaja and Kelod: Balinese Dance in Transition* (Kuala Lumpur: Oxford University Press).
Bateson, G. and M. Mead (1951) Trance and Dance in Bali, https://www.youtube.com/watch?v=Z8YC0dnj4Jw, accessed 6 February 2018.
Cherries01 (2011) Royal MTV DVD #04 – Robam Monimakala, https://www.youtube.com/watch?v=y5osB90S13I, accessed 6 February 2018.
Dhaninivat, H. H. [Prince] (1975) Shadow Play as a Possible Origin of the Masked Play, in Mattani Rutnin (Ed.) *Siamese Theatre: Collection of Reprints from the Siam Society* (Bangkok: Siam Society) pp. 117–20.
Diamond, C. (2012) *Communities of the Imagination: Contemporary Southeast Asian Theatres* (Honolulu: University of Hawaii Press).
Foley, K. (1982a) Of *Dalang* and *Dukun* – Spirits and Men: Curing and Performance in the *Wayang* of West Java, *Asian Theatre Journal*, 1(1), pp. 52–75.
_____. (1982b) Dancer and the Danced: Trance Dance and Theatrical Performance in West Java, *Asian Theatre Journal*, 2(1), pp. 28–49.
_____. (1989) Of Gender and Dance in Southeast Asia: From Goddess to Go-Go Girl, *Progress and Possibilities: CORD 20th Anniversary*, pp. 387–405.
_____. (2015) The *Ronggeng*, the *Wayang*, the *Wali*, and Islam: Female or Transvestite Male Dancers-Singers-Performers and Evolving Islam in West Java, *Women in Asian Theatre* [special issue], *Asian Theatre Journal*, 32(2), pp. 356–87.
Geertz, C. (1980) *Negara: The Theatre State in 19th Century Bali* (Princeton: Princeton University Press).
Giri Komara (2015) *Rama Shinta Kisah Epic Ramayana* (1) (Rama and Sita in the Epic Story of the Ramayana) [SMKI 10 Bandung], https://www.youtube.com/watch?v=OYiYtUnxfL4&t=628s, accessed 6 February 2017.
Holt, C. (1967 *Art in Indonesia: Continuities and Change* (Ithaca, NY: Cornell University Press).

IndonesiaKaya (2017) *Alkisah: Calon Arang*, https://www.youtube.com/watch?v=WJixXShdbpA&t=4s, accessed 10 February 2018.

Indrawan Nur Cahyono [Fakultas Bahasa dan Seni UNNES] (2012) Tari Kandagan Video Angkatan Seni Tari fbs UNNES 2012, https://www.youtube.com/watch?v=MckKcZAOtAg, accessed 6 February 2018.

Jogja Budaya TV (2016) *Tari Langendriyan, Lakon: Menakjinggo Leno Dari Pura Mangkunegaran Surakarta* 1 (Langendryan Dance, Story: Menakjinggo Leno from the Mankunegaran Palace, Surakarta 1), https://www.youtube.com/watch?v=HcioscW6RUk, accessed 6 February 2018.

Kam, G. (1987) *Wayang Wong* in the Court of Yogyakarta: The Enduring Significance of Javanese Dance Drama, *Asian Theatre Journal*, 4(1), pp. 29–51.

Kuman, E. (2016) *Tari Wayang Srikandi vs Mustakaweni ISBI Bandung* (Wayang Dance Srikandi vs Mustakaweni ISBI Bandung), https://www.youtube.com/watch?v=EgCLBtrZs5c, accessed 6 February 2018.

On the Spot – Misteri Tarian Magis Sintren [89939893116992b] (2016), https://www.youtube.com/watch?v=gD0s2VkNhqk, accessed 6 February 2018.

Piayura, P. (2013) Metrosexual Men in Thai Classical Literature, *International Journal of Social Sciences and Humanity*, 3(3), pp. 218–21, http://www.ijssh.org/papers/231-CH030.pdf, accessed 11 September 2017.

Putra, E. (2017) Legong Keraton, Sekha Gandrung Monang Maning, https://www.youtube.com/watch?v=sdhL40WHGBM, accessed 6 February 2018.

Robson, S. (1996) Panji and Inao: Questions of Cultural and Textual History, *Journal of the Siam Society*, 84(2), pp. 39–53.

Rutnin, M. (1993) *Dance, Drama, Theatre in Thailand: The Process of Development and Modernization* (Chaing Mai: Silkworm).

Sawitri, C. (2007) *Widow of Jiah: A Historical Legend*. Trans. S. Boentaran (Jakarta: Gramedia Pustaka Utama).

Soedarsono, R. M. (1990) *Wayang Wong* (Yogyakarta: Gajah Mada University).

Spacoverman (2014) Kuda Kepang – Spellbinding, https://www.youtube.com/watch?v=TwqGp-cmf9I, accessed 10 February 2018.

Stutterheim, W. F. (1956) A Thousand Years Old Profession in the Princely Courts on Java, *Studies in Indonesian Archeology*, pp. 91–103, https://link.springer.com/chapter/10.1007/978-94-017-5987-8_3, accessed 15 September 2017 (The Hague: Martinus Nijhoff).

Sumandhi, I. N. (1979) *A Performance of Wayang Kulit Calonarang* (*A Genre of Balinese Shadow Puppet Theater*) (Middletown, CT: Wesleyan University Press).

Supodo, B. (2016) Tari Topeng Panji Sutra Winangun, https://www.youtube.com/watch?v=L4myDS5V8dM, accessed 6 February 2018.

Tholib, E. (2016) *Diva Seni Pencak Silat Pusaka Mande Muda* (Master of the Art of *Pencak Silat* in the Tradition of Mande Muda), https://www.youtube.com/watch?v=2GhqqIwoVKQ, accessed 6 February 2018.

Tonnum53 (2011) Lakhon Nai Thai Drama Inao Lanangjintala Thai Classical Dance 2, https://www.youtube.com/watch?v=jVl8ilPpfZ0, accessed 6 February 2018.

5

Decolonizing Techno-Art

Praba Pilar

Introduction

Bodies tell stories. Our bodies, which may feel so personal and private to us, exist inside an impersonally established geo-political and social world that produces very different power relations for them.[1] While still in the womb, bodies are inscribed by racism, historical trauma and gender trouble.[2] Once out of the womb, they are further marked by racism; cultural and personal trauma; historical erasure or privilege; experiences of wealth, poverty or degradation; communal and familial memories; religious and spiritual attitudes and practices; multitudes of societal conflicts around gender, identity, sexual preference; and more. For this reason, performance artists work with our own bodies as our material: we transcribe, translate, interpret and relate the narrative texts the world inscribes on our bodies.

For most of my adult life, I have focused my art practice on emerging technologies out of a deep curiosity about the massive impacts information and life science technologies are bringing to our planet. I've engaged in substantial research, and over the years have learned of extremely damaging, dangerous and toxic effects. I have turned this into numerous performance and interdisciplinary projects. I have been, and remain, immersed in the techno-art world.

My perspectives on techno-art were shifted by a relocation that deepened my commitment to my own decolonizing process. In 2013, I moved to the lands of the Cree, Ojibway, Oji-Cree, Dakota, Dene, Inuit and

Métis in Manitoba, Canada. This region is often called the Indigenous heart of the continent. I had to listen and give and ask and hear and let what I thought I knew, about myself and my origin, be destabilized. I had to deepen my understanding of coloniality, modernity and capitalism, and of what a process of decolonizing is over a lifetime. This process spread from my body, to my personal life, to my political engagements, to my practice, and into my techno-art.

In this chapter, I will relate some of the ways my Colombian body's narratives have been written by colonialism, displacement and migration. Paradoxically, these were carved on my flesh as much during my life as hundreds of years before I was born and are not uncommon to Latin American mestizas. Colonialism in the Americas is not the distant past, it is a constant violent collision that transcends linearity. Many people in North America imagine colonialism and slavery happened long ago, and that our societies have progressed beyond State-sponsored murder and land dispossession through treaties, reservations and agreements. For Indigenous bodies of our hemisphere, and for the descendants of African bodies trafficked to and enslaved on our hemisphere, colonialism is present/past lived experience. But we are the descendants of bodies in resistance, and colonialism does not have to be our futurity.

My body has been haunted by colonial violence and hatred from a very young age. My early childhood was in part shaped by my father's nightly ritual of yelling and hurling insults at my mother over our dinner table: 'Yo te rescate. Tu no eres nada. Tu no eres nadie. Tu no eres mas que una India cualquiera (I rescued you. You are nothing. You are no one. You are nothing more than an ordinary Indian)!' He never rescued her; if anything she rescued him and kept him, and us, alive. She was a mestiza Colombian, a category defined at that time as a mixed-race person of Indigenous and European heritage. My father was Argentinian-Italian.

As her daughter, I experienced his nightly racialized attacks as both personal and political. We were her children, also mestizos, also 'Indios cualquieros'. While I understood that in his eyes there was something uncivilized and dirty about her, my sister, brother and I had come from her body. As I saw these same racialized attacks in the public sphere, I decided my mestizaje would embrace my Indigenous roots.

I am a performance artist who asks audiences to question their frames of reference. My experiences living in Manitoba challenged me to unravel my own. I had to ask myself if my Colombian mestiza identity was an accommodation to the hemispheric erasure of Indigeneity, to re-examine the intersections of Colombian criollos, State policies of blanqueamiento (which translates to English as 'becoming white'), and to question how my body is constituted as mestiza.

Incubation

My Colombian mother and Argentinian-Italian father met at work in Bogota, Colombia, in 1958. They were married six months later. My mother came from a very rigid Catholic family, and her marriage was in some ways arranged – my father did not propose to her, but to her parents. She was 27, her fiancé of ten years had recently died of a brain aneurism, and her parents were more than anything relieved that if she married my father, she would not be an 'old barren maid'. My mother was an early feminist, she had studied journalism and was working as a translator. However, in that era, a feminist did not win battles with Catholic parents, and her fate was out of her hands. My father was a computer salesman, much older than her. A complex man, he loved philosophy, literature, opera and war. He was an incredible charmer in public, able to relate stories in six different languages at will. In private, he was violent, unpredictable and seething with uncontrollable rage. She never had a chance to see this private side of him in their brief and chaperoned courtship. They had never been alone.

Colombia was experiencing spasmodic political violence when they married, and they began to migrate around the Americas. After my birth, we went from Colombia to Argentina, back to Colombia, then to Venezuela, back to Colombia, then to Mexico City, to Monterrey, to Nuevo Laredo, and then into the United States. My older sister recounted that we had already lived in twenty-one different locations by the time she was 18 years old. She never moved again. These migrations isolated my family from extended family, lasting friendships and community.

Our home was a racialized battleground. My father claimed he was superior to all of us, as he was from the advanced European civilizations, the Greek and Roman Empires, of a higher intelligence that had no commonality with the Indigenous Americas. He saw the Americas as a land to be civilized, a view shared among many Italian Argentines in that era.

These strangely personalized colonialist battles moved with us wherever we lived. He used genetics to denigrate my mother as inferior. If she drank three glasses of wine, she was a drunk Indian. If she drank none, she was uncultured. If she wore her long black hair down, she was a backwards Indian. If she wore it up, she was a fraud. The attacks were constant and grotesque and pushed my mother further and further into acculturation as a blank spot from no map. No country, no background, no affiliation.

Colourism made it worse. My father and mother were both fair skinned, as was my sister. My brother and I, on the other hand, were darker. We were the visibly repellent Indios of the family, constantly told not to go in the sun, and put in long-sleeved shirts and long pants if we were going outdoors. We tore off these ridiculous garments and spent hours outside. My brother tattooed himself – *Indio Chibcha*. I grew my black hair long and braided it, and clothed myself in what Indigenous textiles I could find, even if they were Mayan. We rejected my father's racist assaults.

I wanted to know where we were from, seeking out family memories, extended family members, people, books, stories and travel. I taught myself to carefully navigate entangled stories. Some absurdly combined blanqueamiento/European ancestry with a pride of not being Gringos, or European, or Indigenous, but mestizos, as if mestizos are not Indigenous. I learned to read between lines, finding Indigenous knowing and cosmovisions outside what I saw as self-rejection and internalized racism.

I rejected the Catholic Church, learned about Indigenous spirituality, history, arts and humour, rejected my father, and legally removed his last name from my identity. This personalized familial colonialist violence was replicated publicly in the different countries and cities I've lived in, one time almost leaving me dead. On a late-night walk down a street in Santa Fe, New Mexico, in my early twenties, a white man in a pick-up truck tried to run me over yelling out the window that he was going to kill me for being an Indian. He thought I was from a local tribe. He was relentless and pursued me as I ran for many street blocks, crossing parking areas, twisting around and around the pumps of a gasoline station, racing across empty lanes, and came within millimetres of killing me.

Ripening

I've lived recurring periods in Colombia, Mexico and the United States, and periods in Argentina, Venezuela, Greece, Spain, India and Canada. Constant migration is my home state. In 2009, I fell in love with a Canadian writer I met at the Bogota, Colombia, *Encuentro* of the *Hemispheric Institute for Performance and Politics in the Americas*. I began to visit her in Winnipeg, Canada; we married, and I subsequently moved there to live with her in 2013.

Winnipeg has the largest urban Indigenous population in Canada, of Cree, Ojibway, Oji-Cree, Dakota, Dene, Inuit and Métis nations. I was generously welcomed and embraced by Indigenous artists, poets, leaders and new friends in Manitoba and the Prairies. With great excitement and interest, I went to numerous exhibitions, performances, readings, discussions, teach-ins and round dances hosted by Indigenous arts spaces and artists. I visited Urban Shaman Contemporary Aboriginal Arts Gallery and saw artworks and performances by Rebecca Belmore and Skeena Reece. I went to Neechi Commons Gallery for exhibitions and poetry readings by Rosanna Deerchild, Katherena Vermette and the Aboriginal Writers Collective of Manitoba. I immersed myself in the presentations, talks, writings and work of Indigenous scholars that included Alex Wilson, Bonita Lawrence, Glen Coulthard, Leanne Simpson, activist Michael Redhead Champagne, and non-Indigenous Native Studies scholar Peter Kulchyski. I became active in the round dances and actions of Idle No More.

I would be asked details about my mestizaje. 'Yes, you are a mestiza, but what are your Indigenous roots? What is your tribal nation or affiliation, your relationship to your land? What are your practices? Who are your relations?' My evasive responses as an urban Colombian mestiza from the capital city of Bogota led to more questions. Though genuinely kind hearted and welcoming, it was unsettling and acutely uncomfortable. It reopened old wounds.

I realized I had more work to do interrogating my mestizaje. My extended family in Colombia is geographically dispersed: we are mestizos, Afro-Colombian, Indigenous and European. We may be rooted in communities beyond these identities, as there have been large Arabic and Asian migrations to our region. However, that has never been part of my extended family lore.

I began a dialogue with other Indigenous bodies in the larger body of the Americas. This dialogue crossed the spectrum of my personal and familial identity, of the brutalizing and politicized enactments of mestizaje, of the historical fictions of our nation/states, of our dispossession, trauma and erasure, of our resistance, survival and persistence. I did not confront, explain or ask questions of Canadian settler culture.

In the midst of this process, I was approached by Urban Shaman Contemporary Aboriginal Arts Gallery, in Winnipeg, to collaborate with performance artist Emilio Rojas and artist Luna on a performance and installation on mestizaje. This was perfect timing. The project was to debut with a performance in late January of 2014, and a month-long installation of artefacts. Unfortunately, Rojas had scheduling conflicts and was ultimately not able to participate.

Luna is an Indigenous/mestiza/Chilean artist based in Winnipeg whose family had to leave Chile after the violent military coup of 1973. They migrated first to Argentina, and after a few years were granted legal status in Winnipeg. We shared the experience of being in families forced to leave our countries to escape brutal violence provoked and supported by foreign intervention. We also shared the experience of being raised with the erasure of Indigeneity through mestiza identities.

We began a series of exploratory meetings to share similarities and differences as mestizas from very different locations in South America – I from the tropical north, the Caribbean Sea, the Pacific, the Andes and the Amazon; she from the Southern Cone, the Atacama Desert, the Andes, Antarctica and Easter Island. We challenged ourselves to recuperate memories, to face our painful dispossession and the violence of our displacement, to excavate our Indigenous pasts. We challenged ourselves to no longer see ourselves as migrants or immigrants or even refugees, but as exiles in Canada. We interrogated ourselves on how we personally benefitted from colonizing settler culture in Canada, and how our presence displaced sovereign Indigenous nations and people.

We touched our hair, our skin, our faces, our ears and verbalized the criticisms, the warnings and the blanqueamiento imposed by our extended families, which I recorded:

> Don't go outside, you'll get browner; stay out of the sun, it will turn your skin dark; you look dirty, you are too dark; do not braid your hair; don't be dirty, don't be an Indian, don't look like an Indian; cut that hair; why are you not wearing make-up? We need to look modern, don't be so Indian; Christ died for you, you owe him better than to be an Indian; I'm doing this to save you.

Through this process, we created a performance and installation titled *Dirty Cochinas of the AMERICAS* [Dirty Pigs of the Americas]. The evening-length performance had three distinct phases. The first phase was a fifteen-minute piece titled *Mestizas*. The second phase was two individual performances of ten minutes – mine was a live 'notecard confessional' on the reasons my family left Colombia and why I was in Canada;[3] Luna's was on Chilean exile. The third phase was on the hidden violence underlying the production and transport of tropical fruits from Latin America to Winnipeg. I will describe the first phase of the performance, *Mestizas*, here.

As can be seen in Figure 5.1, we set up two elevated platforms in the centre of the space. Our platforms were covered with street clothes, Catholic crosses, holy water vessels, lipstick, hair brushes, proper church outfits, woven bags and the clothing of Indigenous people from our regions. I created a fifteen-minute audio track for this section, mixing our own voices with highly distorted and modified audio samples from *Oye Mujer* by Los Aterciopelados, *Matando Gueros* by Brujeria, *Gracias a La Vida* sung by Chavela Vargas, film excerpts, other sound elements and loud pig squeals.

We began the performance standing still on our platforms, draped in our national flags, looking straight ahead as the audio track began. We began moving very slowly, dropping our national flags, wearing only a bra and underwear underneath. We slowly rotated, by putting on, then taking off, three different looks/identities – our street wear, our Catholic wear, and our Indigenous wear. We looked at the audience to make sure each image was registering clearly.

After four minutes, the audio accelerated, and we began rotating through these three looks more quickly, and with less accuracy, mixing elements, increasingly agitated and frantic. After four minutes, the audio again accelerated, and we frantically whipped the clothes on and off, putting them on wrong, mixing them up, pant legs on arms, shirts on heads, slipping, falling, out of breath, agitated, losing all integrity to the identities, and fell to our hands and knees, smashing our national flags into our bodies and faces, crawling over the platform, grunting along with the audio as pigs. At the fourteen-and-a-half-minute mark, the audio went silent and we froze. The audience was completely silent. After one minute, the audio returned with an extremely distorted version of Chavela Vargas singing *Gracias a La Vida*. We moved off the platforms, draping our national flags over them. This ended the *Mestizas* phase of the performance.

Figure 5.1 Performance still of *Dirty Cochinas of the AMERICAS*. Left, Praba Pilar, right, Luna. At Urban Shaman Contemporary Aboriginal Arts Gallery, Winnipeg
Photographer: Karen Asher, 2016

Our artists' statement articulated some of the factors we found most pressing:

> In this work, we share our hemispheric struggle: with our nations, states, histories of colonization, immediate and extended families and cultures, our bodies, our migration, as Mestizas – neither Indigenous, nor European – heirs to nothing, we are the Dirty, The Cochinas, we are the AMERICAS.

The response to this performance was overwhelming. As I looked at the audience, I could see some audience members crying, others visibly upset and others bewildered. Numerous Indigenous women approached me afterwards with very supportive feedback, telling me, 'you were talking to me – you made physical how complex and painful our identities are'. One audience member later emailed me that they connected to the performance as fierce and creative, while disruptive and freeing: 'Thoughtful, creative, fierce, and dignified all at the same time, as if the space/time of the present was disrupted to reveal a much deeper opening, without borders. For a moment in there, I felt the rush of unfettered wind' (Pilar, 2014). Within a week, three Indigenous women artists approached me to ask if I would mentor them in their performance practice. I had not anticipated how my own act of countering a disavowal that removes me from the embodied histories of our hemisphere would connect to Indigenous women of the Prairies.

In Latin America, the concepts of mestizaje, de-Indigenizing and re-Indigenizing are in constant motion. We have been in resistance for 500 years to murderous Spanish colonization, land theft and slavery; had violent independence movements and periods of identitarian nation building; been victims of foreign intervention from the United States and mining corporations from Canada; experienced very large migrations from other regions; and endured racial discrimination, urbanization, military dictatorships and civil war. Political, social and economic structures that reify colonial violence remain in place to this day.

Colombian scholars Chaves and Zambrano trace many of the conflicted meanings of mestizaje, from the racialized hierarchies of blanqueamiento through the contemporary contestation of these categories. They list the reasons for de-Indigenization as 'land-loss, access to rural education, proximity to urban centres, wage labour, and racial discrimination' (Zambrano and Chaves, 2006: 10). They describe contemporary mestizaje in Colombia as a 'mosaic inscribed in the bodies of individuals that permits simultaneous and subsequent affiliations with different groups … multiple crossovers and double or even triple identifications' (Zambrano and Chaves, 2006: 7).

I will briefly review some elements impacting Indigenous identity in Colombia. In 1991, the Colombian constitution was rewritten, and in part promised to significantly alter material conditions for Indigenous and Afro-Colombian people. New rights to territory, education, legislation, language, health care and medical practice were to be granted to those who could attain ethnic recognition. Very strict diacritics were established to regulate identity, often drawing on anthropology texts, and recognition was policed by the State. Only 2 per cent of the Colombian population is recognized as Indigenous. At the same time, material resources in the country remained scarce (Zambrano and Chaves, 2006: 8–9).

This rewriting of the Colombian constitution in 1991 happened within the context of decades of civil war. While some researchers date the beginning of the Colombian civil war to 1964, others to 1948, and others to much earlier, the vicious brutality of this ongoing war is undisputed. The Colombian State, paramilitaries and armed guerrillas are documented as perpetrating 'selective assassinations, torture, extrajudicial executions, forced disappearances, planting anti-personnel mines, bombings, forced displacement, kidnapping, extortion, illicit conscription, massacres, land dispossession, and sexual assault' (Leongómez, 2015: 74). The impact and losses for Colombian people have been profound. Colombia's current population is 49 million (UN Department of Economic and Social Affairs, Population Division, 2017: 18) and over the course of the war, at least 6 million people were forcibly displaced, though that figure is contested as a gross undercount. At least 1 million non-combatants have been killed in the conflict. Colombia ranks second in the world in internally displaced people, and eighth in the world for refugees who have emigrated (Leongómez, 2015: 76).[4]

The civil war, and extreme income and land inequality, has led to conflicts between Indigenous leaders and mestizos over ethnic recognition. Resources remain so scarce that the dilution of fundamental rights for Indigenous communities who have attained them may lead to their death.

Beginning Again – Impact on My Work

After the performance and installation of *Dirty Cochinas of the AMERICAS*, I extended my work into a project focused on reclaiming mapping as a practice of asserting agency, titled *Mapping Myself: Decolonizing Art Practices*. Developed with curator Becca Taylor and Urban Shaman Contemporary Aboriginal Arts Gallery, I worked with Indigenous youth in the Transitional School of the Ndinawe Youth Resource Center on recuperating their identities, connections, strength, persistence and agency. This six-month project resulted in a month-long exhibition of their artworks at Urban Shaman Contemporary Aboriginal Arts Gallery that challenged prevalent stereotypes about urban Indigenous youth. I subsequently developed a video installation of Indigenous voices in resistance from all over the Americas. This piece, titled *Movidas of the Zero Point*, shared cosmologies, challenges and resistance to present-day colonialism from Chile to Canada. While working on these projects, I began to further understand and articulate contemporary techno-culture as a brutal intensification and extension of colonial logics, particularly around extraction. This transformed my techno-art into a decolonizing practice.

When I began investigating the proliferation and impact of emerging technologies in the mid-1990s, I attended numerous conferences, presentations, informal talks and formal events in Silicon Valley. I quickly realized that African Americans, other Afro-descendants, Latinas, Indigenous people and women were not in the room. We were not invited to the dialogue, we were erased. The model human image that the technology sector was oriented to was clearly based on the desires of a middle-class white male.[5] This left a lot of the peopled world out of the aims, intent, design, practices, discourses and creation of a techno-sphere. I began a body of artworks critical of racialization, invisibilization, erasures and the purposive absence of women in the techno-sphere. Begun in 1998, these multi-disciplinary projects have included *The Hexterminators: Super Heroes of the Biozoid Age*, an art-activist collective working to block seed sterilizing technology; *Los Cybrids: La Raza Techno-Critica*, a collaboration with John Jota Leaños and Rene Garcia unpacking the mythologies underlying globalized capitalism in the cyberworld; *Computers Are A Girl's Best Friend*, a solo project on the toxic effects of electronic manufacturing and recycling, and online sex trafficking; the *Church of Nano Bio Info Cogno*, a church satirizing messianic salvation narratives in the Silicon Valley technology world; and *BOT I*, which looked at how emerging technologies keep drawing us in, so that many of us live in a love/hate relationship with our gadgets. My doctoral studies extended this research and embodied practice. My dissertation, *Latin@s Byte Back: Contestational Performance in the Techno-Sphere*, focused on Latina/o/x performance artists who resist and contest negative aspects of the techno-world. I refocused my practice on two new frameworks informed by decolonizing perspectives, Infectious Refusal and Disruptive Poesis.

While I had always touched on coloniality in my work, living in the Prairies led me to make much more direct linkages in my subsequent techno-art projects. In *Enigma Symbiotica*,[6] published in 2016, I created a video and text examining the relationships between technology and coloniality. This included the diagram in Figure 5.2. The core of my current

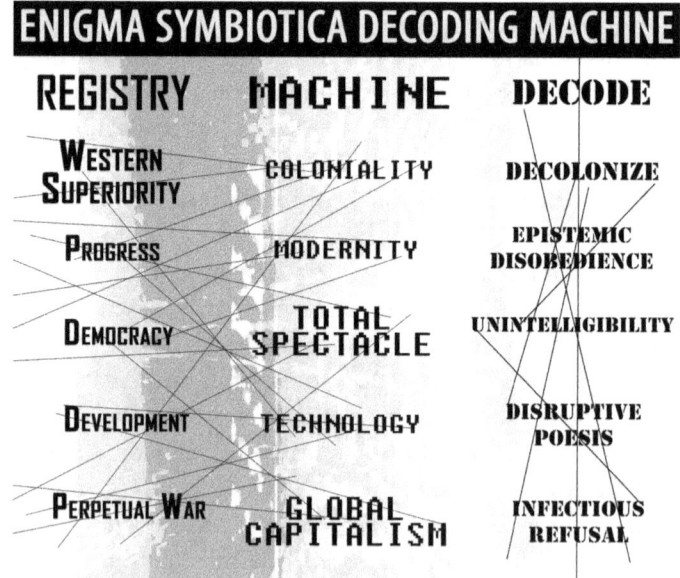

Figure 5.2 Enigma Symbiotica Decoding Machine
Praba Pilar, author archive, 2016

techno-art project, the *NO!!!BOT*, is on resistance to the militarization of human bodies to intensify resource extraction.

Decolonizing critiques and practices have grown prolifically over the last decade, and the definition varies among scholars, activists and geographic areas. A definition that grounds decolonizing work in Indigenous ways of being was shared in the editorial of the first issue of *Decolonization: Indigeneity, Education & Society*:

> The decolonizing project seeks to reimagine and rearticulate power, change, and knowledge through a multiplicity of epistemologies, ontologies and axiologies. Decolonization cannot take place without contestation. It must necessarily push back against the colonial relations of power that threaten Indigenous ways of being.
>
> (Sium et al., 2012: III)

In that same issue, Tuck and Yang define decolonizing always in terms of Indigenous sovereignty and futurity: 'Decolonizing the Americas means all land is repatriated and all settlers become landless' (Tuck and Yang, 2012: 27). Tuck and Yang challenge the use of the term 'decolonizing' as a metaphor for social justice work, warning that this dilutes and unmoors it from Indigenous futurity and instead performs settler moves to innocence.

Conclusion

In my own decolonizing practice and workshops that I lead, I continue to interrogate categories, erasures and invisibilization. I focus on maintaining an awareness of my own, and others', relations to coloniality in the Americas. I ask participants to articulate their presence on the land they are standing on through the processes of colonization. I am committed to interrogating the place of mestizas within critiques of settler colonialism, of displaced Indigenous bodies forced out of our land in the Americas by globalized corporations, of remembering and articulating that the business owners, shareholders, citizens and states of settler cultures benefit vastly from extracting our resources at the cost of our lives. I ask myself, am I an immigrant, a migrant, a refugee, an exile? Displacing others by my presence? Am I Indigenous? Am I Mestiza? I reach for healing of historical trauma and strengthen agency by refusing historic and present-day racist mythologies. I reclaim persistence and endurance by working with Indigenous organizations in the Americas for a futurity not predicated on colonial logics, but on decolonizing ones.

Discussion Questions

1. What narrative texts are inscribed on your body? How would you approach excavating and recuperating these stories? How would you transcribe and relate them?
2. What processes in history have led you to live on the land you are on right now? How do those relate to colonization?
3. How would you broaden your experiences and knowledge to fully include new knowledge you are gaining?

Website

This website contains information on Praba Pilar's decolonizing project and other projects that take place at the intersection of identity, technology and performance:
https://www.prabapilar.com/bio-1/

Notes

1. For a discussion on how power relations are always already established, please see Judith Butler, *The Psychic Life of Power: Theories in Subjection* (Stanford University Press: 1997).
2. For an exploration of the racialization and gendering of bodies, please see Janell Hobson, *Body as Evidence: Mediating Race, Globalizing Gender*.
3. Titled 'my anacondacolombia don't: a notecard confessional', available at https://youtu.be/iG5HhP2zR3M, accessed September 2016.
4. This and all subsequent translations from Spanish by Praba Pilar.

5. I have written about racialization in the techno-sphere in Praise the Lord & Pass the Critical Theory: An Interview with Praba Pilar of the Church of Nano Bio Info Cogno, *H+ Magazine*, R. U. Sirius, 2011; Ruptures in Technoculture: Technophilic Society and Interventionist Performance, *WEAD Magazine*, Issue 4: No Time For Complacency; and BOT I, *Lateral Journal of the Cultural Studies Association*, Spring 2013. Thread: In Search of Digital Feminisms.
6. Enigma Symbiotica is available through the Traversing Technologies issue of *The Scholar & Feminist Online*, http://sfonline.barnard.edu/traversing-technologies/praba-pilar-enigma-symbiotica/, accessed October 2016.

Works Cited and Resource Material

Butler, J. (1997) *The Psychic Life of Power: Theories in Subjection* (Redwood City, CA: Stanford University Press).
Hobson, J. (2012) *Body as Evidence: Mediating Race, Globalizing Gender* (Albany, NY: SUNY Press).
Leongómez, E. P. (2015) Una lectura múltiple y pluralista de la historia. Comisión de Historia del Conflicto y sus Víctimas, Contribución al Entendimiento del Conflicto Armado en Colombia, *Academia Libre*, 12, pp. 151–213.
Mignolo, W. (2011) *The Darker Side of Western Modernity: Global Futures, Decolonial Options* (Durham, NC: Duke University Press).
Pilar, P. (2012) Ruptures in Technoculture: Technophilic Society and Interventionist Performance, *WEAD Magazine*, Issue 4: No Time For Complacency.
_____. (2013) BOT I, *Lateral Journal of the Cultural Studies Association*, Spring. Thread: In Search of Digital Feminisms, K. Behar and S. Ruzanka (Eds).
_____. (2014) Personal Communication via Email, Personal Archive.
_____. (2017) Situating the Web of the Necro-Techno Complex: The Church of Nano Bio Info Cogno, *Performance, Religion and Spirituality*, 1(2), pp. 2–10.
Sirius, R. U. and P. Pilar (2011) Praise the Lord & Pass the Critical Theory: An Interview with Praba Pilar of the Church of Nano Bio Info Cogno, *H+ Magazine*, http://hplusmagazine.com/2011/03/15/praise-the-lord-pass-the-critical-theory-an-interview-with-praba-pilar-of-the-church-of-nano-bio-info-cogno/, accessed 3 July 2018.

Sium, A., C. Desai and E. Ritskes (2012) Towards the 'Tangible Unknown': Decolonization and the Indigenous Future, *Decolonization: Indigeneity, Education & Society*, 1(1), pp. I–XIII.

TallBear, K. (2013) *Native American DNA: Tribal Belonging and the False Promise of Genetic Science* (Minneapolis: University of Minnesota Press).

Tuck, E. and K. W. Yang (2012) Decolonization Is Not A Metaphor, *Decolonization: Indigeneity, Education & Society*, 1(1), pp. 1–40.

United Nations Department of Economic and Social Affairs, Population Division (2017) World Population Prospects: The 2017 Revision, Key Findings and Advance Tables, Working Paper No. ESA/P/WP/248.

Zambrano, M. (2004) Memoria y Olvido en la Presencia y Ausencia de Indígenas en Santafé y Bogotá, *Desde el Jardín de Freud – Revista de Psicoanálisis* (Universidad Nacional de Colombia (Sede Bogotá). Facultad de Ciencias Humanas, Escuela de Estudios en Psicoanálisis y Cultura), 0(4), pp. 56–68, http://revistas.unal.edu.co/index.php/jardin/article/view/8299/8943, accessed 5 June 2016.

Zambrano, M. and M. Chaves (2006) From Blanqueamiento to Reindigenización: Paradoxes of Mestizaje and Multiculturalism in Contemporary Colombia, *Revista Europea de Estudios Latinoamericanos y del Caribe*, April, pp. 5–23.

Part II

Popularizing Performance

6

Steps in Time

The Evolving Role of Dance in the Broadway Musical

Mary Jo Lodge

The history of the musical, particularly the American Broadway musical, is often told as a genius narrative, wherein a parade of uniquely gifted artists used their talents to create and then refine the genre. Most often, these geniuses are composers, like Richard Rodgers, but occasionally, they are lyricists or librettists, like Oscar Hammerstein II. Sometimes, as in the case of Lin-Manuel Miranda, MacArthur Genius Grant winner in 2015, they are all three at once, as he was for his smash hit *Hamilton*. That this shaping of the story of the musical is driven first by the writers makes sense, since many projects, even today, do originate with these artists, but this approach tends to ignore the importance of the contributions of the choreographers and directors to the physical embodiment of the musical. Larry Stempel's lengthy book *Showtime* (2010), for instance, which is billed as 'A History of the Broadway Musical Theater', and clocks in at over 800 pages, dedicates just one chapter out of sixteen (and just over forty pages) to the entire history of dance in the form (in fairness, directors do get more attention). Despite Stempel's approach, however, there is a way to view the history of the American musical as driven by the changing role of dance in the art form which might warrant a rethinking of this composer/lyricist origin story he and others espouse. This history begins, as most of the American musicals do, with the 1866 production of *The Black Crook* at New York City's Niblo's Garden, which is considered by many musical theatre historians to be the first musical. *The Black Crook* would otherwise be a footnote in musical theatre history as a struggling burlesque extravaganza with a convoluted book by Charles M. Barras and interpolated music from a variety of composers of the day were it not for a fateful union of dance with the show. *The Black Crook* became a smash hit, running for a then unheard of 474 performances (a long run even today), when dance, specifically in the form of a scantily clad troupe of French ballerinas who were stranded in New York after a fire destroyed the theatre where they were meant to be performing, was included in the show after its opening. The inciting incident in the birth of the American musical, then, was the addition of dance to the form. One could argue, therefore, that it is the geniuses in the realm of dance who have made the most notable contributions to American musical theatre, not the least of which was the creation of this new, hybrid art form. As with the composer-driven narrative of musical theatre history, the people creating the innovations are important, but the innovations themselves are even more significant. While today few but the most dedicated dance enthusiasts know that David Costa created the dances (and performed in) *The Black Crook*, many theatre fans who embrace the form today also indirectly embrace Costa's innovation of merging song and text with dance (see Figure 6.1). Examining the dance geniuses of the musical theatre, as well as their ground-breaking innovations, provides a new way to shape the musical's historical narrative and offers a distinct lens through which to view the evolution of narrative show dance in the American musical.

In this chapter, in addition to reconsidering the history of the American musical by examining its use of dance, I examine the ways in which the musical was shaped by a uniquely American dance vocabulary. I also explore the role star dancers, dance directors and later choreographers played in creating and defining dance as a key element of the American musical. Next, I examine the part director/choreographers played in making dance equal to its counterparts of song and speech in the American musical, and how the increased importance of dance spawned a new breed of musicals which are dance driven. I also explore how the increasing dominance of the triple threat performer in American musical theatre has affected the prominence of dance in the modern musical. Finally, I examine the evolving symbiotic relationship dance has

Steps in Time: The Evolving Role of Dance in the Broadway Musical   93

Figure 6.1   David Costa in costume for the Pas de Demons from *The Black Crook* (1867)
Photographer: Courtesy of New York Public Library

helped the musical forge with popular culture, particularly in America, which has helped to assure its continued contemporary relevance.

Charting the Innovations in Theatre Dance History

As noted above, a history of the American musical that considers dance innovations to be especially significant starts, as much musical theatre history does, with *The Black Crook* in 1866. After that, there were certainly notable developments, though as Richard Kislan notes: 'The show dance of the American stage absorbs its predecessors gradually and by degrees' (1887: 23). Despite this gradual progress, certain major innovations can be identified which mark important advances in the development of dance in the Broadway musical. While a longer study could include a more nuanced analysis, three innovations in the history of the musical that involve dance will be discussed in greater detail below, as they mark especially significant milestones for the Broadway musical. These include, first and most importantly, the development of a unique vernacular for dance on the American stage. The second innovation is the arrival of storytelling dance sequences on Broadway, typically in the form of dream ballets which were staged by the newly christened choreographers who descended from earlier dance directors. The third innovation was the ascension of the triple threat performer, brought about by the newly minted director/choreographers, starting in the 1950s, which ultimately led to both the increased dominance of dance in the musical, as well as a rise of productions in which dance was either (or often both) subject matter or central element. These three innovations mark key milestones in musical theatre history and offer a clear way to view musical theatre history as being shaped by dance.

The Creation of an American Show Dance Vernacular

Perhaps the most significant of the innovations listed above is the one which came first, the creation of a uniquely American vocabulary of dance steps for this new American art form. While dance did exist in American theatre prior to the advent of *The Black Crook*, Richard Kislan notes that: 'The earliest American show dance mirrored the nature and customs of eighteenth-century England' (1987: 3). While this was true for many early musicals (though *The Black Crook* reflected a more continental influence with its imported French ballet dancers), by the late 1800s, American theatre began to draw on dances created in the United States, a legacy that relied heavily on the art forms that spanned the years from approximately 1850 through the early part of the 1900s and that served as direct antecedents to the Broadway musical: burlesque, vaudeville and minstrelsy.

Early American show dance found its roots in burlesque (*The Black Crook* is classified as one), which at the time meant comic variety shows which featured racy and/or bawdy acts, and the dance specialties that appeared in early vaudeville acts (these were nearly always choreographed and performed by their creators). Vaudeville shows, which were viewed as a more family-friendly form of burlesque, were made up of a series of unrelated acts. At least some of those were dance performances which featured a range of movement styles including toe dancing (early American ballet), eccentric dancing (dances done by comedians like Ray Bolger) and acrobatic dancing (including early American ballroom dances that included lifts). Ethnic dances, which featured the steps drawn from various immigrant cultures, were also popular, though Richard Kislan notes that such specialties were typically 'of the more approximate rather than authentic variety' (1987: 38). These early performance types carried over into early musicals, and effectively formed the vocabulary for American dance.

Ballet, first evident in *The Black Crook*, remained a staple of early musicals, particularly in the form of women's dances done in pointe shoes. Early stars like Adelaide Dickey and Marilyn Miller epitomized the form, and appeared in numerous revues on Broadway, including Shubert's *The Passing Shows* in the early teens, and for Miller, in *The Ziegfeld Follies* and later as the star of a series of musicals in the early 1920s (Kislan, 1987: 35). However, as Long reports: 'in 1900, no American ballet companies existed', so most toe dancers who came from the vaudeville circuit had few other options for where to perform (2001: 15). In addition to ballet, American ballroom dance, often called exhibition dancing at the time, also rose to prominence in early musicals, particularly after the premiere of Franz Lehar's *The Merry Widow* (1907), which famously included a waltz performed by the leading characters, 'The Merry Widow Waltz', at the close of its second act. The show was a smash hit and glorified ballroom dancing, and opened the way for Vernon and Irene Castle, an early American ballroom dance team (who did not appear in the show), but instead, and perhaps more importantly, helped 'popularize dancing by making it a fad in high society' (Stearns and Stearns, 1994: 97). Ballroom and partner dancing, which, like ballet, were once considered scandalous (ballet because it exhibited ladies' legs in tights, and ballroom because of the close holds required between partners, who might not be married), also became a staple of Broadway dance by the 1920s.

In addition to ballet and ballroom, America's most enduring contribution to show dancing is undoubtedly tap dancing, which still appears regularly in new musicals, even today. Tap dance emerged first in vaudeville, and was typically performed by African Americans, though its roots on stage date back to minstrelsy. Kislan reports: 'The tap dancing of American show business derived its movement vocabulary from the folk dances of England and Ireland and the American Negro step dances that evolved during the era of minstrel entertainment' (1987: 157). The minstrel show, a uniquely American institution (though productions were later exported to Europe), was 'the most popular form of entertainment in the United States for more than half a century – from 1845 to 1900 approximately' (Stearns and Stearns, 1994: 43). Today it is rightly viewed as an overtly racist entertainment in which white performers donned blackface makeup and gave performances that were full of exaggerated stereotypes about African Americans and glorified the days of slavery. Still, despite their deeply flawed foundations, minstrel shows, which were later performed by black actors (who still wore blackface makeup), were among the first entertainments to embrace the dances that emerged from African American traditions (melded with elements of Irish clogging and jigs), namely tap dance, which emerged once vaudeville came into prominence.

Tap dance quickly became a staple of the Broadway stage, and rose to even greater prominence when African American performers finally began appearing in Broadway shows. Richard Kislan observes:

> That black American tap dance evolved into a unique and long-lived show business commodity was due to an emerging black cultural identity that found a common, expressive language in the street tradition of step dances, and to an increased acceptance of that dancing in popular American entertainment.
>
> (1987: 33)

Shuffle Along (1921), the first musical which was written and created by an entirely African American team (a re-worked version of the show, known as *Shuffle Along, or, the Making of the Musical Sensation of 1921 and All That Followed* ran briefly on Broadway in 2016), used tap dance extensively (see Figure 6.2). Brian Seibert of *The New York Times* points out, in speaking of the 2016 version: 'The new "Shuffle Along" argues that one of the ways the original "changed Broadway forever" is that the chorus girls, in contrast to the promenading showgirls of white revues, really danced, throwing around their hips and feet in jazz rhythm' (2016).

Yet the tap dancing female chorus of *Shuffle Along* was not the only place where tap's dominance was apparent. Black star tap dancers like Bill 'Bojangles' Robinson and the Nicholas Brothers were wildly popular – Bojangles reportedly made '$6600 per week for an appearance in motion pictures' – and insured that tap would have a long history in the theatre (Kislan, 1987: 33). Both Bojangles and the Nicholas Brothers were notable for their contributions to the form, as well. Stearns and Stearns report that, 'Bill Robinson's contribution to tap dancing is exact and specific: he brought it up on the toes, dancing upright and swinging. (Clogs, jigs

Figure 6.2 Scene from the stage production *Shuffle Along* (1921)
Photographer: Courtesy of New York Public Library

and reels had been danced on the toes, but they did not swing.)' (1994: 186–7). The Nicholas Brothers, known more for their film rather than stage appearances, brought an athletic, acrobatic, masculine style of tap dance, known as flash dance, which featured 'a furious array of spectacular floor and air steps like the flip, spin, knee drop or split' to the forefront (Kislan, 1987: 32). Later Caucasian dancers like Fred Astaire carried on Robinson's more precise stylistic choices (Astaire infamously performed in blackface to portray Robinson in the 'Bojangles of Harlem' number in the 1936 film *Swing Time*), while Gene Kelly embodied the Nicholas Brothers' flash dance legacy in films like *It's Always Fair Weather* (1955), where he famously tap danced on roller skates.

Ballet and ballroom, and particularly tap, formed the foundational elements of the vernacular of American show dance, which later expanded to include what became known as jazz dance. Choreographer Jack Cole, who began staging dances on Broadway in 1943 after a career as a dancer, is often hailed as the father of American jazz dance (which he developed from a variety of influences, including ballet, Latin dance and Indian dance). Dance historian Constance Hill noted that 'Cole's updated and cooled-down movement aesthetic distinguished "modern" jazz dance from anything that had come before it' (2009: 244). American show dance (and even theatre dance training) is dominated today by a combination of jazz and tap dance, demonstrating the staying power of these forms.

The last addition to the dance language of the American musical, and a far more recent one, is hip-hop, which, while far from dominant on Broadway stages yet, was first hinted at in Savion Glover's choreography for *Bring in Da' Noise, Bring in Da' Funk* in 1996. Historian Errol Hill called the show's dance style, 'tap/rap (tap dancing informed by hip-hop and funk rhythms)' (2003: 439). Of the four remaining shows to date that have reached Broadway with hip-hop staging, one, a short-lived 2014 musical called *Holler if Ya Hear Me*, based on the music of rapper Tupac Shakur, featured hip-hop choreography by Broadway veteran Wayne Cilento, while the other three, *In the Heights* (1999), *Bring it On* (2011) and *Hamilton* (2015), all of which were penned, at least in part, by Lin-Manuel Miranda, featured hip-hop choreography by Andy Blankenbuehler. Hip-hop, which first emerged, like early tap dance, as a street rather than studio dance style in the late 1960s, took almost thirty years to appear on the Broadway stage. Veteran dancer turned choreographer Blankenbuehler has said that he finds hip-hop to be 'a natural extension' of Jack Cole's jazz style from the 1950s, perhaps indicating that hip-hop is absorbing that show dance which came before it (Cramer, 2013: 43). Today, jazz and tap stand as the dominant forms of dance on Broadway stages, while hip-hop is slowly entering the vernacular, and ballet and ballroom still do appear, particularly in revivals. These movement styles are all now widely accepted as the language of show dancing in America, which marks a significant development of the Broadway musical.

From Dance Directors to Choreographers: Narrative Dance Arrives on Broadway

Tap, ballet and ballroom dance were widely in use on the Broadway stages by the early 1920s, though prior to that time, dancers, particularly specialty dancers, both choreographed and then performed their own dances. The rise of chorus girls, who were featured in large numbers particularly in the revue and extravaganza shows like Shubert's *The Passing Shows* and *The Ziegfeld Follies* between the early 1900s and the early 1930s, created a need for someone to stage the dance sequences in which they appeared. These artists became known as dance directors (they are considered the precursors to choreographers), and Richard Kislan notes that, 'while modern choreography strives for expressive, particularized movement, dance direction strove for clever new ways to present the old routines' (1987: 41). In general, the movements staged by dance directors 'relied on simple steps within a kaleidoscopic array of geometric patterns' (Kislan, 1987: 43). Kislan notes that 'dance directors subscribed to the notion that precision dancing constituted the right and proper action within the chorus line formation' (1987: 43). Busby Berkeley famously brought this philosophy to his film musicals, and his elaborate musical staging, which values precision and geometric patterns, offers prime examples of the work of the dance director (Berkeley previously staged numerous Broadway musicals between 1925 and 1930, before heading to Hollywood, where his work is better known).

Ned Wayburn was considered 'the most prolific, outspoken and influential dance director of his day' (Kislan, 1987: 47). He served as dance director for both *The Passing Shows* and *The Ziegfeld Follies*, and is credited both with creating the couple's version of the popular Charleston and with popularizing the female dancing chorus which became a staple of the American musical theatre (Cohen-Stratyner, 2009: 220). Other important dance directors of the era include Bobby Connolly, who served in that role on many stage shows, and notably on the film of *The Wizard of Oz*, and female pioneer Albertina Rasch, who was famed for her use of ballet-inspired movements with her troupe of dancers called 'The Albertina Rasch Girls', who appeared in many musicals between 1925 and 1945 (Kislan, 1987: 60).

Classically trained ballet master George Balanchine was the first to claim the title of choreographer for his work on *On Your Toes* (1936), the ballet-inspired musical by Rodgers and Hart. Balanchine approached dance differently from his dance director predecessors. In fact, Kislan credits him with starting 'a revolution that would change forever the nature, scope and function of American show dancing' and he goes on to say that Balanchine 'insisted that his work for the commercial theater be integral to the show's intent, not merely its decorative accessory' (1987: 71). *On Your Toes* featured two lengthy ballets, 'Princess Zenobia', which was a 'spoof of classical ballet' and 'Slaughter on Tenth Avenue', which was 'a dark jazz ballet that would be the climax of the story' (Miller, 2007: 38). A 1936 *Theater Arts Magazine* review recognized the ground-breaking nature of Balanchine's choreography, saying, 'We may have come unknowingly upon a successor to the old musical form, a musical show that is not a comedian's holiday, but a dancer's' (cited in Miller, 2007: 38). With his ballets, Balanchine was a pioneer because he used dance, more specifically ballet, to further a show's narrative. Balanchine choreographed many additional Broadway musicals between 1936 and 1954 before he turned his attention almost exclusively to the ballet concert dance world. Balanchine may have shifted his focus because he chafed at his role, which afforded him little control of the show beyond the dance sequences with which he was specifically charged.

While Balanchine was the pioneer for narrative ballet in the musical, Agnes De Mille brought the potential he uncovered to fruition in Rodgers and Hammerstein's *Oklahoma!* (1943), a ground-breaking musical often credited with fully integrating song, dance and text in service of the plot of musical. De Mille's 'Dream Ballet', which segued out of leading lady Laurey's rendition of 'Out of My Dreams', depicted Laurey's struggles to make up her mind between two suitors (with a ballet dancer doubling as 'Dream Laurey'). De Mille's 'Dream Ballet' used ballet specifically to advance the plot of the musical and spawned countless imitators over the next few decades. In fact, self-contained ballet sequences came to be expected in Broadway shows (nearly all of Rodgers and Hammerstein's shows post *Oklahoma!* feature them). So popular were these ballets, staged by De Mille and other choreographers, including rising star Jerome Robbins, fresh off his success with *On the Town* (1944), that ballet superseded tap as the dominant form of American show dancing in the 1940s and 1950s. Still, as Kislan notes, 'choreographers of the stature of Jack Cole and Agnes De Mille documented the practical and artistic liabilities of staging and choreography made secondary and serviceable to other elements of a musical' (1987: 93). The choreographer on Broadway had come a long way from the days of the dance director, but there were still distinct limitations on his or her ability to contribute to the narrative progression of a musical through dance.

Equality then Dominance for Dance: The Triple Threat Performer and the Director/ Choreographer

Most historical accounts of the musical acknowledge that certain musicals mark turning points in the development of the form. Both *The Black Crook* and *Oklahoma!* are usually cited as two of these, as noted above, in large part because of the role dance played in their creation. Another landmark musical appeared in 1957 with *West Side Story*, when Jerome Robbins, who had previously directed or choreographed major musicals, now filled both roles on one show as a new hyphenate: the director/choreographer. Kislan articulates succinctly what the innovations of the director/choreographer were:

> What they did, and to critical and commercial success at that, was to redefine the role of movement in stage entertainments, magnify its importance, and reverse the chain of command that governed the various artists during the preparation of a musical show.
>
> (1987: 93)

Kislan goes on to summarize the significance in this change in leadership regarding dance: 'The dance director follows, the choreographer adapts, but the director-choreographer leads, and that has made all the difference' (1987: 93). Thus, *West Side Story*, a retelling of *Romeo and Juliet* set during a gang turf war in contemporary New York City, became a landmark musical for numerous reasons related to its use of dance, but one of the most critical was its introduction of the director/choreographer.

Positioning a choreographer as director *and* choreographer on a single show made musical theatre more integrated, in terms of its structure, since the director/choreographer could use song, story *and* dance to advance a show's plot. Jerome Robbins introduced another innovation in integration in *West Side Story*: he integrated the musical in the bodies of its performers, as well. Whereas shows previously had separate singing and dancing choruses, Robbins combined both of those into one group, and, in fact, required all of his performers to be equally strong singers, dancers and actors. The musical now no longer required a convention like a dream ballet to justify why the leading lady wasn't dancing a principle role; all performers were up to the song *and* dance demands of the project. In *West Side Story*, for instance, Paul Laird notes that 'even the romantic leads, Carol Lawrence and Larry Kert, had extensive dance training' (2008: 225). Other director/choreographers embraced this trend, which has become known as the rise of the triple threat performer. In fact, since *West Side Story*, the triple threat performer has gone from being an anomaly on Broadway to being the norm.

Robbins served as director/choreographer for several major Broadway shows between 1957 and 1964, but like Balanchine before him, after that, he worked more extensively in the ballet world. In fact, given his stature as a giant in the field of musical theatre, it is somewhat surprising to note that he did not create new work as a director/choreographer on the Broadway stage after 1964 (though he did restage his biggest hits *Gypsy*, *West Side Story*, *Peter Pan* and *Fiddler on the Roof* in numerous revivals and later in his retrospective Broadway show, *Jerome Robbins' Broadway* in 1989). Robbins' director/choreographer successors include such musical theatre giants as Bob Fosse, Michael Bennett, Gower Champion, Tommy Tune, Susan Stroman, Kathleen Marshall and Andy Blankenbuehler. While each contributed unique elements to the legacy of the musical – such as Fosse's distinctive, precise choreography, Champion's pioneering use of Labanotation to accurately record choreography, and Blankenbuehler's introduction of hip-hip to the Broadway dance vocabulary – it is the use of triple threat performers that all of these artists adopted that was their most significant contribution to the form (Kislan, 1987: 113).

Michael Bennett, as director/choreographer, created the next major landmark musical after *West Side Story*, in terms of its use of dance, with his 1975 production of *A Chorus Line*, a 'veritable celebration of Broadway dance and dancers' (Laird, 2008: 220). If *Oklahoma!* used dance to tell the story, at least in part, and *West Side Story* used dance to tell all of the story, with *all* of the performers, in *A Chorus Line* dance *was* the story and everything else was in its service. Bennett employed dance as both subject (the characters are at a Broadway audition, vying for coveted positions as members of a Broadway chorus) and chief form of expression in *A Chorus Line*. The show was revolutionary on several fronts, for not only did it assert the primacy of dance in the American musical, but Bennett literally created it in a new way, utilizing the workshop, in which he 'begins with an idea, allows the writers to write, be wrong and rewrite, provides the time and opportunity to see and hear the material on the performance and the option to abandon the project if it never really works out' (Kislan, 1987: 130). Like the triple threat performer, the workshop model of development has become far more standard for creating musicals today than the older composer/lyricist, out-of-town-trial model.

A Chorus Line, and its runaway success (it ran for over fifteen years), marked the start of a new era for the dance musical. No longer were dance scenes relegated to the singular ballets of *Oklahoma!* but dance now shaped and informed entire musicals. For example, Bob Fosse created *Dancin'* in 1978, just three years after the premier of *A Chorus Line*, and he used pre-existing music (and no composer or lyricist) for it and served as its director/choreographer/auteur. *Dancin'* was the focus, and dancing was both the subject and the means to tell the story, which jettisoned a traditional book for a revue format. Other dance musicals followed, including the aforementioned *Bring in Da Noise, Bring in Da Funk* (1996), which used tap dance to tell the story of the African American experience in America, and director/choreographer Susan Stroman's *Contact* (2000), which, like *Dancin'*, used pre-existing music, and no composer, to tell three short stories almost entirely through movement. In 1999, Lynne Taylor-Corbett directed and choreographed *Swing!* which brought swing dance back to Broadway in a revue style format, and featured separate singers and dancers, while in 2002, ground-breaking concert dance choreographer and director Twyla Tharp premiered her *Movin' Out*, a musical created from the songs of rock star Billy Joel, on Broadway. It was sung by an onstage singer-pianist and danced by a company of dancers who, as in *Contact*, did not sing. While these shows, sometimes referred to as dancicals for their prioritization of dance above all else, might seem to indicate that the triple threat performer is no longer the priority, shows like these have become rarer over the last decade, as triple threat performers have continued to dominate.

Of note, the use of the triple threat performer has grown with the casting of excellent dancers into triple threat roles, even if their singing was not generally considered as much of an attraction as their dancing (thus, the triple threat requirements may be different for extraordinarily talented dancers). In effect, gifted dancers, even as far back as Marilyn Miller, had shows created for them (like her 1920 Cinderella musical *Sally*) which showcased their dancing and required little from them vocally. In 1939, *The Hot Mikado* (a jazz version of the Gilbert and Sullivan operetta) was created as a vehicle for tap dancer Bill 'Bojangles' Robinson, though he was not particularly known for his singing. Later dance standouts like Gwen Verdon and Chita Rivera had numerous musicals built for them, including *Chicago* (1975), in which they co-starred, even though their vocal ranges were less notable than their dance abilities. Musicals that focus solely on dancers are rarer today (unless, like the above, they are constructed as dance revue shows with separate singers), but this does not mean that dance has lost its importance. This, on the contrary, seems to demonstrate how intertwined the elements of song, dance and speech have become in the modern musical, such that the triple threat performer is needed to communicate most musical theatre narratives.

Beyond Innovation: Dance and Popular Culture

Viewing the history of musical theatre through the lens of its dances clearly provides a new perspective for appreciating and understanding the art form. Broadway, and show dancing, do not, however, occur in vacuum, but are instead deeply affected by the popular culture that surrounds them. The early development of tap dance, from street dance and ethnic movement to dominant show dance form, at least for a time, is a great example of popular culture's influence on Broadway dance, while the myriad videos on YouTube of musical theatre fans attempting to recreate the dance steps from their favourite productions demonstrate Broadway's influence on popular culture. Placing musical theatre dance in its historical context among Broadway musicals is only half of its story, then; understanding how musical theatre dance is deeply connected to, and interdependent on, popular culture, particularly American culture, helps to more clearly define how dance played a major role in shaping both the musical and, in the process, American popular culture.

In the early days of the musical, dance crazes started regularly, exploding from musical stages into the popular culture realm. The previously mentioned 'Merry Widow Waltz' certainly launched American ballroom dancing, while 'The Charleston', the dance that even today still defines the 1920s in popular culture, originated in the 1923 musical *Runnin' Wild* and then swept the country (Cohen-Stratyner, 2009: 221). More recently, Michael Jackson's 1982 smash hit album *Thriller*, born in the early days of MTV, featured numerous influences pulled from Broadway in his choreography for the album's music videos. His video for the *Thriller* track 'Beat It', for example, which centred around a fight between rival street gangs, harkens back to the choreography of Jerome Robbins. Dance historian Sherril Dodds notes that in the 'Beat It' video 'as the gangs enter into battle, with the two leaders poised with knives, their movement is reminiscent of the choreographed fight scenes from the Jerome Robbins' film musical *West Side Story* (1961)' (2009: 252). (Since Robbins had recreated his Broadway staging for the film, the stage influence here is clear as well.) Precursors of Jackson's famous moonwalk, a series of smooth, dragging, backward steps, can be seen in the moves of early tap dancers like the Nicholas Brothers and Gene Kelly. In addition, Jackson's video for the 'Billie Jean' track drew heavily from Bob Fosse's dance vocabulary and even featured Jackson dressed in short pants, light socks, black shoes and a dark hat, similar to what Fosse's dancers wore onstage in 1954 in his iconic 'Steam Heat' number from *The Pajama Game*.

Jackson was not the only artist to prominently quote Bob Fosse's work. Pop diva Beyoncé Knowles released her hit song 'Single Ladies (Put a Ring on It)' in October of 2008, and the song went on to win extensive critical and popular acclaim, and was chosen as 'Song of the Year' at the Grammy Awards that year. The lauded music video, which features black and white footage of complex choreography performed by Knowles and two other dancers was also a runaway success, earning numerous 'Video of the Year' awards. It has become one of the most imitated videos on YouTube, with dancers of all genders, ages and sizes emulating Knowles' smooth moves, but it ignited a storm of controversy when a variety of internet bloggers noticed it was very similar to a live performance given by Broadway star Gwen Verdon and two backup dancers on *The Ed Sullivan Show* in 1969. The Verdon number, called 'Mexican Breakfast', featured choreography by the legendary Bob Fosse. The story is even more complicated, since the Verdon clip first re-emerged when it was paired, once again on YouTube, with the song 'Walk It Out' by rapper Unk. Beyoncé noted in several interviews, after the controversy arose, that she saw the Verdon/Unk video on YouTube and was inspired to attempt the choreography for her 'Single Ladies' video. Putting aside the issue of whether the 'Single Ladies' video is an homage to Fosse and Verdon or outright theft (both have been alleged), the fact remains that one of the most recognizable pop music videos in recent history, by one of the most famous singers, has a Broadway pedigree.

Dance doesn't only move from Broadway into pop culture, however – the reverse is also true. A recent example of this is in the introduction of steps drawn from hip-hop dance into the world of Broadway. Hip-hop's roots are far from musical theatre; dance scholar Halifu Osumare traces the trajectory of hip-hop 'as a cultural extension of the Africanist dance continuum from traditional West African dance through American tap and early jazz dance to the 1970s street corner b-boy competitions' (2009: 263). Osumare notes that many styles fall under the umbrella of hip-hop, ranging from 'popping, locking, electric boogie, house and b-boying/b-girling (break dancing)' (2009: 262). This is the physical language that Blankenbuehler used to great success in *In the Heights*, *Bring it On* and, most recently, *Hamilton*. In fact, Blankenbuehler, in an interview with Lyn Cramer (2013: 39), notes that in his creative process to introduce authentic hip-hop into the musicals he stages, he would 'bring these fierce hip-hop dancers into the room, and I would say, How can this be better? How can this look like a real hip-hop step?' This reciprocal relationship between Broadway and popular culture affirms that show dancing has continued to have contemporary relevance and reinforces the importance of American musical theatre dance both onstage and off.

Conclusion

While the developments in narrative show dancing are absent from or glossed over in many musical theatre history texts, prioritizing them yields a new lens through which to understand the musical's development. Considering how important innovations like the development of the American show dancing vernacular are, or the role choreographers played in helping dance to serve the story of musicals moves the focus away from the approach to musical theatre history which favours composers and librettists. Exploring how director/choreographers contributed to the rise of both the triple threat performer and the dance-driven musical can yield a deeper understanding of the fundamental role that dance has played in creating the modern musical. Re-telling the story of the Broadway musical by prioritizing the dance innovations throughout its history and placing those innovations in the context of the popular culture that they influenced, and were simultaneously shaped by, provides a more complete way to view the history of the American musical.

Discussion Questions

1. Why do you think dance is not typically the focus of historical narratives of musical theatre? Should it be? Why or why not?
2. Is there any modern equivalent to the Broadway dance director (as opposed to the choreographer)?
3. How is the dramatic narrative of musical theatre similar to or different from other theatre and dance forms?
4. Do you see influences of Broadway dance in other dances, beyond the Beyoncé ones discussed, in current popular culture?

Website

http://musical101.com/

Works Cited and Resource Material

Cohen-Stratyner, B. (2009) Social Dance in Broadway Musical Comedy, in J. Malnig (Ed.) *Boogie, Shimmy Sham, Shake: A Social and Popular Dance Reader* (Urbana and Chicago: University of Illinois Press) pp. 217–33.

Cramer, L. (2013) *Creating Musical Theater: Conversations with Broadway Directors and Choreographers* (London: Bloomsbury Methuen Press).

Dodds, S. (2009) Music Video and Popular Dance, in J. Malnig (Ed.) *Boogie, Shimmy Sham, Shake: A Social and Popular Dance Reader* (Urbana and Chicago: University of Illinois Press) pp. 246–60.

Hill, C. V. (2009) Jack Cole's 'Modern' Jazz Dance, in J. Malnig (Ed.) *Boogie, Shimmy Sham, Shake: A Social and Popular Dance Reader* (Urbana and Chicago: University of Illinois Press) pp. 234–45.

Hill, E. (2003) *A History of African American Theatre* (Cambridge: Cambridge University Press).

Kislan, R. (1987) *Hoofing on Broadway: A History of Show Dancing* (New York: Prentice Hall Press).

Laird, P. (2008) Choreographers, Directors and the Fully Integrated Musical, in W. A. Everett and P. Laird (Eds) *The Cambridge Companion to the Musical* (Cambridge: Cambridge University Press).

Long, R. E. (2001) *Broadway, the Golden Year: Jerome Robbins and the Great Choreographer-Directors 1940-Present* (New York: Continuum).

Miller, S. (2007) *Strike Up the Band: A New History of Musical Theater* (Portsmouth, NH: Heinemann).

Osumare, H. (2009) The Dance Archeology of Rennie Harrie: Hip-Hop or Postmodern, in J. Malnig (Ed.) *Boogie, Shimmy Sham, Shake: A Social and Popular Dance Reader* (Urbana and Chicago: University of Illinois Press) pp. 261–81.

Seibert, B. (2016) In Savion Glover's Shuffle Along, Tap's Reach Has Its Limits, *The New York Times*, 23 May, accessed 3 June 2017.

Stempel, L. (2010) *Showtime: A History of the Broadway Musical Theater* (New York: W.W. Norton & Co.).

Stearns, M. and J. Stearns (1994) *Jazz Dance: The Story of American Vernacular Dance* (Boston: Da Capo Press).

7

The Multiple Narratives of Cirque du Soleil

Katie Lavers and Louis Patrick Leroux

Introduction

> Cirque du Soleil [is] one of the biggest brands in show business. It has 19 productions globally, with eight in Las Vegas alone. The company sells 11 million tickets worldwide annually, more than all Broadway shows combined, while turnover in 2013 was $750 million (down from $1 billion in 2012).
>
> (Hunter-Tilney, 2015: 5)

As the above extract demonstrates, Cirque du Soleil is now a major producer of live events, a hugely successful company that in 2015 was sold by founder Guy Laliberté to a consortium for a reported 1.5 billion dollars (Peterson-Withorn, 2015; Leroux, 2016). The net worth of founder Guy Laliberté himself, who still retains a 10 per cent holding in the company, was reported in 2016 as being 2.18 billion dollars (*Canadian Business*, 2015). Cirque du Soleil has a huge reach, performing 'to more than 160 million spectators in more than 400 cities on six continents ... [and with] close to 4,000 employees, including 1,300 performing artists from close to 50 different countries' (SAP, 2015).

The question is how Cirque du Soleil has achieved this unprecedented level of international success in circus. In this writing, the authors propose that one of the major driving factors contributing to the company's success is its broad-spectrum approach to narrative in not only the dramaturgy employed in its shows but also the entrepreneurial narratives permeating the multinational's promotional materials; the narrative arc of the company's founding story; and the overarching narrative of the life of the company's founder and director Guy Laliberté.[1] In this chapter, we argue that it is Cirque du Soleil's use of narrative, in particular the metanarrative structure of the 'quest', which distinguishes the company's work and brand, and that this use of narrative has fundamentally changed and broadened audiences' understandings of what circus can be.

Background

With the emergence of 'new circus' in Europe and Australia in the 1970s, many of the traditional and iconic foundational elements of traditional circus were abandoned or contested. In particular numerous circus workshops and eventually circus schools were set up, successfully democratizing the teaching of circus skills and thus breaking the hold, and the almost feudal dominance, of the traditional family circuses on the transmission of circus skills. This created an influx into the art form of new people including artists from outside the realm of circus. These artists brought with them new ideas and approaches from other disciplines including theatre, visual arts and dance. Notable new circus companies created largely by artists coming originally from outside the traditional circus families included Circus Oz in Australia in 1978, Archaos in France in 1986, and Cirque du Soleil in Canada in 1984. These companies all created new, audacious circus aesthetics. Circus Oz created a radical circus with a strong political agenda engaging with women's rights and Indigenous land rights, and working for the banning of uranium mining in Australia; Archaos created an anti-consumerist industrial punk aesthetic introducing cars and motorcycles in place of the traditional horses, performing aerial acts suspended from cranes, and performing juggling acts with chainsaws; Cirque du Soleil, however, took an altogether different path, a resolutely commercial path with an innovative approach to narrative as one of the foundational, distinguishing core elements.

Dramaturgical Narrative in Cirque Shows

In Cirque du Soleil shows, the performers' bodies, in line with David Graver's classification, are presented as 'character bodies', where the spectators accept that the performer is playing a character. The 'character body' consists of all the physical characteristics, that is, the gestures, postures and expressions performed by the actor to convey 'the life and experiences of a fictional character in a fictional world' (Graver, 2005: 159).

As theatre scholar Karen Fricker points out, the performers in Cirque du Soleil shows 'are understood to be playing fictional roles, something so important to Cirque that it insists on musicians and ushers being in role' (Fricker, 2010, para. 16). Fricker writes that this focus on 'character bodies' draws attention away from individual performers, instead drawing focus towards the show itself which guarantees that the productions are not dependent on any specific artist or troupes, and are thus able to outlast any cast changes. For Cirque du Soleil the show itself is the star. Although there are specific acts featuring the physical attainments of each individual performer, which draw attention to the 'performer body', this usually takes place 'within the context of an overall narrative and metaphor' (para. 16).

On stage, Cirque du Soleil artists embody 'performative exceptionalism' (Leroux, 2016: 21) in their performance of their 'tricks' and acts. Traditional circus has always relied on tricks and prowess and, in spite of the fact that it is the artistic goal of much contemporary circus to be able to surmount the act-based structure, at its foundational core, circus for the most part remains an act-based form. The technical and physical achievements of the performers are often emphasized, and the level of difficulty underscored, through the age-old tradition of 'chiquer un ratage' in which artists fail at their first two attempts at a trick and, with mounting anticipation from the audience, succeed with their third try. Individual acts are developed by artists over years and these become calling-cards or, indeed, autonomous pieces which producers and directors fit into their succession of acts. From the moment that these acts are organized in incremental and increasing difficulty, a dramaturgy of virtuosity emerges. This organization of acts is an ever-present physical narrative trope in Cirque du Soleil shows. However, in addition to this physical narrative, Cirque du Soleil also engages in a through-line, a narrative that is often presented as a journey or a quest. As renowned circus scholar, Peta Tait, points out, the narrative arc of Cirque du Soleil shows is frequently about 'an innocent protagonist, often female, helped by an older identity, seemingly male, to face a challenging journey or search for identity' (Tait, 2005: 128).

After almost forty years of Cirque du Soleil shows, the idea of presenting a circus performance as an archetypal journey, or a quest, may now be commonplace, but at the time this was an innovative and audacious creative step. Peta Tait writes that these narratives or 'conceptual throughlines provide an invaluable structure for creating image-based work' (Tait, 2005: 128). However, we argue that as well as providing an important structural device for the creation of physical and image-based work, the narrative element of a journey or quest moves circus into new territory. To use the Homeric narrative of a protagonist on an odyssey moving through episodic experiences was an extraordinary flash of brilliance, creating a perfect narrative structure for the essentially episodic nature of the various circus acts. This not only gave the Cirque du Soleil show coherence and cohesion, but also archetypal resonance. With this shift, circus was able to move beyond tricks and individual acts into an area where physical exceptionalism was brought in touch with mythic resonance through the show's narrative structure.

One definition of the 'quest' is:

> a journey in the course of which one advances spiritually and mentally, as well as physically travelling miles. The quester leaves the familiar for the unknown. The nature of the goal may not be clear at first and may only become fully apparent at the end of the quest.
>
> (Irwin, 2011)

Drawing on this definition, the multiple narratives of Cirque du Soleil can best be encapsulated as the narrative of the 'quest', complemented by the quest's component parts – 'experience', 'forward motion' and 'risk-taking'. Many of the Cirque du Soleil shows use the narrative of a quest. Karen Fricker describes the show *Kà* (2005) as 'a classic quest tale, in which a hero undertakes an initiatory journey from innocence to experience and must fulfill an extraordinary task after suffering separation from his/her natural environment' (Fricker, 2010, para. 11). Cirque du Soleil describes the show *Joyà* (2015), which is the first Cirque du Soleil resident show in Mexico, in this way, writing, 'JOYÀ tells the story of an alchemist and his granddaughter embarking on a quest to uncover the secrets of life' (Cirque du Soleil, 2017a).

The Quester

While there are exceptions, many of the Cirque du Soleil shows present the episodic narrative of the quest of a character, a protagonist or 'quester', who is introduced into the world of the show and travels through a series of events, and experiences, to later re-emerge transformed. This quester functions as a form of 'audience-avatar' (Leroux, 2010) whose role is to undertake a journey through the world of the show and to stand in for, and to represent, each and every audience member, in order to allow for a collective metaphysical transformation by the end of the show. As Ame Wilson, writes 'Cirque [du Soleil] subverts the mythical notion of personal heroism in favor of tales of metaphorical collective transformation' (Wilson, 2002: 135). This quester or audience-avatar can take a variety of forms.

One of these forms is 'the man/woman of the people' which is the character most often favoured by director Franco Dragone. Dragone is an important figure in the development of the Cirque du Soleil aesthetic and narrative drive as he directed most of its shows during the formative period of the 1980s and early 1990s, directing 'no fewer than 10 productions: *Cirque du Soleil* (1985), *La Magie Continue* (1986), *Cirque Réinventé* (We Reinvent the Circus, 1987), *Nouvelle Expérience* (1990), *Saltimbanco* (1992), *Mystère* (1993), *Alegría* (1994), *Quidam* (1996), *La Nouba and O* (1998)' (Cirque du Soleil, 2017b). His initial contribution in the form of an audience-avatar was in *Nouvelle Expérience* which premiered in 1990, in which a person (a performer who is placed in among the spectators as a plant) is pulled out of the audience, and represents the audience member moving through the world of the show and experiencing exceptional things.

In *O*, the water-based extravaganza in Las Vegas, 'the man/woman of the people' (again a plant) emerges from the audience to become 'the hero of an exploration of a "magical realm," and is spectacularly flown up and over the watery stage' (Leroux, 2012). The person pulled out of the audience may perform and do a few tricks and be portrayed as doing extraordinary things, but is shown as not having the level of excellence of the performers in the show, and, by the end of the show, we come to understand that the quest for performative excellence is a long one, and we will only ever match the exceptionalism of the performers if we ourselves undergo years of training.

Another manifestation of this central quester is the figure of 'the innocent'. In *Kooza* we see the innocent encounter the episodic events in the show and emerge transformed by the experience. The innocent becomes 'the master magician (or maybe the ringmaster of old) with power over the whole spectacle of KOOZA; it is he who in the end, turns out the lights' (Hurley, 2016a: 72).

In *Kà*, the Las Vegas show directed by Robert Lepage, the two central characters of the royal twins are the two innocents carried on an extraordinary adventure through the world of the performance. When a royal ceremony comes under attack from an enemy tribe, the young prince and princess become separated. 'A variety of adventures follow, most involving perilous escapes from bad guys with flaming arrows and fierce-looking body tattoos' (Isherwood, 2005), until, finally, the twins are happily reunited at the end of the show.

Quest narratives, however, do not always have to feature successful quests. Author Robert Irwin describes his own life journey or quest which:

> began in the 1960s when I travelled out from the home counties in search of the meaning of life and self-knowledge. I hitchhiked across North Africa and in a zawiya (a kind of Sufi monastery) in Algeria I saw miraculous things and experienced ecstasy, but ... my own Memoirs of a Dervish is uniquely an account of ultimate spiritual failure.
>
> (Irwin, 2011)

Varekai, directed by playwright and director Dominique Champagne, features the figure of the quester with resonances of Icarus who seeks to transcend his limits and at the end falls, and ultimately fails. The central image in *Varekai* is based on falling from the height of the big top and is based on Champagne's own fall in the first play he produced, a decade earlier, when he fell from a high point in a tent and was seriously injured.

Another form that this figure, so central to the quest narrative, can take is that of 'the traveller', and this can sometimes take the form of a combination of the figure of the clown and the innocent. In Cirque du Soleil, as in traditional circus, clowns reappear throughout the show in addition to the central figure, in a functional role preparing the next apparatus or the next set change; sometimes mocking or attempting to replicate the act that has just been presented, and reminding us, the audience members, of our own physical limitations, and of the physical exceptionalism of the performers. In *Luzia* (2016), directed by the renowned theatre director, Daniele Finzi Pasca, the two figures, that of the clown and of the innocent, are combined to become the traveller, and it is the journey of the traveller through the world of the show that we follow. The traveller in *Luzia* arrives on set via a parachute. The sound of a plane is heard as the lights dim and then a parachutist is spotted free-falling down into the space. The parachutist stands and looks about him taking in his surroundings, and then begins his journey through the events of the show. 'His impeccable timing and wit play well with his curiosity, which seems to mirror that of the audience's as he becomes a traveler weaving his way through act after act with a child-like sense of wonder' (Vandewart, 2017). It is the traveller's experience, sometimes even the traveller's gaze itself, which animates the show:

> There is a distinctive Finzi Pasca moment towards the end of the show, when people are seated, feasting, around a long table laden with fruits and delicacies, and for just a moment, as [the traveller] walks amongst them, this moment freezes. [The traveller's] gaze highlights the transience of physical enjoyment and by implication the transience of life. As [the traveller] turns towards the audience and gazes at the spectators, a shiver of memento mori moves through the crowd for just a moment before the fiesta, and the show itself, resumes.
>
> (Lavers, 2016)

The World

The dramaturgical narrative of the quest allows the quester to explore and experience a new world, and it is the creation of these new theatrical worlds and landscapes which drives the design, sound and thematic of each show. Circus scholars Jennifer Harvie and Erin Hurley have referred to the new world created for each Cirque du Soleil production with its own transnational population of performers and crew, as an 'imagi-nation'. They write:

> Taking what it needs from the national and the international spheres, the Cirque generates its own geographically and ideologically coherent space … its non-territorial 'realm of imagination,' populated by an international cast of performers and financed by sell-out crowds and corporate investment. It is this new imagined community—the 'imagi-nation'—that the Cirque creates for itself and for its audiences each time it produces and tours a new show.
>
> (Harvie and Hurley, 1999: 309)

Cirque du Soleil develops a new world and invites the audience to enter into it, and, to travel through and to explore it through the audience-avatar of the quester, and most importantly to experience it. The kind of experience on offer can vary from a cultural exploration such as in *Luzia* which immerses itself in the culture of Mexico. For *Luzia*, director Daniele Finzi Pasca worked with Eugenio Caballero, the Mexican designer, who won an Oscar for best art direction in Guillermo del Toro's film *Pan's Labyrinth*, and it is his work which manifests the world and creates the extraordinary visual strength of the show:

> Luzia draws on the mythology and culture of Mexico as a source of inspiration and the show features a sizzling colour palette of vibrant pinks, oranges and yellows … surreal silver headdresses in the form of crocodiles, insects, birds and fish; and a huge orange circular curtain referencing the Mexican art of paper cutting.
>
> (Lavers, 2016)

The word 'Luzia' is created from two words 'luz' (light) and 'illuvia' (rain) and it is this conjunction of light and water that is explored throughout the show to create the world for the journey:

> Featuring water as a central image the show involves a circular hi-tech waterfall with each drop of water computer controlled. At one point in the show, a 15 metre high curtain of falling water, that turns through 180 degrees, creates shimmering patterns of blossoms and vines in midair in different densities of falling water as it moves across the stage.
>
> (Lavers, 2016)

The music for *Luzia* is based on traditional Mexican music; however, during moments of spiritual intensity the composer Simon Carpentier, at the suggestion of Daniele Finzi Pasca, draws on the vocal abilities of the Indian classical singer, Mahesh Vinayakram (Everett-Green, 2016). This kind of mix and match of cultures has led Hurley to say that what Cirque du Soleil presents, with their world-beat aesthetic and narrative of free movement, is a 'fantasy of globalisation' (2016a: 72). The diverse acts in their shows are 'deterritorialized from their originary location and then reterritorialized firmly within the logic of Cirque du Soleil's unified production aesthetic' (Harvie and Hurley 1999: 313). Fricker has also commented on the problem of 'Orientalism' in *Kà*, 'the setting's vagueness and its somewhat ad-hoc mingling of cultures opens the production to a critique of exoticism and Orientalism' (2010, para. 12).

However, at their most extraordinary, Cirque du Soleil's worlds also move beyond the 'fantasy of globalisation' and the aesthetic of 'Orientalism' and tap into powerful archetypal worlds. Nowhere is this desire to transcend the earthly and move into the mythical made more manifest than in the worlds created for the shows *O* and *Kà*, which both create theatrical worlds which abolish the conventional fixed and stable surface of the theatrical stage, or the circus ring. With the abolishing of a constant terra firma these shows enter new territory. The characterizing and common feature of both shows is a retractable stage and the fact that characters most often do not simply exit or enter, but rather disappear into the void, to reappear later. This remains the defining image that links both productions:

> The centerpiece of O's stage is a 53 x 90 foot, 1.5 million-gallon pool which descends 25 feet below stage level. Much of the production's action takes place in and above the pool, with performers swimming, diving, and acting in the water, thus defying the convention of circus and theatre productions taking place on static stage surfaces.
>
> (Fricker, 2010, para. 20)

The performers explore the experience of diving through space and plunging into water, offering the spectators the kinaesthetic experience of entering a new realm.

With *Kà* Cirque du Soleil wanted 'to offer spectators an experience that's larger than life' (Le Page, cited in Cirque du Soleil, 2017c). The designer of the production was Mark Fisher, a top British architect, who specialized in designing spectacular stage shows and had previously designed shows for the Rolling Stones, Pink Floyd, Lady Gaga, Madonna and U2. He also designed the opening and closing ceremonies for the Beijing Olympics. In *Kà*, as in *O*, there is no stage floor, instead there is a hidden pit, or a void, 51 feet deep. The action takes place on or around two stages, one is a 35-foot square tatami deck which moves backwards and forwards in a way that Mark Fisher likens to 'a kitchen drawer mechanism but on a grander scale' (Fisher, 2005, cited in Fricker, 2010, para. 20). Fricker describes the other surface, the sand cliff deck, as the pièce de resistance, 'a 25-by-50-foot, 100,000-pound monolith operated by a gantry arm that allows it to spin on an axis, tilt back and forth, and raise up and down, sometimes simultaneously' (Fricker, 2010, para. 20).

Kà offers repeated images of the performers throwing their bodies into space from these platforms, images of falling, and plunging freefall into the void. As director Robert Lepage notes:

> Je sens que ma vie est truffée d'occasions, d'invitations à me jeter dans le vide. Pas le vide au sens de la vacuité. Le vide dans le sense du risque. Ce spectacle de Cirque du Soleil, et l'ambition de ce spectacle-là, est un énorme appel au vide. (I have the feeling that my life is filled with opportunities,

with invitations, to throw myself into the void. Not the void in the sense of emptiness. Void in the sense of risk. This show for Cirque du Soleil, and the ambition of this show, is a huge gesture towards the void).

(Lepage, 2005, cited in Fricker, 2010, abstract)

In some senses this kinaesthetically powerful image of free-falling into a void is a metaphorical image for stepping into the unknown, which is one of the essential experiences of embarking on a quest. These elements of risk, danger and the embracing of 'experience', including kinaesthetic experience, can be seen as forming essential parts of the quest narrative in Cirque du Soleil.

Entrepreneurial Narrative

In parallel with the central importance of narrative in the dramaturgical structure of its shows, narrative can also be seen as being central to Cirque du Soleil's branding. The company's press releases and promotional materials repeatedly emphasize the core narrative, that is, of a quest or a journey. At a talk for the 'Tomorrow Awards' Conference in Montreal in 2011, Cirque du Soleil's brand manager, Jean Guibert, explained how the company, 'never uses superlatives in its press releases or promotional material. Instead, the brand focuses on emotional words like "wonder" and "journey"' (Levy, 2011).

The other element of the quest narrative that Cirque du Soleil repeatedly emphasizes in its marketing materials is 'experience'. As Nigel Hollis, the chief global analyst at marketing research agency Millward Brown, comments, 'Cirque du Soleil's meaningful difference comes from giving people an authentic, amazing experience' (Voight, 2013).

Although the essential Cirque du Soleil experience is the show itself, this experience can be heightened by building the anticipation and expectation leading up to it. The company manages and builds the anticipation and expectation of the show through the development of awareness of Cirque du Soleil as a brand. The Cirque du Soleil brand reinforces the perception of the company as the epitome of an innovative pop cultural phenomenon – a new form of circus without animals, packed with world-class circus skills and artistic vision with popular appeal. The brand perception of Cirque du Soleil in the 1990s was of a company that, despite all of its risk-taking, could not fail; a company redefining North Americans' understanding of what circus could be. During the early 2000s Cirque du Soleil became associated with the wider occupation of cultural and popular space. The company had helped to completely transform Las Vegas, with many of its permanent shows running for years, and also toured widely with tent shows and arena shows. Cirque also moved beyond its live shows, and became visible on television, on the wide-screen in 3-D, in the Grammys, the Oscars and the Super Bowl. The Cirque du Soleil spectator, through this developed sense of this brand awareness, feels expectation and anticipation for the 'experience' of attending the show, and this before-show expectation is managed carefully to increase the impact of the show. Spectators on arrival for a Cirque du Soleil show undergo an immersive cross-pollination of many brands and managed expectations in a very effective 'brandscaping' environment (Klingman, 2007). Although the show is the actual experience, the products, the programme, the popcorn, the beer, the souvenirs with a sliding scale of price tags, the co-branding with automobiles, luxury goods, the optional VIP events, all contribute to creating a narrative of expectation and experience in which the environment allows for the selling of products. In her review Lindsay Vandewart focuses on how this sense of anticipation forms part of the essential experience of the show, describing how audience members are treated to free popcorn and drinks as they wander among the huge range of *Luzia* souvenirs, and how dancers move to a live mariachi band, 'while a stilt-walker parades the grounds in character as a puppeteer with a lively, mime-like puppet performer moving delicately beneath her strings' (Vandewart, 2017). She goes on to describe how anticipation is further built when the audience enters the big top itself, with curiosity piqued by a huge suspended golden sun, marigolds circling the stage, and an oversized key placed front and centre.

This entrepreneurial narrative of 'experience' combined with 'wonder' and 'journey' has been taken further in *Toruk* through the development of immersive digital technology which enables spectators to have a 'personalized experience' delivered direct to their mobile devices (SAP, 2015).

Louis Malafarina, senior director, corporate alliances at Cirque du Soleil, describes these new personalized experiences:

> Before spectators even enter the arena, they can download the TORUK – The First Flight mobile app ... and immerse themselves into the world of Pandora to learn more about the characters and mythical storyline inspired by James Cameron's movie 'Avatar.' Throughout the performance, the SAP HANA platform will facilitate communication between spectators and the show's visual effects control system, creating a personalized experience delivered directly to their mobile devices based on their interaction with the app and location in the theater.
>
> (SAP, 2015)

As well as emphasizing the motif of journey or experience in relation to its own shows Cirque du Soleil has also been on the cutting edge of experiential marketing, and has leveraged its brand image to build branding partnerships, as Cirque du Soleil CEO Daniel Lamarre says, 'Today, people aren't looking for transactions. They're looking for experiences. At Cirque, everyone—whether they're in a costume shop or our executive offices—is in the business of creating unforgettable experiences' (cited in Target, 2017). Experiential marketing has now become the cutting edge of marketing. Global marketing analyst David Moth at Econsultancy writes that the premise of experiential marketing is to create a closer bond between the consumer and the brand by immersing them in a fun and memorable experience. If a brand event stirs genuine positive emotions within people then they are more likely to associate those emotions with that brand, which is more effective than just showing them a Facebook ad (Moth, 2014).

The role of 'experience' in marketing is a relatively new area of research. Bernd Herbert Schmitt, Professor of International Business in the Marketing Department at Columbia Business School, points out:

> consumer and marketing research on experience is still emerging. Experience, as a concept and as an empirical phenomenon, is not as established as other consumer and marketing concepts such as choice, attitudes, consumer satisfaction, or brand equity. This needs to change.
>
> (Schmitt, 2010)

Cirque du Soleil CEO Daniel Lamarre, discussing the relationship between the 'Cirque du Soleil experience' and branding partnerships, is quoted as saying: 'With our background in entertainment, we are seeking to create artistic experiences—or content—that help brands appeal to their key audience' (cited in Voight, 2013). An example is Cirque du Soleil's collaborations with technology companies such as a partnership with Google promoting the Chrome Browser 'by creating a game-like app, Movi.Kanti. Revo, in which the user makes his way through a surreal world, encountering Cirque characters along the way' (Voight, 2013). The ideas of quest, with its implied values of risk-taking, experience and crossing boundaries all remain pivotal to Cirque du Soleil's entrepreneurial narrative.

Cirque du Soleil's Founding Narrative

The 'founding narrative' forms an important part of many companies' identities including Cirque du Soleil. Founding narratives are:

> carefully crafted, revised, reiterations of defining moments. Cirque du Soleil's founding narrative relies on its communal, street performer origins in the backwaters of rural Québec, leading to its explosion on the world scene made possible by ambition, talent, charm, invention, and a series of calculated risks.
>
> (Leroux, 2012)

Guy Laliberté, Cirque du Soleil's founder, talking about the company's survival in the early stages of its history, states: 'It was only with the courage and arrogance of youth that we survived' (cited in Hunter-Tilney, 2015), although, '[g]overnment grants and a substantial overdraft from a Quebec community bank also helped' (Hunter-Tilney, 2015). The company's self-narrative firmly focuses on the importance of risk-taking and audacity rather than the government support it received, as Daniel Lamarre reiterates: 'We like to take risks. It's part of who we are. Every time we come in a comfort zone, we will find a way to get out, because being comfortable in our business is very, very dangerous' (quoted in Tischler, 2005).

The company also cites its successes within the context of an ongoing search for innovation: 'We are constantly researching new artistic avenues and innovating within our organization and we intend to carry on taking such risks and inventing with audacity' (Laliberté, cited in Pittman, 2009). The company's self-narrative positions the company as being in constant forward movement, on a journey or on a quest through innovation and audacity to exceptionalism: 'If innovation and audacity are to be the determining criteria of the product (the shows), the process (both artistic and administrative), and in ensuring the continued existence of the company, the only possible movement is forward' (Leroux, 2012).

In spite of the creation of Cirque du Soleil's Global Citizenship and Social Responsibility Division which coincided with its stratospheric economic success in its Las Vegas ventures, and in spite of the company pledging to devote 1 per cent of its revenue to programmes managed by their public, social and cultural affairs service, the organization's philanthropic profile is low. Very little mention is made of the fact that Cirque du Soleil contributes funds to the National Circus School; to La TOHU, which is Canada's first performance venue with a subscription series and an international festival devoted exclusively to the circus arts; or of the fact that the company encourages its own employees' artistic projects; funds Arts du Monde and Cirque du Monde, two programmes for youth at risk around the globe; and supports One Drop, an organization aiming to provide clean water to people around the world. The company has rarely promoted its philanthropic activities and has only recently begun to mention them in press releases. Guy Laliberté has said: 'We are now taking a more prominent public role in an effort to inspire other companies and individuals to make a similar commitment to citizenship' (cited in Pittman, 2009). Instead of widely promoting these philanthropic ventures Cirque du Soleil has always elected to place focus on the ideas of risk-taking, innovation and audacity and experience, all of which act to reinforce the quest as being central to the company's narrative.

Guy Laliberté

The life of Cirque du Soleil's founder Guy Laliberté can perhaps be seen as exemplifying the company narrative, through the presentation of his life as a journey through experience to exceptionalism, '[a] former busker, he became one of Canada's richest men and the world's first billionaire fire-breather … His employees call him the "roi soleil"' (Hunter-Tilney, 2015). However, in 2009 Cirque Du Soleil celebrated its 25th anniversary and Guy Laliberté was miserable:

> It's not the emotion you'd expect. Laliberté had [gone] from a fire-breathing performer on the streets of Montreal to the billionaire owner of the venerable Cirque Du Soleil franchise […] Laliberté had fame, stability, mansions, fast cars and more money he could ever need. But he was missing two things: Freedom and a challenge. So he bought a $35 million ticket to space.
>
> (Bertoni, 2011)

His life journey from small town boy to billionaire creator and 'Guide' for Cirque du Soleil reached a mythic peak with the journey into space. This high-risk form of travel, or quest, can be understood as an essential element of the metanarrative of the company, and of the brand:

> Laliberté's privately funded journey into space aboard Russian spaceship Soyouz and onto the International Space Station in October 2009 … developed a title: 'The Poetic and Social Mission into Space,' as well as a theme, a logo, products, a web page, a blog, press conferences. A number of Cirque employees suddenly mobilized in Russia and, of course, an international live show directed by Fernand Rainville which featured performances in fourteen cities by various world music acts or philanthropic-minded pop bands such as U2. The billionaire's caprice had become a Cause.
>
> (Leroux, 2012)

The narrative theme of the quest and the value placed on experience resonates clearly in Laliberté's response during an interview undertaken while he was in space, in which, when asked how he is feeling, he responded: 'I feel great, it's been an amazing journey so far, an experience of a lifetime' (Bevan, 2009).

Laliberté takes centre stage, as the original Cirque du Soleil individual of exception, rising from the backwaters of rural Québec to outer space, after having conquered hyper-America, and seducing much of the world with the company's touring shows. The return on investment for this could be teased out over time through Cirque du Soleil's recent business developments in Russia, but it is mostly intangible economically and can rather be understood to have strengthened the brand equity through the exemplary daring singularity of its founder and principal brand 'personality' Guy Laliberté, who has referred to himself as 'the first clown in space' (Bertoni, 2011).

Laliberté's official title at Cirque, in contrast to most CEOs, is 'the Guide', a term which reflects his mythic role in leading the company on the quest to success. Laliberté's interest in quest is further exemplified in his new partnership with Alexandre Amancio, one of the creative team involved in the gaming franchises Assassin's Creed and Far Cry 2. With this new company, Reflector, Laliberté is focusing on generating original gaming content, and setting new narratives in innovative virtual worlds (Lodderhose, 2017).

The narrative arc of the life journey of Cirque du Soleil's founder Guy Laliberté, (from street busker, to billionaire, to company 'Guide', to self-described 'clown in space', to creator of new virtual worlds) and his embodiment of the quest, or life-journey, through experience to exceptionalism, can be seen as exemplifying the metanarrative of the 'quest' which underpins the multiple narratives of Cirque du Soleil.

Conclusion

In this chapter we have investigated the role of narrative in the success of Cirque du Soleil and have pointed to the importance of the quest as a metanarrative which has archetypal resonance and is vital to the company's success. The quest, with its essential core elements of the importance of experience, forward motion and risk-taking, has been shown to be of pivotal importance, underlying the multiple narratives of Cirque du Soleil, not only the dramaturgical narratives, but also the entrepreneurial narratives, the founding narrative of the company, and the narrative of the life-journey of company founder, Guy Laliberté, effectively giving archetypal resonance to the company and the global success it enjoys. It will be interesting to see how these narratives – dramaturgical, thematic, commercial and foundational – evolve over the next few years under the company's new stewardship which now includes not only the entrepreneurial founding members, but also private equity firms from the USA and China. Will the current existing narratives remain in place in light of their proven international success and their ability to communicate with such a wide audience, or will new narratives emerge?

Discussion Questions

1. How does Cirque du Soleil exemplify a concept of a broad-spectrum approach to narrative?
2. Discuss how Cirque du Soleil disseminates the metanarrative of 'quest' and the supporting narratives of 'experience', 'forward motion', 'risk-taking' and 'boundary crossing' in its online publicity and in interviews with creatives.
3. Examine another performance company's work and business practice through the lens of a broad-spectrum approach to narrative.
4. How does the broad-spectrum approach to narrative introduced in this writing change understandings of narrative and its function in relation to performance companies?
5. Can a broad-spectrum approach to narrative be applied to a pop cultural icon or a celebrity? Can this approach be identified in social media narrative self-representations and the performance of celebrity?

Websites

Primary Cirque du Soleil website: https://www.cirquedusoleil.com/
Numerous sections of Cirque du Soleil performances on YouTube.

Note

1. The term 'broad spectrum' in this essay in relation to narrative is used to denote an extended continuum of narrative that extends beyond the narrative devices used in the theatrical performance to include narratives such as

those used in company promotion, and in the company founding narrative. The use of this term 'broad spectrum' references Richard Schechner's (2013) notion of a 'continuum' or 'broad-spectrum' approach to the inclusive analysis of performance to extend beyond normative theatrical or performance practice. Schechner's approach to the inclusive analysis of performance acts as an inspiration for Lavers' and Leroux's broad-spectrum approach to the analysis of narrative, which is used to drive this chapter, 'The Multiple Narratives of Cirque du Soleil'.

Works Cited and Resource Material

Bertoni, S. (2011) Why Cirque Du Soleil Billionaire Guy Laliberté Traveled To Space, *Forbes*, https://www.forbes.com/sites/stevenbertoni/2011/06/09/why-cirque-du-soleil-billionaire-guy-laliberte-traveled-to-space/#5762e607cb2c, accessed 20 June 2017.

Bevan, S. (2009) Space Tourist May Have Last Laugh, *The World Today*, ABC Radio, http://www.abc.net.au/worldtoday/content/2009/s2706042.htm, accessed 20 June 2017.

CB STAFF (2015) Canada's Richest People: Guy Laliberté', *Canadian Business*, http://www.canadianbusiness.com/lists-and-rankings/richest-people/rich-100-guy-laliberte./, accessed 20 June 2017.

Cirque Du Soleil (2017a) An Experience for the Senses, Cirque du Soleil website, https://www.cirquedusoleil.com/joya#about, accessed 20 June 2017.

_____. (2017b) Franco Dragone Biography, http://www.fampeople.com/cat-franco-dragone, accessed 4 July 2018.

_____. (2017c) Meet the Team, Cirque du Soleil website, https://www.cirquedusoleil.com/en/jobs/casting/team/mentor/robert-lepage.aspx, accessed 20 June 2017.

Everett-Green, R. (2016) Cirque du Soleil's Luzia is a Magical Mexican Spectacle, *The Globe and Mail*, https://www.theglobeandmail.com/arts/theatre-and-performance/cirque-du-soleils-luzia-is-a-magical-mexican-spectacle/article29837400/, accessed 20 June 2017.

Fricker, K. (2010) Le goût du risque: Kà de Robert Lepage et du Cirque du Soleil (Risky Business: Robert Lepage and the Cirque du Soleil's Kà). Trans. Isabelle Savoie. *L'Annuaire Théâtral*, 45, pp. 45–68, https://www.erudit.org/fr/revues/annuaire/2009-n45-annuaire3893/044274ar/, accessed 20 June 2017.

Graver, D. (2005) The Actor's Bodies, in P. Auslander (Ed.) *Performance: Critical Concepts in Literary and Cultural Studies* (New York: Routledge) pp. 157–74.
Harvie, J. and E. Hurley (1999) States of Play: Locating Québec in the Performances of Robert Lepage, Ex Machina, and the Cirque du Soleil, *Theatre Journal*, 51, pp. 299–315.
Hunter-Tilney, L. (2015) Guy Laliberté, Cirque du Soleil Co-founder, *The Financial Times*, https://www.ft.com/content/5156e710-e99a-11e4-a687-00144feab7de?mhq5j=e3, accessed 20 June 2017.
Hurley, E. (2016a) Performance Services: The Promises of Cirque du Soleil, in L. P. Leroux and C. R. Batson (Eds) *Cirque Global: Quebec's Expanding Circus Boundaries* (Montreal: McGill-Queen's University Press) pp. 71–8.
_____. (2016b) The Multiple Bodies of Cirque du Soleil, in L. P. Leroux and C. R. Batson (Eds) *Cirque Global: Quebec's Expanding Circus Boundaries* (Montreal: McGill-Queen's University Press) pp. 122–39.
Irwin, R. (2011) Robert Irwin's Top 10 Quest Narratives, *The Guardian*, https://www.theguardian.com/books/2011/apr/21/robert-irwin-top-10-quest-narratives, accessed 20 June 2017.
Isherwood, C. (2005) Fire, Acrobatics and Most of All, Hydraulics, *The New York Times*, http://query.nytimes.com/gst/fullpage.html?res=9F07E2DD113B-F936A35751C0A9639C8B63, accessed 20 June 2017.
Klingman, A. (2007) *Brandscapes: Architecture in the Experience Economy* (Cambridge, MA: MIT Press).
Lavers, K. (2016) Luzia: Cirque du Soleil at Its Best With New Show, Luzia, *ArtsHub*, http://performing.artshub.com.au/news-article/reviews/performing-arts/katie-lavers/luzia-251791, accessed 20 June 2017.
Leroux, L. P. (2009a) Le Québec à Las Vegas: peregrinations postidentitaires dans l'hyper-Amérique, *L'Annuaire théâtral*, 45, Spring, pp. 9–20.
_____. (2009b) Zumanity: la spectacularisation de l'intime ou le pari impossible d'authenticité au Cirque', *L'Annuaire théâtral*, 45, Spring, pp. 69–91.
_____. (2010) Zumanity: The Spectacularization of Intimacy, or the Impossible Gamble of Authenticity in the Cirque, Presentation, Concordia University.
_____. (2012) Cirque in Space, Presentation, Duke University.
_____. (2016) Introduction: Reinventing Tradition, Building a Field: Quebec Circus and its Scholarship, in L. P. Leroux and C. R. Batson (Eds) *Cirque Global: Quebec's Expanding Circus Boundaries* (Montreal: McGill-Queen's University Press) pp. 3–21.
Levy, D. (2011) Branding Emotion: Video Q&A with Cirque du Soleil's Jean Guibert, http://sparksheet.com/branding-emotion-video-qa-with-cirque-du-soleil's-jean-guibert/, accessed 20 June 2017.

Lodderhose, D. (2017) 'Cirque Du Soleil' Creator Guy Laliberté & Alexandre Amancio Form Reflector Entertainment – Cannes, http://deadline.com/2017/05/cirque-du-soleil-creator-guy-laliberte-assassins-greed-alexandre-amancio-reflector-entertainment-1202102235/, accessed 10 July 2017.

Moth, D. (2014) 10 Very Cool Examples of Experiential Marketing, *Econsultancy*, https://econsultancy.com/blog/65230-10-very-cool-examples-of-experiential-marketing, accessed 20 June 2017.

Peterson-Withorn, C. (2015) Billionaire Guy Laliberté Cashes Out as Investors Acquire Majority Stake in Cirque du Soleil, *Forbes*, https://www.forbes.com/sites/chasewithorn/2015/04/20/billionaire-guy-laliberte-cashes-out-as-investors-acquire-majority-stake-in-cirque-du-soleil/#64553d4d7c72, accessed 20 June 2017.

Pittman, C. (2009) First Poetic Social Mission in Space: Guy Laliberté, founder of Cirque du Soleil and the One Drop Foundation, Begins Training for Travel on Board SOYUZ TMA-16 to ISS, Cirque du Soleil Global Citizenship website.

Productions Conte, Ka Extreme, by Cirque du Soleil, Montreal, Quebec. Promotional/documentary DVD, https://www.amazon.com/Cirque-Du-Soleil-Extreme-Creation/dp/B002G7MYV8, accessed 20 June 1017.

SAP, Systemanalyse und Programmentwicklung (System Analysis and Program Development) (2015) SAP Makes Audience Part of Cirque du Soleil's *TORUK – The First Flight* with New Interactive Mobile Experience, http://news.sap.com/sap-makes-audience-part-of-cirque-du-soleils-toruk-the-first-flight-with-new-interactive-mobile-experience/, accessed 20 June 2017.

Schechner, R. (2013) *Performance Studies: An Introduction* (New York and London: Routledge) p. 2.

Schmitt, B. (2010) Experience Marketing: Concepts, Frameworks and Consumer Insights, *Foundations and Trends in Marketing*, 5, pp. 55–112.

Tait, P. (2005) *Circus Bodies: Cultural Identity in Aerial Performance* (London and New York: Routledge).

Target (2017) Flying High: Cirque du Soleil CEO Daniel Lamarre Swings By Target, https://corporate.target.com/article/2017/05/cirque-outer-spaces, accessed 20 June 2017.

Tischler, L. (2005) Join the Circus, Fast Company, https://www.fastcompany.com/53331/join-circus, accessed 20 June 2017.

Vandewart, L. (2017) Review: Cirque du Soleil Sets New High with Luzia, *303 Magazine*, http://303magazine.com/2017/06/cirque-du-soleil-luzia-denver/, accessed 20 June 2017.

Voight, J. (2013) Brands Are Eager to Partner With Cirque du Soleil: It's a Balancing Act, *Adweek*, http://www.adweek.com/brand-marketing/brands-are-eager-partner-cirque-du-soleil-150147/, accessed 20 June 2017.

Volz, J. (2010) *How To Run a Theatre: A Witty, Practical and Fun Guide to Arts Management*, 2nd edition (London and New York: Bloomsbury).

Wilson, A. (2002) Cirque du Soleil Reimagines the Circus: The Evolution of an Aesthetic, PhD Thesis, University of Oregon.

8

Personal Agency and Community Empowerment
Moth Style Engagement

Judith Halebsky

Introduction

The Moth is a storytelling organization based in New York City that hosts events and workshops in which everyday people are invited to narrate their stories in front of an audience.[1] Moth-style stories are a genre of personal narrative where people tell stories about the events of their own lives. The stories are generally planned but not scripted, memorized or aided by notes. A story, like a memory, is revised and made anew at each telling. The way a story changes in the process of remembering can help us make sense of not just the past but also the present. Narrative storytelling is relatively accessible through open mikes and community group workshops. It requires lived experience, of course, but also willingness to examine that experience and share it with others. As with many acting techniques, improvisation asks the performer to be fully present physically and mentally. It also opens the possibility for gaining insight in the moment of telling and seeing the story anew as it is evoked onstage. The Moth offers narratives that we label as true but it is the empowerment of voicing individual experience and the larger resonances of these stories with our human condition that gives them theatrical power. It is in these moments of revelation and vulnerability that the art of personal narrative, popularized through the Moth, can be a transformative social force.

Novelist and Moth founder George Dawes Green hosted the first Moth event in his home in 1997. He was inspired to recreate the nights of his youth spent telling stories on a porch in Georgia. He explains, 'I just loved the idea of a community of people that would be able to gather and tell stories. Life for everybody in that group was richer' (Ziv, 2015). After refining a few aspects of hosting a live show that included imposing strict time limits on storytellers, the show moved from his home into public venues such as bars and coffee shops. Since then, the Moth has produced over 2,000 live shows on six continents, two books of Moth stories, multiple CD volumes, and a weekly show on National Public Radio. The podcast has 30 million downloads per year. The Moth runs the Justice Project that offers storytelling workshops to people affected by the criminal justice system and has an initiative for storytelling in spaces that support gender-based equality. They run a Teacher Institute to train educators to bring Moth-style storytelling into their classrooms. The popularity of the Moth has spawned many other storytelling groups including Porchlight in San Francisco. The name of the Moth comes from Green's nights sitting on a porch in Georgia telling stories while moths fluttered toward the light. San Francisco's Porchlight makes a direct connection to the Moth in both name and the general structure of their events.

The Moth hosts StorySLAMs, GrandSLAMs and Mainstage events. At a StorySLAM audience members willing to tell a story put their name in a hat. Names are drawn at random and the people are invited up to the stage to tell their story. There is no script and no audition. The set is minimal and the costumes are street clothes. An emcee introduces the storyteller by their name and the title of their story. There is a musician onstage who serves as timekeeper. After five minutes, the musician will make a gentle sound as a sign that the time is up. If the storyteller goes a full minute overtime, the musician plays a note or a chord more aggressively. Before the show starts groups in the audience volunteer to judge the stories. Points are tracked for each story and the winner goes on to tell a new story at a Moth GrandSLAM event. While the StorySLAM is open to any member of the audience lucky enough to have their name pulled from the hat that night, a GrandSLAM presents storytellers who have previously won a StorySLAM. Mainstage shows are carefully curated by an artistic director and held in performance venues such as theatres and concert halls. Narratives included in the Moth podcast have been selected from multiple Moth events. There are events monthly in multiple cities across the country and around the world. The ones that make it onto the podcast have been chosen from hundreds, if not thousands, of stories.

A Moth show is fun, inspiring and moving but it also has a social purpose. Moth StorySLAMs make a space for individual voices to tell their story and their experiences even when these stories differ from commonly held beliefs, ideas or shared narratives of historical events. In this way, Moth stories have the power to speak against official narratives and, through their telling, can shift dominant ideas to reflect the experiences of those who live these stories. We see this in many Moth stories including two discussed below: Kimberley Reed's *Life Flight* and Robert Zellner's *Poitier and Brando, Mississippi, 1964*.[2] The thrill of Moth storytelling comes not just from the content and delivery of the story, but also from the act of voicing a distinctive perspective. It is a means to claim the ways our individual experiences do not fit expectations, rules and established images. Moth storytelling creates a space of connection where representations are malleable and where storytellers are making anew their past for how it can illuminate and change the present.

Crafting a Narrative

Crafting a narrative to tell live onstage is a personal journey that involves the interior work of reflecting on the experiences of our lives. When Catherine Burns, artist director of the Moth, is drawing out a story from someone to perform on stage, she starts by asking, 'Tell me about yourself. Tell me how you became *you*' (2013: 2). To find a narrative requires figuring out how certain experiences and moments have shaped us. On a personal level, we know that a particular story is significant or meaningful. As storytellers, we need to find ways to tell our story to an audience so that it transmits the significance and meaning of these events. This is where the work of crafting a narrative begins. While the improvisational quality of the stories might make it seem as though the storyteller is just speaking from memory, most often Moth narratives have been carefully developed with the help and feedback of peers, other storytellers or a director. Devising a story draws on both writing and acting techniques but at its core requires examining the experiences that have shaped our lives.

Burns works with storytellers through the personal journey of developing a story for the stage. Burns describes this journey as a willingness on the part of the storyteller to be vulnerable, to examine their failures, regrets and weaknesses. This point of view requires the perspective of time or personal change to see how we are shaped by past actions and events. In looking for narratives for the Moth, she explains:

> We ask people to share the biggest moments of their lives — the moments that changed them for the better (or worse). And while many of our favorite stories are about moments of triumph, stories about our *mistakes* can often be more revelatory. The number one quality of a great storyteller is their willingness to be vulnerable, their ability to tell on themselves.
>
> (2013: 2)

The risks that storytellers take onstage is part of what makes a Moth show dynamic and thrilling. Due to these risks and the personal work of storytelling, preparing a narrative for the stage requires a supportive atmosphere.

When I teach, I aim to create a space for our best narratives to be revealed. On the first night of class, we get in a circle. I ask students to introduce themselves by telling us how they came to study at this university. Each student takes a turn talking briefly about how they chose Dominican University or ended up at this institution through a series of events. I also share my personal narrative. After everyone has spoken, I point out that they have now each told a story. This highlights how creating a narrative is part of our everyday lives and something that we each practise regularly. Generally, in creative writing classes we read all works submitted to the class as fiction. While we might guess that the narrative within a written story reflects the personal experience of the author, we discuss the work as though it were imagined. This provides for a degree of separation between the writer and their work that we do not have in the storytelling classroom. For this reason and others, it is important that the classroom emphasizes respect, empathy and support for each member of the class. One way to establish this atmosphere is for me to be open and supportive. As a group, we agree that we will not share the stories people tell in class with people outside the class. This provides for security in trying out stories and sharing personal stories. Doing this on the first day of class also establishes the classroom as a place to take risks. I ask students to offer any other ideas or requests for ground rules. This helps the group cohere and gives students the agency to shape the parameters of our class experience. Once the ground rules are established, I remind the class of our agreed upon parameters and occasionally ask if anyone wants to add to them or revise them.

Over the course of the semester, the length of narratives increases from a two-minute story to a five-minute story to a ten-minute story. In class, students work in small groups and take turns 'drafting' their narrative by telling the story to this small group (two to four students). This sets up a benchmark due-date on creating a story that does not necessarily have a written or audio-recorded version. It provides an opportunity for the storyteller to practise performing to a small audience and to receive individual feedback. They can also tell a revised version the next week to a new classmate who has not yet heard it. When we have a class sharing night where students perform, most of the audience is hearing these stories for the first time. This structure allows students to practise and revise a narrative and at the same time preserves the energy of a storytelling session where students share work that is largely new to the audience.

As discussed earlier, the material of these narratives are the experiences of our lives, which means we each already have more material than we could ever use. However, developing memories into a compelling narrative requires reflection and an active process of going back into the details, images, sights, smells and feelings of the memory. To keep an open and exploratory mind in searching for a story, it helps to develop multiple options of possible stories to tell. At our first class meeting, I ask students to come to the next class with three ideas for stories to tell. They brainstorm each story in rough notes in a journal. We take bits of memories and the reflections on events and develop a narrative structure.

Educational guidelines from the Moth instruct, 'Stakes are essential in live storytelling. What do you stand to gain or lose? Why is what is happening in the story important to you' (Storytelling Tips & Tricks)? For the audience to invest in the narrative, there needs to be something to risk or lose. Another part of structuring a story is to emphasize a theme or repeated motif that can bring the narrative together and reveal its significance.

Once the material for a story has been remembered by the storyteller, a creative process of how best to evoke the experiences of the storyteller in ways that can be imagined and accessed by the audience begins. In our personal experience, the stakes of what we stand to gain or lose might come near the end of the story but to engage an audience, the narrative needs to offer the risks of the story near the beginning. We often remember events in sequence but the story does not need to be bound to a particular chronology. I ask students to consider what will establish the stakes of a narrative early on. Should the story start at a moment of realization, at a low point or at the end? Perhaps the story is best started in the middle of things. This requires switching from telling a lived experience in the order of events as they happened to telling a lived experience through how it best reveals a revelation or lesson learned for an audience.

At the Moth, the stories gain authority through the concept of the personal narratives as true, lived experience. Foregrounding these performances as true stories diminishes the audience's awareness of the ways that they are constructed. In general, the performers are not professional actors or trained theatre artists. However, actors and writers are attracted to the form and it is not unusual for a StorySLAM winner to have pursuits as a screen writer, novelist or stand-up comedian. In learning how to develop a Moth-style story, the activity of engaging in a narrative analysis (breaking down a story through chronological events, themes, repeated motifs) helps to reveal the art of creating a performance. Kimberley Reed's story *Life Flight* offers an example of setting stakes, shifting expectations, establishing characters and settings, and employing a repeated motif.

At the beginning of *Life Flight*, Reed sets the parameters of the tale and imparts the information needed for the audience to connect with the significance of the story. Writers often call this the contract; it sets the expectations of the story that the storyteller agrees to fulfil. Reed's story begins with an urgent call from her mother with news that her father is being airlifted to a hospital for an emergency organ transplant. Her mother offers reassurance that everything will be fine. Reed, in a gesture that establishes the distance between spoken words and their implied meaning, describes her mother as 'perennially optimistic' and tells the audience that the situation is urgent (2011). This sets the frame for her story: her father is at death's door. She establishes a *what's at stake* through the question of whether or not she can get to his bedside before he dies.

As the narrative unfolds, the frames shift suddenly. The next sentence reveals that the father has passed away. With the first hook resolved, we risk losing interest in the story. But just as quickly, Reed introduces new, more complex stakes. The narrative goes on to focus on Reed's return to her hometown for the funeral, which is complicated because she left home as a son and is returning as a daughter. Now the story is about a pressing need to return to a place she planned never to go back to and whether or not a family member, neighbours and old friends will accept her.

A storyteller needs to choose how to most effectively and efficiently evoke the key aspects of the story. Green describes this as 'condense and tweak and reshape and condense some more' (Green, 2013: xx). Characters and settings are communicated through providing specific details. In Reed's story, she efficiently creates vivid moments through well-chosen bits of information. Reed describes her brother Mark as conservative and short-tempered. They are estranged not because they had a falling out but because our narrator has not found the courage or opportunity to tell her brother about her transition. She explains, 'I just kept putting it off'. She creates an image of her brother with information that builds on what is revealed elsewhere in the story: growing up in a small town in Montana with a professional, hardworking father and a caring mother (2011). The narrative is revealed through descriptions of precise details and specific moments of Reed's return to her hometown and meeting her brother after their father's death.

As the family gathered in the hours after her father's death, she described going to Applebee's with her mother and siblings to celebrate what would been her father's sixty-fifth birthday. They order apple pie with a candle in it. Reed focuses her narrative on her brother Mark and the expression on his face while he blows out the candle. In this moment Mark is coming to realize that their father has died and at the same time gaining perspective into why his sibling, our narrator, has been out of touch. She reflects on his facial expression: 'He was trying to process my father's passing. He was figuring out why it had been so long that the two of us hadn't talked … and it was just all kind of coming together' (2011). Reed's story establishes layers of conflict and shares them through carefully chosen images and details.

A narrative needs a theme, a transformation or a repeated motif. The stakes of a story often connect to the theme. For Reed, her theme functions as a repeated motif around the idea that her father was someone who worked in the background fixing things. She describes how he grew up on a farm and became an eye doctor, pointing out that he can fix both farm equipment and eye problems. She stresses that he was modest about these skills and his ability to fix problems, saying, 'he was always doing it behind the scenes' (2011). At an early point in the story, Reed realizes that she and her mother will now have go to through this difficult situation without his assistance. By the end of the story, Reed's estrangement with her brother and her exile from her hometown have both been resolved. This narrative conclusion is paired with a formal device of again evoking the repeated motif of the loving father, even after his death, fixing problems from behind the scenes. Reed quotes her mother saying, 'You know, Dad was always fixing things, and it looks like he fixed this too' (2011).

Moth performances are revealed as personal truth in the first person. However, there are two points of view, the storyteller in the present speaking onstage, and an earlier, younger self, naïve to the events that unfold. This creates two perspectives. While there are no set rules other than the guidelines of a true story told live, the Moth website and educational materials set out some parameters. One of their storytelling tips instructs, 'stories have a *change*. The main character (you!) has to change in some way from beginning to end' (Tips for Storytelling, Safety and Best Practice). This change creates the two points of view in the story. The events of the story or the reflection on these events function as a catalyst for insight and growth. In the guides for educators, a similar catchphrase is used with students: scars not wounds. They ask students to tell a story that they have distance from rather than a story about an ongoing conflict or issue. In part, this is so that the storytelling event does not become fuel for ongoing conflicts within the school. But more importantly, working with a story of the past gives students the tool of perspective in developing and sharing the story. The storyteller is performing the self and also reconstructing an earlier self through narrative. The art of evolving the narrative involves actively working with the material of memory and reflection.

Remembering Onstage

One common assumption about memory is that it works as a recording with an archive of events stored away within our minds that, when called up, emerge as unchanged records of experience. If this were the case, remembering would be a straightforward process. However, as scholars in psychology and philosophy explain, we remember events based on our prior experience and our needs in the present. In *Searching for Memory: The Brain, the Mind, and the Past*, Daniel Schacter writes: 'many of us still see our memories as a series of family pictures stored in a photo album of our minds. Yet it is now clear that we do not store judgment-free snapshots of our past experiences but rather hold onto the meaning, sense, and emotions these experiences provided us' (1996: 5). Our emotional experience of an event shapes how we remember that event. At the same time, our present situation also shapes how we remember events of the past. Scholar Sue Campbell explains that memory is generated in two phases. The first phase is 'encoding experience as memory' and the second phase is 'retrieving the memory from storage' (2014: 13–14). Campbell points out that the needs of our present shape how we remember the events of our past. The process of remembering involves an ongoing shifting and improvising with our earlier experiences that we have encoded as memories.

Moth performances are true to the storyteller's memory; in this way they stress emotional truth over what some might label factual or journalistic truth. Campbell disputes concepts of accuracy in memory and puts forward a concept of *good remembering*:

> good remembering often involves getting something right about the significance of the past as judged from the standpoint of the present. In remembering, we often care that we are appropriately guided by our experience of the past, and this concern reflects the nature of memory as the set of capacities through which we learn by experience.
>
> (2014: 14)

Here, Campbell's concept of good remembering connects with the elements that make for a riveting Moth story: a narrative that reflects on the significance of past events in terms of how these events shaped the storyteller in the present.

We live in social spaces with values and expectations that are shaped by powerful forces such as the government, educational institutions, family units and the media. Campbell writes about the power of remembering in structuring and controlling groups: 'political projects of nation building and destroying are infused with attempts to shape and control the significance of the past in order to legitimate and serve a future vision' (2014: 91). At the Moth, these power structures are disrupted for a few minutes or a few hours. Storytellers and audience members can feel the shift in this power as individual memory and experience that does not conform to dominant narratives is voiced and validated onstage. One Moth event with the theme *American Myths: Stories of US* directly addresses the dissonance between images and ideas of American experience and the reality of a US lived experience. This Moth event, held on 23 October 2002 in New York City, asked personal narrators to address myths held about the United States. In the video recording of that night, Zellner talks about his work as a member of the Student Nonviolent Coordinating Committee (SNCC) in his story, *Poitier and Brando, Mississippi 1964*.

Zellner's narrative focuses on Freedom Summer, a civil rights mobilization in 1964 that aimed to increase voter registration among African Americans in Mississippi. This effort built on a growing civil rights movement and earlier voter registration efforts that were frequently met with violence. Zellner explains: 'people were getting killed because they were black and wanted to vote. Many of our organizers were shot, some of them were killed' (2002). His narrative stresses the difference between how history is remembered in the public imagination and his first-hand experiences. He points out how some representations of those events such as the film *Mississippi Burning* present a view of the US government at that time that conflicts with events as Zellner lived them.

In planning Freedom Summer, Zellner and others believed the federal government would offer some degree of support or protection for civil rights workers. As a movement committed to non-violence they needed this support (Umoja, 2003: 202). They found out otherwise when J. Edgar Hoover, then director of the Federal Bureau of Investigation, made public a statement on 10 July 1964 saying: 'we most certainly do not and will not give protection to civil rights workers ... protection is in the hands of local authorities'. This statement was most likely welcomed by segregationists in Mississippi (Umoja, 2003: 209). In Zellner's telling, the murder of three young men, James Chaney, Andrew Goodman and Michael Schwerner, is directly connected to the public statement from the US government that it would not protect the civil rights workers. Weeks later, the young men were found dead, buried in an earthen dam.

Zellner points out that the film *Mississippi Burning* positions the FBI as heroes of the civil rights movement. Zellner's first-person history, however, disputes the representations of *Freedom Summer* in a major motion picture. Zellner says, 'they participated in the mythic misrepresentation of American history when they made the FBI the heroes of the civil rights movement' (2002). Zellner aims to reveal complicity on the part of the US government in segregation, oppression, violence and murder in the south in 1964. This central thrust is carried along by endearing and humorous antidotes. He describes joining the civil rights movement after meeting Martin Luther King and Rosa Parks and 'they got me started on a life of crime' (2002). Zellner makes himself vulnerable to the audience. He performs his story in an open, unguarded way. He speaks to the collective memory of the summer of 1964 as mythic and points out ways that the federal government's complicity in the violence and brutality of that time has been ignored, glossed over or diminished. He is challenging mythic presentations of US history and allows the audience to contemplate it from a different perspective.

The risk and aesthetic power of Moth narratives have many sources, but one we see time and again in the stories of Reed, Zellner and others is the authority of first-person experience to speak against dominant narratives. This is one of the ways that the formal structure of the Moth creates change and greater agency for the storyteller and the audience. The practice of telling these narratives makes a space for people to talk frankly about their experiences in ways that are personal. They voice feelings of shame, regret or failure. At the same time, the stories, our stories, are connected to larger social issues.

Author and Moth storyteller Adam Gopnik roots the dynamic power of Moth in the transmission of the storyteller's first-person narrative to the audience and their connection with the narrative. He writes: 'If "I'll never feel the same" is the moral of every good story, "We're all in this together" is the moral of every Moth occasion' (2013:XV). He goes on to explain that the audience connects to the performer through the first-person narrative: 'You can stand up and tell a story that is entirely, embarrassingly, of "I's" and a listening audience somehow turns each "I" into a "me"'(2013: XV). Gopnik sees the ways that the audience enters into someone else's first-person narrative as grounded in the vulnerability of the storyteller and supported by the audience. Remembering is a social activity. How we remember is shaped and supported by interactive listeners. Scholars describe the process of remembering as a socially constructed practice. Paula Reavey and Steven D. Brown explain that it 'transcends a neat opposition between the individual and the social since personal "memories" maybe co-constructed and elaborated by others' (2006: 180). In this way, the audience is an important component of storytelling not as passive receivers, but as active responders through laughing, sighing, clapping and voting for stories. This role is even stronger in a workshop setting when people draft personal narratives or work with a director. Improvising a story about a memory aligns the formal aspects of an improvised performance with the process of remembering in retrieving, reviving and revising. We construct memories for the present and the people who guide our stories as listeners and responders have an active role in the process of remembering.

The text of a Moth performance is not set. The words, body gestures, vocal tones and timing are improvised. This is central to the art of the Moth. The delivery relies on the storyteller to evoke again the source of the narrative with their mind and body. The improvisational aspects reflect how we store and recall memories. Rather than a fixed archive of established information, memory changes through our work of remembering. Each time we recall or call up a memory, we interpret it again through our current point of view in the present. This in turn changes how we remember a particular incident or event. The act of remembering relies on the pressures and concerns of the present, and Campbell would add the future, to shape how we remember. An improvised story without a concrete plan of what words to say, how to hold the body, and how to shape the tone of voice, allows the storyteller to dynamically interact with that past memory in the present. It allows the performer to find new meaning in the story at the exact moment of delivery and to inscribe a new understanding onto the story informed by the present situation. A script might offer greater eloquence and precision; however, at the Moth a manicured script and rehearsed performance is traded for the risk, concentration and dynamic energy of improvisation.

From its inception in 1997, Moth has continued to grow. Their website lists upcoming events by region and many National Public Radio stations air the 'Moth Radio Hour'. There is a pitch line that people can call to leave a recorded message of their story idea. Sometimes these recordings are included in the Moth podcast. Some stories from the pitch line are developed through guidance from the Moth's artistic director and later performed onstage. Burns, as artistic director, offers feedback and support during the development process of these performances and knows full well that the performer will walk onto the stage alone passing from her hands to the waiting audience. She describes this moment as a 'high-wire act' and, like Gopnik, attributes the energy of a Moth performance to the dynamics between the performer and the audience. This energy is fuelled by the risks of telling the story and the support the audience gives to the performer in being heard. 'The audience's faith in the storytellers becomes a safety net that allows them to explore the most intense moments of their lives onstage in front of a room full of strangers' (Burns, 2013: 2). At the Moth, everyday people share the stories of their lives and the larger issues of which they are a part. Reed and Zellner share their vulnerabilities with us as a way of asking us to connect with them, to invite us into their story. This asks us to form a community with them. And as listeners and audience members, we do.

Discussion Questions

1. Listen to Zellner or Reed perform their Moth story. As you listen, investigate how they employ the narrative building blocks of establishing character, setting, theme/motif, risk and change. What key images and details do they use as building blocks? Trace the chronology of the story. Where does the order of events as presented in the story depart from the chronology of events in the life of the storyteller? Why does the storyteller structure their narrative in this way?
2. Has a narrative ever changed your way of thinking? Give an example of a meaningful story that has stayed with you.
3. If you were asked to perform your own narrative onstage, what would you tell?

Websites

The Moth, True Stories Told Live: https://themoth.org/
Video of Bob Zellner performing *Poitier and Brando, Mississippi, 1964*: https://www.youtube.com/watch?v=fB7HLJCDF6o
Recording of Kimberley Reed performing *Life Flight*: https://themoth.org/stories/life-flight

Notes

1. Author note: Thanks to Arline Klatte and Beth Lisick who taught me storytelling in a Porchlight workshop at Intersection for the Arts in San Francisco in 2011. Also thanks to Scott Whitehair of Chicago's Story Lab for guidance on the range of storytelling groups in the USA and internationally.
2. Key aspects of these stories will be revealed in this chapter. Readers may wish to listen to these stories online as preparation for reading this chapter.

Works Cited and Resource Material

Burns, C. (Ed.) (2013) *The Moth: 50 True Stories* (New York: Hachette Books).
Campbell, S. (2014) *Our Faithfulness to the Past: The Ethics and Politics of Memory* (New York: Oxford University Press).

Fact Sheet (2017) The Moth, https://themoth.org/media-kit, accessed 1 July 2017.
Gopnik, A. (2013) Preface, in *The Moth: 50 True Stories* (New York: Hachett Books).
Green, G. (2013) Foreword, in *The Moth: 50 True Stories* (New York: Hachett Books).
Reavey, P. and S. Brown (2006) Transforming Past Action and Agency in the Present: Time, Social Remembering, and Child Sexual Abuse, *Theory and Psychology*, 16(2), pp. 179–202.
Reed, K. (2011) *Life Flight*, The Moth, https://themoth.org/storytellers/kimberly-reed, accessed 28 June 2017.
Schacter, D. (1996) *Searching for Memory: The Brain, the Mind, and the Past* (Basic Books: New York).
Storytelling Tips & Tricks (2017) The Moth, https://themoth.org/share-your-story/storytelling-tips-tricks, accessed 8 April 2017.
The Moth: True Stories Told Live (2017) https://www.themoth.org/, accessed 1 July 2017.
Tips for Storytelling, Safety and Best Practice (2017) The Moth, PDF, https://themoth.org/education/resources, accessed 10 April 2017.
Umoja, A. (2003) 1964: The Beginning of the End of Nonviolence in the Mississippi Freedom Movement, *Radical History Review*, 85, pp. 201–26.
Zellner, R. (2002) *Poitier and Brando, Mississippi, 1964*, The Moth, https://www.youtube.com/watch?v=fB7HLJCDF6o, accessed 28 June 2017.
Ziv, S. (2015) Have We Got a Story for You: 18 Years of Storytelling at The Moth, *Newsweek*, http://www.newsweek.com/2015/07/10/moth-storytelling-turns-eighteen-348443.html, accessed: 22 June 2017.

9

Narrating and Negotiating Identity in World of Warcraft

Jonathan Osborn

A Quest for Dance

My name is DianaTaylor, and I am a female Tauren shaman. I appeared spontaneously in a burst of light near Camp Narache in Southern Mulgore six weeks ago. Since then I have been traversing the continent, gradually increasing my regional and global knowledge, meeting hostile and friendly creatures, developing my shamanistic abilities and practical skills and probing the limits of my agency. I have worked diligently and often long into the night pursuing these goals while accruing an ever-increasing collection of gold, magical objects and sacred artefacts. Despite these concrete personal and material gains, my own reason for existence – to explore dance in this realm – has been met with frustration; for I have not developed my dancing abilities nor had contact with many individuals who wish to dance with me. I have heard rumours of group dances – at festivities where dance is an integral part of ceremonies and during spontaneous moments of collective triumph – but sadly I have not attracted the attention of admirers, been fortunate enough to meet long-term collaborators, or been invited to gatherings where dance is a focus. I must declare that dancing in this magical world has been an exceedingly lonely venture. I have made concerted efforts to dance in a multitude of contexts, settings and geographies, and have subsequently become well versed in both site-specific performances and personal ritualistic dances, both of which were potentially witnessed by many.

I was able to dance immediately upon my birth near the ceremonial hearth in Camp Narache. My dance is quite simple and consists of twenty unchanging, and always perfectly executed steps. The sequence of these steps is:

1. Four steps to the right beginning with the right hoof and an off-centre clap of the hands;
2. Four steps to the left beginning with the left hoof and an off-centre clap of the hands;
3. Three steps backwards beginning with the right hoof followed by a tap with the left hoof and an off-centre clap of the hands;
4. One step back with the right hoof and a tap with the left hoof and then a step forward on the right hoof and tap with the left hoof and an off-centre clap of the hands;
5. Four steps to the front to begin again with an off-centre clap of the hands.

This simple pattern of movements can be repeated for as long as I wish. The general quality is one of energetic ease and nonchalance, and I never appear outwardly disengaged or disinterested. While I was initially amazed at my virtuosic performance (considering my lack of experience and training – there seems to be some inkling of 'blood memory'[1] at work) as well as my limitless endurance (I was once able to dance for more than thirty minutes without tiring), I appeared to be the only one impressed.

Reasons for this became clear only later, when I realized that all females of my people can dance in this one specific fashion, and thus this particular action is not interesting, exotic or meaningful in itself – perhaps more akin to breathing than a creative endeavour. Similarly, the males of my race also dance in one specific fashion – although their movement is considerably different in terms of the quality, dynamics and form. Despite our huge accumulation of cultural knowledge and our frequent direct contact with benevolent ancestral spirits which guide us throughout our lives, the true origin of these dances is elusive to the Tauren people.

All members of our culture are able to dance in only one of two fashions, depending on the sex of the performer, from the dazzling moment of conception. We are not unique in this regard, as dances here are unteachable, unalterable and unforgettable birthrights – gifts and curses bound directly to race and biological sex. One may attempt to dance with a member of another race, although if one hopes to find synchronicity or unison during this encounter, one will be sorely disappointed due to the specific repertoires encoded deep into our blood. These repertoires, when compared with one another, consist of wildly different forms, rhythms and durations. Although I dream daily of somehow contesting this legacy, it seems that, despite the proliferation of magic here, there are things that are beyond possibility. Clearly the ancestral spirits dictate that it remains this way.

After satisfying my immediate fervour for dance, I began exploring. I was initially surrounded by other Taurens, many of whom were also new arrivals. The village I appeared in was part of a grassland landscape of plains bordered by cliffs where soothing pipe music filled the air. Encircling me were a series of buildings made out of hide, wood and cloth decorated with symbols which resembled geometric animals. Senior members of my community were stationed near the entrances, or just inside them. These generous and wise individuals taught me about my tribe's history, mentored me in skill acquisition, and offered opportunities to gain wealth and power through quests. According to these elders, our tribe had recently returned to our ancestral land, but only after we had joined a consortium of races called the Horde. Comprised of orcs, trolls, blood elves, goblins and undead, the Horde (in return for access to our natural resources and our assistance in their seemingly unending conflict against another group called the Alliance) enabled us to end our slavery to the Centaurs, and to reclaim some notion of our sovereignty. Whether or not this arrangement is merely another form of servitude, or indeed a path to future self-determination and permanent freedom, is yet to be established. Regardless, quests for the cleansing of our land, the protection of our borders, and the search for tribal artefacts were of top priority. It was through these adventures (which often resulted in the death of ancestral enemies, neighbouring creatures or marauding invaders) that I slowly developed as a shaman and an apprentice herbalist. My understanding of magic increased from knowledge of only one spell to mastery of ten, including the power to transform into an invisible wolf (who oddly enough could also dance in only one fashion).

Despite my zeal for dance, the majority of my time here has been spent engaged in practical quests – a situation which I suspect may parallel the status of dancers in other realities – is it not common for a dancer to sustain themselves with a second career? However, I did try to dance during these adventures: I would dance with my elders when they offered me quests and when I returned to them in triumph bearing feathers, sinews and sacred documents. Perhaps my performances were substandard, because without exception, none offered any remarks, preferring to speak about history and other more practical concerns. Undaunted, I continued to try to dance with the different beings I would meet while exploring Mulgore, attempts which were met with various reactions – the most common of which was complete indifference.

On two occasions though, the situation was different – one ended in an exchange of information and a small performance, and the other resulted in my untimely but not permanent demise. The former situation consisted of an extended dance between myself and a male Tauren warrior named Wolfback that occurred immediately after we defeated 'Pokey' Thornmantle (a member of a local rival group). Wolfback introduced himself and after we exchanged pleasantries, I invited him to dance. Wolfback had no idea how to dance and asked how it was done. After a brief explanation, Wolfback and I danced triumphantly around the battle site, keeping our respective internal rhythms perfect despite a perceivable lack of a strong beat in the pipe music which filled the air around us. Eventually Wolfback departed and I unfortunately never had the good fortune to share his company again. The latter situation (which resulted in my demise) was a result of my lack of attention while I was beset with the desire to perform for another Tauren. After following her around and asking repeatedly if she would like to dance, I paused momentarily to demonstrate my dancing abilities. Unfortunately, this devotion to art and lack of concern for my immediate welfare resulted in my death by two large wolves. In my fervour, I had crossed an unseen barrier which separated a relatively safe area from a more dangerous landscape. I immediately woke up in a burial ground, miles from my dismembered and partially digested body. It may be of note that in Azeroth, the dead definitely can't dance (however, the undead certainly can). I never did get to hear what she thought of my dancing.

After my revival (and a succession of seemingly doomed efforts to dance with others in Azeroth), I gradually decided to contemplate dance on a more personal level and develop a practice as a solo artist. I stopped insisting on the participation of others and focused on my own experience. I noticed that I began to feel the urge to dance when I had completed a particularly hazardous expedition, or had acquired new abilities or new possessions. Thus, dance in many respects became an individual celebratory ritual related to successfully navigating trials of passage and an action acknowledging personal growth; often there would be others present when I commenced dancing, but I no longer expected their attention, applause or recognition. Indeed, considering that dance was becoming more of an external sign marking the completion of inner goals, how could others even be expected to understand the meaning behind my dancing? Having fully accepted this new perspective my dancing has become quite spectacular: I have danced in the red desert sands dwarfed by technicolour skies, in glowing crystal caverns under massive granite mountains, in ornate fountains dripping with water which bestowed health and power, and on high cliffs overlooking the majestic landscape of my ancestral homeland. I think few performers have graced better stages.

Dancing in Azeroth

World of Warcraft (WOW) is a massive multiplayer online role-playing game (MMORPG) launched by the Blizzard entertainment company on 23 November 2004. It is set in the virtual world of Azeroth – the site of an ongoing battle between the multicultural armies of the Alliance and the Horde. Populated by various Tolkienesque 'races' which exist in cooperative and combative relationships in a diverse range of environments, WOW enables players to create a narrative based on individualized characters for the purposes of developing wealth and abilities, participating in quests, combating fantastic creatures, exploring exotic geographies, and participating in online relationships and communities. Categorized as a virtual world by both secular and academic sources, WOW was quickly recognized as a complex site for action, interaction and representation.[2] Accordingly, WOW has attracted the attention of contemporary researchers interested in a diverse range of subjects including culture, race, class, geography, gender and communication who have credited the game as a rich site for the production, interpretation and contestation of meaning. One focus of contemporary research has been the examination of Azeroth as an intertextual world – a space comprised of narratives drawn from thousands of real and fictional sources. These narratives are found in the textual form of game lore, racial histories and quests but they are also found in the game's visual, aural and kinetic components. These components when combined together create context for players – a means through which to inhabit this virtual space – and they also create connections between the game and the outside world where players' bodies exist.

When I entered Azeroth and created my character DianaTaylor in order to do research about dance in WOW, I also brought myself and my own personal narratives into the game. My identity as a dance researcher and dance artist framed my online identity, my online expectations and my online behaviour. I named my character after a prominent performance scholar who researches indigenous theatre of the Americas and brought with me an interest in aspects of living (and modes of play) that others might find of minor importance. Rather than discounting this experience a unique anomaly, I believe that this is actually the basis for all player experience of WOW and other virtual worlds. This chapter will explore this facet of player experience through an analysis of dance within WOW and the way it relates to embodied action demonstrated through performance by players.

Despite the abundance of recent critical attention, the subject of dance within the context of WOW has been under-examined. Present in the guise of an 'emote' (a performative gesture visible during gameplay), dance is an action available for characters during practically any moment of play. Although players cannot choreograph the set of movements which comprise a character's dance, they may choose when and where they dance, and may therefore use the dance function to perform a variety of communicative actions dependent on context. Although not integral to basic gameplay, instances of dance within Azeroth demonstrate salient connections to fantastical meta-cultures, twentieth- and twenty-first-century popular and global cultures, and bodies, both virtual and real.

The Genetic Dances of WOW

How is dance designed into the matrix of WOW? As alluded to previously, WOW characters may only perform one dance which is determined by their race and biological sex (which players choose). Interestingly, unlike other signs of cultural heritage such as clothing, language, history and belief systems (in which noticeable similarities between the different aspects and artefacts of culture reinforce a distinct sense of homogeneity and coherence), the dances that characters perform are distinctly different from the reigning aesthetic of any region. For example, the Tauren race that DianaTaylor is a member of is frequently cited as being a composite of various Indigenous peoples from North America and is perhaps a vivid example of the concept of 'Indianness' advanced by Jacqueline Shae Murphy in her work *The People Have Never Stopped Dancing* (2007).[3] In the essay 'The Familiar and the Foreign: Playing (Post)Colonial in World of Warcraft' (2008), Jessica Langer states:

> There are many Tauren hairstyles and accessory styles available that echo those worn in many commercial photographs, made for a white audience, of Native people. The near-ubiquity of Native American/First Nations styling suggests that the images of the Tauren, like those old photographs open them to real or imaginary appropriation as private property by non-Indians. Their literal fusion of human and animal may also be read as a physical conflation of Plains Tribes and the buffalo they hunted for their livelihood ... Tauren dwelling structures are, in essence, giant tepees modelled very closely on those sturdy yet portable dwellings made by the nomadic, herd-following people of the American and Canadian plains. The painting on these structures also resembles closely the geometric and colour scheme of the most well-known traditional Native art ... Tauren NPC names are modelled heavily on stereotypically Native names.
>
> (95–6)

Despite the deliberate effort by programmers to create visually cohesive and homogeneous cultural material for the Tauren race, the dance performed by DianaTaylor, as representative of those of Tauren females, illustrates a conception of dance which is philosophically intertwined with essentialist notions of culture and genetics but unrelated to the visual and textual aesthetics. Diana Taylor does not perform any sort of movement that could be associated with 'Indianness'. Instead, she performs a version of 'The Electric'[4] originally choreographed by Ric Silver for a 1976 performance by the Silver Star Dance Troupe at VAMPS NYC to disco/reggae artist Marcia Griffiths' 'Electric Boogie' (1976). His basic choreography, colloquially referred to as the *Electric Slide*, has also been adapted for fitness, social dance and music video contexts.

Although a departure from the exact form described by Silver, the female Tauren dance is still recognizable as a modified version of the original dance. While Blizzard is not explicitly forthcoming with information regarding design inspirations or explicitly interested in potentially contentious crediting of sources, the use of the song 'Electric Boogie' at performances at BlizzCon 2008 (a Blizzard fan conference) testifies, in an oblique manner, to the origins of this dance.

As indicated previously, male Tauren characters do not dance like the female Taurens. Rather, they perform a dance strikingly similar to 'Peanut Butter Jelly Time', a viral visual meme of a dancing banana created by Ryan Gancenia Etrata and Kevin Flynn as a flash animation in 2002. Consisting of alternating glances to the left and right combined with raising and lowering both arms and the simultaneous bending of both knees, the 'Peanut Butter Jelly Time' banana 'danced' to a song of the same name produced by The Buckwheat Boyz, a musical group from Miami, Florida.

Despite being part of a racial group within WOW which is explicitly linked with the 'natural world', and consciously represented through visual, aural and textual means as affiliated with existing representations of Native American culture, both of the sex-specific dances Taurens perform are based on recent inventions of popular culture, albeit from wildly different cultural sectors. This pattern is continued through all the dances of WOW's playable inhabitants and all twelve races are associated with substantial cultural material in visual (clothing, architecture, art, material objects) and text form (lore, quests, non-player character names) which reinforce a specific cultural identity based on a conflation of Tolkien/Dungeons and Dragons inspired fantasy and aspects of real-world cultural identities. However, all perform dances apparently 'borrowed' from various contemporary sources including dance franchises such as Riverdance, films such as *Saturday Night Fever* and *Napoleon Dynamite*, and specific video performances from Beyoncé, Justin Timberlake, Daler Mehndi, Shakira, Lady Gaga, Britney Spears, MC Hammer, Alizée and Michael Jackson (see Table 9.1).[5]

Numerous fan-made videos on YouTube, including *World of Warcraft: Dancing* (animpinabox, 2007) and *World of Warcraft Dance Origins* (NeynuSaloo, 2012), animate these connections through featuring the characters dancing accompanied by either the specific artist's songs and/or alongside video footage of the original artists performing the dances.

A heavily repeated theme within WOW research is the examination of Azeroth as a site featuring representations of culture that emerge from real-world discourses.[6] Within these conversations, there

Table 9.1 Popular culture origin of character dances

RACE	CULTURE	MALE DANCE	FEMALE DANCE
Human	European	*Saturday Night Fever*	'Macarena'
Dwarf	Northern European	*Saturday Night Fever*	Riverdance
Gnome	Science Fiction	Bloodhound Gang	Pussycat Dolls
Worgen	Eastern European	Justin Timberlake	Lady Gaga
Draenei	Persian	Daler Mehndi	Shakira
Night Elf	East Asian	Michael Jackson	Alizée
Pandaren	Chinese	LMFAO	Caramell
Orc	African	MC Hammer	Juvenile
Troll	Caribbean	Capoeira	Shakira
Forsaken	European	Air Guitar	Liquid Dancing
Tauren	Native American	'Peanut Butter Jelly Time'	Electric Slide
Goblin	Jewish	Soulja Boy	Beyoncé
Blood Elf	Drug Addicts	*Napoleon Dynamite*	Britney Spears

is a discernible lack of agreement between sources regarding the exact meanings embedded within WOW. Some researchers find WOW a site loaded with intentional stereotypes and explicit Western representations of dominant and subaltern cultures. For example, Jessica Langer (2008) argues that:

> these bodies [within WOW] deliberately suggest not the actual bodies of people from real-world cultures but rather stereotypical representations of those bodies. Here then is the crux of the problem with Blizzard's cultural borrowing: if in-game races are closely identified with real-world races, and those same in-game races are treated as biologically distinct species rather than socially categorized races then the implication is that real-world race is also biologically determined – an outdated and destructive implication that belongs to a racist discourse.
>
> (104)

Other researchers forward theoretical speculations that fall outside an explicitly postcolonial discourse through an examination of the mechanics of gameplay. Scott Rettberg, in his essay 'Corporate Ideology in World of Warcraft' (2008), argues convincingly that:

> on the level of real world economy, the millions of players of World of Warcraft are, through their subscription fees, supporting a multinational corporation. Blizzard, the developer of World of Warcraft, is a subsidiary of Vivendi Games, a subsidiary of the conglomerate Vivendi, which owns a range of telecommunications, television, and entertainment companies. Within the confines of the game world, players are also active in a simulation of a society driven by allegiance to one of two multinational conglomerates, the Alliance or the Horde. Players have further allegiance to particular localities and racial groups, guilds and raiding parties. While each business unit functions with a great deal of autonomy, and certain goal-oriented quests might cross established lines in pursuit of targets of opportunity, the social structures of World of Warcraft are in fact very similar to the interlocking and shifting hierarchies of multinational corporations like Vivendi … the game itself trains players how to function within the market economy, of which World of Warcraft is a product, and for which it serves as a heuristic device. World of Warcraft players are both

participating in the globalized economy as consumers and learning how to efficiently operate as 'players' and good corporate citizens.

(34)

In light of these observations the phenomena of dancing within WOW simultaneously problematizes a metanarrative regarding monolithic appropriations of cultural heritage (and contemporary sociological conceptions of the transmission of dance within culture), and elaborates on a metanarrative regarding capitalism, consumerism and globalized culture. Unlike other cultural markers which are used in WOW as signs of relative difference and distinction, the borrowed pop culture dances of the characters clearly implicate WOW within a unified contemporary corporate discourse where consumerist fantasies of youth, replicability and star worship conspire to conceal an insidious reality of global cultural relativity. This cultural relativity, while giving lip-service to traditional and conservative cultural narratives by fabricating extensive and intricate histories of heritage, in fact denies the possibility for differences in meaning and cultural values through the promotion of a devotion to repetitive labour and acquisition. Thus, while one may be an orc warrior or a blood elf magic addict or a Pandaren monk within Azeroth, the actual differences are only skin (or pixels) deep. Modern dance icon Martha Graham is credited with the statement 'movement never lies'; in this case the character movement imbedded with WOW reveals deep connections to a global entertainment economy.

Players Dancing Difference

Despite this rather grim reading which implicates and subsumes dance within a narrative of neoliberal corporate subservience, there is evidence that the dances within WOW effect and affect real bodies within the physical world. Through real-world performances players actively perform their own identities through their characters' movement vocabulary. This action creates new embodied connections that in turn create alternative narratives which challenge the encoded hermeneutic prescriptions described by game researchers.

On YouTube there are many videos featuring individuals dancing at official Blizzard sponsored dance contests held at gaming conferences. Here, players perform movement phrases associated with their favourite characters and clearly demonstrate a disavowal of racial, sexual and formal prescriptions that audiences respond to and emphatically support. Thus, a static virtual and 'genetic' repertoire gleaned from pop culture consumer archival sources is reinterpreted and invested with new meaning through live performance. Interestingly, official winners for each category rarely replicate dances faithfully, or resemble standard physical types present in WOW. This is in distinct discordance with other competition categories for costume and voice, where winners are rewarded by crowd applause for verisimilitude. In her book, *The Archive and the Repertoire* (2003), Diana Taylor outlines a theoretical perspective regarding the constant embodied negotiation between ephemeral lived reality and canonical knowledge in which information and ideas absent from archived histories are made manifest by the cultural performances of groups and individuals.[7] Examples from the BlizzCon performances give credence to the validity of this idea, although rather than revealing buried or suppressed histories, the dances unveil subversive connections and disruptive interpretations of the encoded and regulated dances.

In *Blizzcon 2011 Dance Contest Tauren Female 2* (joeyboy680, 2011), a young man named Casey Powers from Rapid City, South Dakota performs the female Tauren dance, (re)introducing the turns present in the original choreography. Casey Powers demonstrates an eschewal of both the concept of in-game gender prescriptions and formal verisimilitude, clearly preferring the performative ideas of the real Diana Taylor over faithful replication of a virtual 'DianaTaylor'. Similar performances are given by men in the videos *Night Elf Female Dance Blizzcon 2010* (Barrenschatblog, 2010), *Blizzcon 2010 Dance Contest Dwarf Female (male contestants)* (Almus, 2010) as they perform the movements explicitly associated with female game races. This disruption of game narrative is furthered by performances of women performing the dances of male characters, people of smaller stature embodying 'large' characters (and vice versa), and people of a variety of ethnicities clearly ignoring the racial prescriptions supposedly firmly embedded within Azeroth (vilemgf, 2011).

A particularly spectacular performance by a woman in the video *Undead Female Dance Contest Winner 2008* (KandiLandia, 2008) elaborates on this trend and clearly demonstrates how personal identity and history affect an individual's negotiation with WOW. The female Forsaken (or undead) dance is one of the most lacklustre dances within the game, consisting of a rotting yet graceful character waving their hands and hips slowly and slightly in a sequential manner; however, the dance is interpreted by the player as a liquid, transitory series of movements charged with dissonance, disruption and grace. Beginning with a fairly faithful replication of the character's in-game dance, the standard movements are then used as a coda which is returned to periodically while slipping in and out of various contorted positions with ease and authority. Spurred on by an enthusiastic audience, clearly both engaged and supportive of her interpretation, the player's performance (informed by her imagination and perhaps past dance experiences) continues for far longer than any others performed during the contest.

Comments on the associated YouTube page are positive, supportive and a testament to popular understanding of the game as an object involved in cultural play (rather than a final arbiter of cultural meaning), and dance as a lived interpretive act: 'I really hope they take some of her moves and add them to the way the female undead dances' (Mark Miles); 'undead female is all about the arms movement!!! and she did it her way!!!!' (Leonia Cunha); 'I'd be STOKED if they remade the undead female dance to her version' (OnlySuzyV); and: 'She rocked the dance and the auditorium! I have a level 70 undead female and just WISHED she could dance like this!" (Kandi Landia).[8] Clearly, although 'playing' in a world where dance is prescribed and regulated, players both appreciate and understand dance (and likely gameplay in general) as a more adaptable, personal and creative phenomenon. Ignoring game world associations with race, and sex and dance, performers at BlizzCon embody dance as an embodied practice subject to change, interpretation and negotiation. Unlike the unalterable 'genetic' archive of dances programmed into WOW, the players demonstrate, through their performances, a desire to disrupt rigid categories firmly entrenched within the game's matrix and embody an open and fluid poise towards personal form, identity and agency.

From game to virtual world, to racist and colonialist discourse, to corporate training tool, the World of Warcraft (like the real world) is a site for divergent agendas, narratives and interpretations. However, unlike our mundane reality, the creators of this world are known, and the origin of its inhabitants, geographies and cultures are recoverable and traceable to existing and persisting political, economic, aesthetic and social phenomena. Although the abode of pixelated gods, demons and monsters, the players of this game are not mere somnambulists operating under a wizard's spell, but rather the active negotiators of their own experiences and the real source of magic within this silicon dream.

Discussion Questions

1. What is the role of dance in creating the narrative evolution of a character in WOW? How is this related to the quest narratives of WOW?
2. The dances that many of the WOW characters perform have been 'borrowed' from figures in popular music and films. What was the narrative role of these dances in the films?
3. How do those who play WOW use dance to create an identity and related narrative to fashion performances for BlizzCon?
4. What is the role in the creation of narrative between popular musical performance, WOW and BlizzCon?

Websites

World of Warcraft: https://worldofwarcraft.com/en-us/
Almus (2010) Blizzcon 2010 Dance Contest Dwarf Female (male contestants): https://www.youtube.com/watch?v=510LoEHRt-U
Animpinabox (2007) World of Warcraft: Dancing: https://www.youtube.com/watch?v=066_q4DIeqk
Barrenschatblog (2010) Night Elf Female Dance Blizzcon 2010: https://www.youtube.com/watch?v=85t2BJtniEw
KandiLandia (2008) Undead Female Dance Contest Winner 2008: https://www.youtube.com/watch?v=e2PoIXQA5Mw

Notes

1. *Blood Memory* is the title of Martha Graham's autobiography.
2. Scholarship regarding WOW was originally limited to articles in game-related publications. However, in 2006 the appearance of a *Games and Culture* journal devoted entirely to WOW anticipated the publication of three academic texts compiled or written by sociologists and game researchers in the years 2008–10.
3. In *The People Have Never Stopped Dancing*, Jacqueline Shea Murphy provides an account of the appropriation and alteration of aspects of Native American and First Nations culture by intellectuals and modern dance artists. In the text, she coins the term 'Indianness' to describe the aesthetic results of this appropriation.
4. The full title of the choreography is *'The Electric', a Four Wall Dance Fugue*.
5. This table outlines connections between the game's racial categories, visible markers of real-world ethnicities and identities, and the popular music and film inspirations for WOW's dances. The table was generated after viewing numerous related fan-made videos, studying a similar table on the WOW wiki site regarding 'Dance', and the examination of a number of articles regarding identity in WOW cited in this chapter.
6. Academic literature is readily available in print and digital formats, and includes books, collections of essays and entire journal special editions devoted to World of Warcraft. Please see the WOW edition of the journal *Games and Culture* and books such as *My Life as a Night Elf Priest: An Anthropological Account of World of Warcraft* (Nardi, 2010); *Digital Culture, Play and Identity: A World of Warcraft Reader* (Corneliussen and Rettberg, 2008); and *The Warcraft Civilization* (Bainbridge, 2010).
7. Diana Taylor studies the cultural performance output of communities found within the Americas and her ideas are consistently linked to art produced by groups lacking documented histories. In this chapter, the players of WOW are imagined as semi-colonial subjects within the corporatized landscape of WOW, searching for agency and attempting to produce personal meaning through in-game performance.
8. All comments are taken directly from the comment section of the *Undead Female Dance Contest Winner 2008* YouTube page, https://www.youtube.com/watch?v=e2PoIXQA5Mw.

Works Cited and Resource Material

Almus (2010) *Blizzcon 2010 Dance Contest Dwarf Female (male contestants)*, https://www.youtube.com/watch?v=510LoEHRt-U, accessed 29 July 2017.

Animpinabox (2007) *World of Warcraft: Dancing*, https://www.youtube.com/watch?v=066_q4DIeqk, accessed 29 July 2017.

Bainbridge, W. S. (2010) *The Warcraft Civilization: Social Science in a Virtual World* (Cambridge, MA: MIT).

Barrenschatblog (2010) *Night Elf Female Dance Blizzcon 2010*, https://www.youtube.com/watch?v=85t2BJtniEw, accessed 1 July 2017.

Corneliussen, H. and Rettberg, J. W. (Eds) (2008) *Digital Culture, Play, and Identity: A World of Warcraft Reader* (Cambridge, MA: MIT Press).

joeyboy680 (2011) *Blizzcon 2011 Dance Contest – Tauren Female 2*, https://www.youtube.com/watch?v=8EWiTNAZth4, accessed 29 July 2017.

KandiLandia (2008) *Undead Female Dance Contest Winner 2008*, https://www.youtube.com/watch?v=e2PoIXQA5Mw, accessed 1 July 2017.

Krzywinska, T. and H. Lockwood (2006) Guest Editors' Introduction, *Games and Culture*, 80(1).

Langer, J. (2008) The Familiar and the Foreign: Playing (Post)Colonialism in World of Warcraft, in H. Corneliussen and J. Walker (Eds) *Digital Culture, Play, and Identity: A World of Warcraft Reader* (Cambridge, MA: MIT Press) pp. 87–108.

Murphy, J. S. (2007) *The People Have Never Stopped Dancing: Native American Modern Dance Histories* (Minneapolis: University of Minnesota Press).

Nardi, B. A. (2010) *My Life as a Night Elf Priest: An Anthropological Account of World of Warcraft* (Ann Arbor: University of Michigan Press).

NeynuSaloo (2012) *World of Warcraft Dance Origins*, https://www.youtube.com/watch?v=2Sb94BZtz3A, accessed 29 July 2017.

Rettberg, S. (2008) Corporate Ideology in World of Warcraft, in H. Corneliussen and J. Walker (Eds) *Digital Culture, Play, and Identity: A World of Warcraft Reader* (Cambridge, MA: MIT Press) pp. 19–38.

Silver, R. (2006) '*The Electric Slide' The Basic Choreography*, http://the-electricslidedance.com/home-page.html, accessed 1 July 2017.

Taylor, D. (2003) *The Archive and the Repertoire: Performing Cultural Memory in the Americas* (Durham, NC: Duke University Press).

Vilemgf (2011) *Blizzcon 2011 – Dance Contest (Full Video)*.

Part III

Rocking the Boat:
Revolutionary Integrations

10

Ellen Lauren
The Art of Extreme Acting

Scott T. Cummings

Ellen was an equestrian athlete for many years in her youth, and the physical and mental discipline she developed during those years dovetailed into her work as an actor. The fact that she had to dialogue with an animal using physically generated energy, gesture, and action also opened up a certain sensitivity in her perceptive abilities. For this reason, more than many actors, my particular method of training actors resonated with her soon after she encountered it. It took her some time to absorb the training into her instrument, and her performance of Agave in Dionysus was an integral part of that. Now, because she has gone through this experience, she is one of the few performers outside of the company able to teach the training.

Tadashi Suzuki

You don't look at Ellen in, say, Chess Match No. 5, and go, 'Oh, she's trained in Suzuki and Viewpoints.' You don't see the training in her body or her acting. It's not visible. That's the sign of a master. She is the most differentiated actor I have ever met in my life. She can be outrageously funny. She can be deeply tragic. And she is always doing things she's never done before. We'll be doing a Viewpoints session with a bunch of actors, and I will see something interesting happening over there and wonder, 'Who is that person? Oh, that's Ellen.' She is a transformative actress. That's why people don't recognize her when she comes out after a show.

Anne Bogart

In May 2017, renowned Japanese theatre director Tadashi Suzuki brought his Suzuki Company of Toga (SCOT) to Saratoga Springs, New York, to perform his version of *The Trojan Women* and to participate in a four-day symposium focusing on his influential method of actor training. It was SCOT's first visit to the USA in sixteen years. The company travelled from their home base in the remote village of Toga-mura via Tokyo and New York City to the campus of Skidmore College, stayed for six days, and then turned around to head to Beijing for an international theatre festival at the National Center for the Performing Arts. There are any number of reasons why the 78-year-old Suzuki might want to take the time and trouble to make such a trip. One reason, perhaps at the top of the list, is Ellen Lauren.

Ellen Lauren is one of the unsung heroes of the American theatre. She is a consummate performer, an actor of prodigious range and skill who commands attention onstage simply by the quality of her presence. She began her career in the resident regional theatre, and then in the early 1980s she was introduced to the rigorous performance techniques being developed by Suzuki and his company. She began to travel to Japan in the summers on an annual basis, first to train with fellow American actors and eventually to work with SCOT as an associate artist and master teacher. She played Juliet in Suzuki's *Waiting for Romeo* (a piece created for her), Lady Macbeth in his adaptation of *Macbeth*, Goneril in *The Tale of Lear* and Jocasta in *Oedipus*. Off and on for eighteen years, she toured the world as Agave in Suzuki's celebrated production *Dionysus*, performing at such historic sites as the Moscow Art Theatre, the Teatro Olimpico in Vicenza, and the first-ever Theatre Olympics in Delphi. And in 2015, as part of SCOT's fiftieth anniversary season, she assumed the role of Clytemnestra in his *Electra*.

Lauren's sustained work with Suzuki is significant and, for an American actor, unique, but she has spent most of her time for the past twenty-five years as a founding member of the SITI Company. In the late-1980s, Suzuki was looking to establish an outpost in the USA, partly as a place for American disciples such as Lauren to create work and spread his teaching. In 1992, he and director Anne Bogart teamed up with this group of artists to found the Saratoga International Theater Institute as an annual international forum for exchange, training and performance. Over the next several years, as Suzuki withdrew from direct involvement, the summer institute morphed into the year-round SITI Company with Bogart as artistic director, Lauren as associate artistic director, and a mission based on the collective creation of original work, international collaboration, and theatre training that practises the Suzuki Method of Actor Training alongside Bogart's revision of the Viewpoints originally articulated by Mary Overlie. Ellen Lauren became SITI Company's leading lady – if an ensemble such as theirs can be said to have one – playing key roles in such early company-generated pieces as *The Medium*, *Culture of Desire*, *Going, Going, Gone*, and *Cabin Pressure* as well as in Bogart's productions of *Picnic*, *The Adding Machine*, *Miss Julie*, *Private Lives* and *Hay Fever* at Actors Theatre of Louisville. She went on to act in SITI's collaborations with the playwright Charles Mee, Martha Graham Dance Company, Bill T. Jones/Arnie Zane Dance Company, the playwright Jocelyn Clarke, New York City Opera, and installation artist Ann Hamilton. She has been instrumental in shaping SITI's training programmes, including the four-week Summer Intensive held on the campus of Skidmore College every summer since 1993. In 2014, after two decades of shorter term workshops and programmes, SITI established a nine-month conservatory programme in New York with Lauren as director. Around this time, the company reorganized its leadership structure, making Lauren and long-time company member Leon Ingulsrud co-artistic directors with Bogart.

When the SITI Company was founded, no one could have predicted the result of harnessing the Suzuki and Viewpoint practices as a training regimen and basis for creating original work. While both practices are essentially corporal, they are opposite in ethos and aesthetic. The Suzuki training, at least in its early stages, focuses inward on the mind, body and spirit of the individual actor in order to develop the ability to focus outward in performance on an external 'fiction'. Highly athletic, it demands hard physical work in pursuit of established forms that test stamina, endurance and the resilience of the mind–body connection. The goal is to develop the actor's control of the centre of gravity, the flow of energy, and breathing as a preparation for animating speech and movement (and by extension silence and stillness) with dynamism and power. From the beginning, the Viewpoints focuses outward on what surrounds the actor in order to increase sensitivity to what is already present onstage and to promote the ability to act in response to external stimuli with spontaneity and definition. It offers a playful approach to deepening perception and cultivates a freewheeling flow of energy within a group onstage. In spirit, Suzuki is diagnostic, absolute, vertical and individual; Viewpoints is improvisational, relative, horizontal and social. In their different ways, each practice enhances an actor's ability to command attention by refining the ability to pay attention, to take notice and respond with interest to what is already happening, and thus to take responsibility for composing her own performance.

I have followed the work of Ellen Lauren with fascination ever since I first saw her in the SITI Company's *Going, Going, Gone* at the 1996 Humana Festival of New American Plays. More than any actor on the planet, she can be seen as the living embodiment of the uncanny synergy between the Suzuki Method of Actor Training and the practice of the Viewpoints. Neither Tadashi Suzuki nor Anne Bogart is an actor. Each of them can be said to recognize their work – its pulse, its shape, its impact – in her, specifically in her body in action, and it seems reasonable to think that her acting has added to the meaning, value and substance of both practices. With this in mind, I asked Lauren if she would participate in a series of interviews over the course of a year geared towards articulating some of the knowledge that she has developed onstage over decades. We decided to focus on her three most recent acting projects at that moment. The interview here is a composite of conversations that took place between August 2016 and July 2017. For the sake of clarity and concision, it combines sentences, ideas and trains of thought from different sessions and even interpolates material from other interviews dating back to 2001. The goal is to explore how this unique performer thinks about her art and the two physical trainings on which it is based. It offers a rare first-person reflection on acting as an embodied practice that ultimately focuses not on the self but on the audience, who gathers to observe it.

* * * * * * * * *

The daughter of Mary Ball and Naval officer Marcellus Pitz, Ellen Lauren grew up in a number of places. She attended West Virginia University, and after graduation she toured federal penitentiaries for a year in a government-sponsored improv company. In the 1970s, she studied in the MFA acting programme at Temple University. She left there to join the resident acting company of the Milwaukee Repertory Theatre, where she played such roles as Beatrice in Much Ado About Nothing, *Laura in* The Glass Menagerie, *and Shelly in* Buried Child. *Around this time, in partnership with Milwaukee Rep, a newly created professional actor training programme at University of Wisconsin-Milwaukee began to bring Tadashi Suzuki to the USA to demonstrate his work. Before too long, a cadre of American actors, including Lauren, was traveling to Suzuki's mountain retreat for more extensive training.*

I was one of the first generation of Americans to go to Toga-Mura, in the mountains of western Japan. I responded to the camaraderie of the shared experience, how unique it was. You're on the compound for ten weeks and you don't really leave. We got up in the morning for breakfast duty and trained and cleaned the dorms and put our feet in the river and watched rehearsal. We all felt very special to be there.

We were Americans, tall, healthy, gregarious, loud and outgoing, different from the Japanese sensibility. And our bodies could go fast, we were strong. Suzuki was interested in what happened when our American, Stanislavsky-based training met his work. We were all, in some sense, engaged in a heady process of experimentation.

It was like nothing I had ever experienced. I had never been to Japan. I had no points of reference for that culture. I was a young, decent looking, moderately skilled regional theatre actress at the time. I had been doing it for about eight years, and I had a great life. I was successful enough, but something was missing for me, some kind of risk or edginess, some kind of marriage of rigor and expression, cutting-edge technique and traditional form. I think I was looking for a way to become a theatre artist, in a holistic sense, and not just an actor.

In Toga, I began to see work unlike anything I had ever imagined. So, instead of a regional theatre season made up of a sleek concept for *Measure for Measure*, a solid *Arms and the Man*, a delightful *Blithe Spirit*, a not half-bad *Christmas Carol*, and then a new play series, there I was exposed to Gardzienice from Poland, Butoh dancers, Bow Gamelan, Robert Wilson, Meredith Monk, Yuri Lyubimov's Taganka Company, Chorus Repertory from Manipur, and Tadeusz Kantor, just to name a few. It opened up the world for me. I began to develop an understanding of my own artistry and the possibilities of what theatre could be as an art form. I went for six or seven years for the entire summer. I couldn't be there enough. The world of Toga – the ethos of the SCOT Company, the rigor of the training, the genius of Mr. Suzuki, the quality of what you were watching onstage, the night sky in the summer, the unique architecture, the sheer majesty of those mountains, the safety and the freedom of it – these were all extremely heightened experiences. Once I had a taste of that, there was no going back for me. It made me who I am as an actor.

Lauren had been working with Suzuki for thirty years when he asked her to take over the pivotal role of Clytemnestra in his Electra, *making her the fifth actor to play the part since it first entered his repertoire in the mid-1990s. Hiroko Takahashi played the part in the inaugural production. Over the years, Suzuki made changes in the cast each time he prepared the piece for another tour. Toshiko Takeuchi played the role on a 2001 US tour. Russian actor Lyubov Selyutina took the role at the Taganka Theatre in Moscow in 2007. SCOT leading actor Chieko Naito played Electra in a 2009 version with a largely Korean cast. And then, in 2015, Suzuki turned to Lauren.*

In the summer of 2015, I spent ten weeks in Toga training, building the role of Clytemnestra, and rehearsing *Electra* with the SCOT Company. When I first got there, I was given an incomplete and rough script that, as translated into English, was stilted and a bit impenetrable. I was given carte blanche to fix it, which I had to do quickly so that the SCOT actors could learn their cues for this bilingual production.

Once the text was set, I was left in a room to figure it out without a lot to go on. That's often the way that Suzuki works early in the process. I had the script, some props, my wheelchair, and a recording of the cues in Japanese (a language I don't speak). I knew the basic score that he wanted, but what happened between the entrance and the exit was really up to me. I also needed to incorporate the actor playing my nurse in my structure, for while she doesn't speak, her presence onstage makes for a highly choreographed duet between us.

On any given day, everyone started off with group training, and then I would do my own training in an effort to develop a body with the rigor to speak so that the sound of the words – the focus and the ferocity with which they are directed toward the imaginative space – is as much the story as the content of the words themselves. I had to figure out the body's relationship to the words, how to allocate energy and concentration to the language and the message I am conveying, and how far and in what direction to send my energy. These are hard things to achieve, particularly because I don't live and train with the SCOT Company year-round. Before arriving in Toga for *Electra*, I spent a month doing strength training in the morning and long runs in the mountain roads near my house in upstate New York. Then, I would train for another hour in my barn with the summer sounds coming in from the back meadow. Even then, arriving in Toga, which is a much higher elevation than upstate New York, I felt I was starting at the bottom. The actors of SCOT are so accomplished and strong, it takes a great deal of will power to believe you can get to a place to hold your own onstage with them.

With Suzuki, in performance or rehearsal or just in front of him alone, everything comes at you so fast that you have to work with all of your wits. At first, you're just trying to breathe. Then you are trying not to forget how to pull together all the things you need to concentrate on. And then you want to get to that place where you are actually performing your crisis, going deeper and deeper into it in order to take the audience to a place they do not often go. It also has to have a light touch, believe it or not. You are looking for ease – what is sometimes called flow – or the audience just becomes uncomfortable. That's what Suzuki's performances do for me as a spectator. When they really get there, they pull you in with their curiosity and uniqueness, and then you turn around to get out and you cannot. You are trapped in this unrelenting relationship to the stage. It takes over your whole life for that sixty minutes. Suzuki's *Electra* is a theatrical punch in the gut that lasts just over an hour. As in other Suzuki works, the ostensible setting is a psychiatric ward or insane asylum, with characters situated in wheelchairs that symbolize their isolation and derangement. Japanese composer and percussionist Midori Takada sits onstage surrounded by instruments and provides a live score that sets the tempo and tone for the production. The spoken text is pared down to a minimum, much of it belonging to Clytemnestra. She makes her first appearance standing on the arms of her wheelchair pushed on at dizzying speed by her attending nurse. In a short speech, she admonishes Electra and then is wheeled out backwards, laughing with false confidence. In her second appearance, Clytemnestra unleashes a savage thirty-minute monologue that anticipates with dread and defiance the return of Orestes to consummate the revenge that Electra covets so desperately. The scene ends in a rapid-fire stichomythic exchange with

Electra – with Electra's lines being spoken in precise unison by the chorus as Electra crouches nearby. Finally, Clytemnestra is wheeled offstage babbling in anticipation of her imminent murder, which is soon confirmed by a blood-curdling scream.

In 2015, Lauren performed in Electra *eight times as part of the festival celebrating the fiftieth anniversary of SCOT (founded in Tokyo as the Waseda Little Theatre by Suzuki in 1965). Lauren felt the work that summer was moderately successful, but neither she nor Suzuki was fully satisfied. Suzuki asked her to return to Japan in December to perform the role for an engagement at the Kichijoji Theatre, a black box theatre in a hip area of northwest Tokyo where Lauren had played Goneril in SCOT's* King Lear *two years earlier. Rehearsals began at the compound in Toga, which in winter is pristine with snow and even more isolated than in summer. With only the company on site and only the plays for Kichijoji to focus on, the atmosphere was more intimate. It seemed to make a difference to Lauren.*

In the summer, the festival time in Toga is very stressful. In the winter, Toga becomes so quiet, and I found a deeper concentration. When we got into the space in Kichijoji, something fresh happened. I figured out the breathing. Intellectually, I understood it, but I had to find it on a cellular level. I started to connect some sensibilities and Suzuki was affirming that. So, if he gave me a note saying 'It's too Beethoven. It needs to be more Mozart', I knew what he meant. It had to do with stopping. Technically, if you come to a stop and emphasize the stop or show the audience you are stopping, it is cheating in a way, as opposed to 'I'm stopping and my brakes are on so hard but I'm not going to let you know what it's costing me and I have to gear down and take another breath and pull out smoothly'. I was pushing so hard in Toga, and now I was beginning to discover more of a pulling sense, how to manage the silences and the timing. I was beginning to discover how to move much less and get more done in the stillness.

It's a matter of finding an inner concentration toward the self where first and foremost you're chasing a feeling inside that will affect the outside space. Not the outside space in general, but a specific distance and direction that includes the audience. You're trying to get them to change their breathing and to move in on an animal level. You are creating an atmosphere around your body, and thus the space is becoming denser between you and the audience. It has a great deal to do with timing and finding the widest range of expression with the body and the language at the same time in very restricted containers, like a wheelchair. Clytemnestra is very animal, very crazy, very extreme. Her psychological state is complex and that has to be felt on a visceral level. She is terrifying, and pathetic, and also a little bit of a clown. In the end, you are creating a portrait of qualities that every human has the potential to tap into, so it is also about creating something that the audience can recognize in themselves, disturbing as that is. So, I'm showing them 'Ellen's' inner world, not a character in the way we think of character in most people's understanding of that word (see Figure 10.1).

When I am making this thing called Clytemnestra, I am counting all the time. It is all part of the math of building a performance. Say, for example, that my movement is to put my forearm on the arm of the wheelchair. I have to figure out if I do the movement as I say the line and what word to start on. Or do I take the breath, move the arm, stop the arm, count three seconds, then say half the line, lay down the arm, count one second, and speak the rest of the line? I am always timing how long

Figure 10.1 Ellen Lauren as Clytemnestra in the SCOT Company production of *Electra* directed by Tadashi Suzuki

Photographer: Zhang Tian

do I hold a breath; how far do I push the breath. This is another aspect of Suzuki's aesthetic: using all your air, working in states of apnoea without the audience consciously knowing it. You start to play with the ability to get them into this state of apnoea as well. There is a great example that Suzuki uses to demonstrate the fact that we can change the way an audience breathes. If you are onstage and you hold a needle and thread inches apart and move to thread the needle, half the audience will hold their breath. That phenomenon is hardwired in us and you can play with that as a performer. You can use it as part of the material of the performance. You literally form a physical relationship with an audience. You can feel it when the audience gets there right when you get there. Their timing gets better because your timing is sharp and in tune with them. You are curating the silence and stillness as much as the movement and sound to seduce them into this state.

Lauren returned to Toga in September 2016 to re-rehearse the play for SCOT's engagement later that month at the Chinese tourist resort known as Wtown a couple hours from Beijing. Performances took place in a 3,000-seat, outdoor, Greek amphitheatre set directly against the Simatai Great Wall, which dates from the Ming Dynasty. The contrast to the intimacy of the 300-seat Kichijoji Theatre called for adjustments.

Suzuki is a genius at placing his work in different spaces. His company has toured the world and developed the facility to expand or compress their choreography and energy to fill the space at hand – the way a great dance company can. The only places that I had played comparable in size to the Simatai Great Wall Theatre were the Herod Atticus in Athens and the ancient theatre in Montpellier, France. You go out and you are facing this sea of 5,000–7,000 people who you cannot see because there is extremely high-powered lighting focused on you. I was young, and I made the mistake at first of trying to fill those spaces with force. Suzuki would tell me I looked like a hysterical housewife. I would get it after a few performances, but never consistently in those big arenas, and rarely if ever on the opening night. I learned that the bigger the space, the more refined you have to be, the straighter your line has to be, the calmer you have to be. You are going to have more success pulling the audience in to you than going out and trying to fill the space the whole time. You have to pick two or three places where you really go for it, but otherwise you need to ratchet things down and show the audience the potential that could erupt at any moment. It is a simple lesson, but it is really difficult to do. And it takes a toll, physically, emotionally, intellectually, spiritually. You cannot go out and do eight performances a week. The work is not built that way.

Suzuki likes to say that Stanislavsky's work deals with the moment after the crisis, the emotional and psychological fallout, whereas his work takes place in the moment of crisis, the emotional and psychological collision. That point of impact is what interests him, and that requires an all-in kind of acting, a bare-faced pressing into the crisis. You are not re-creating an emotional state from everyday life for the audience to look at. You have to go to an extreme place physically and psychologically and use your body and voice in a way that is not called upon in daily life. You have to get to a point where you are not really controlling yourself as much as perhaps you think you should onstage. You cannot hold anything back. This is a question of magnitude and exploring the reaches of the human psyche under pressure in a way that sneaks up on an audience and captures them unawares, whether they like it or not. Suzuki's work is like walking into a museum gallery and seeing Picasso's *Guernica* on the wall. For a second, you stop breathing.

* * * * * * * * *

Anne Bogart has an insatiable intellectual curiosity. She is a voracious reader, and the pieces she conceives for the SITI Company are often inspired by the echo of something she has been reading. Some pieces have a secret cause that takes the form of a probing thematic question around which material is gathered. Others use an important cultural figure as an organizing principle, such as 'The Medium' (Marshall McLuhan) or 'Culture of Desire' (Andy Warhol). One artist and sensibility of enduring fascination to Bogart is the novelist Virginia Woolf, whom she discovered and read extensively at age 14 and has returned to again and again. In 1977, as a fledgling director in New York, she created a piece based on The Waves. *In 2009, she directed SITI Company in* Freshwater, *Woolf's Bloomsbury comedy and only play. In 2015, SITI collaborated with artist Ann Hamilton to create a performance installation called 'the theatre is a blank page', which included a performer reading Woolf's* To the Lighthouse *out loud from start to finish. But Bogart's most significant rendering of Woolf is the solo performance piece titled* Room, *created in 2000 with Ellen Lauren.*

Room *was the second in a trilogy of SITI solo pieces that premiered at the Wexner Center for the Arts at Ohio State University. Each one featured a founding member of the company performing texts selected by Bogart from the writings and interviews of a major twentieth-century artist and then arranged by Irish playwright and dramaturg Jocelyn Clarke. Will Bond took on visionary theatre director Robert Wilson in* Bob *(1998); Lauren voiced Virginia Woolf in* Room *(2000); and Tom Nelis presented composer and conductor Leonard Bernstein in* Score *(2002). None of these is a historical impersonation in the manner of Hal Holbrook as* Mark Twain *or Julie Harris in* The Belle of Amherst. *They are more akin to abstract performance essays that juxtapose the spoken text with movement, design and sound scores in a way that creates perceptual gaps and contrapuntal rhythms.*

Lauren began her preparation for Room *by immersing herself in the writing of Virginia Woolf. Then, in the summer of 2000, she and Bogart set to work in rural upstate New York, where each of them has a second home.*

> We started in a room in Anne's newly acquired house. We would not go in there unless we were working. The rule was that she would go upstairs and wait for me, and when I was ready, I would mount the steps and walk in and say, 'Hello', and begin to speak certain passages of Woolf that Anne had asked me to memorize. When I needed a break or I was out of text, I would say, 'Thank you', and leave. And she would come downstairs and we would talk a little bit or just stare out the window, maybe have a snack, and then after a while, she would go back up to the room, and I would go up, and we would continue working. She would give me assignments before I came up. So, for the very first rehearsal, it was 'Come upstairs. There's going to be a chair and a small table and a stack of books. And there will be a book on the top and I want you to read that book aloud to me until you are tired, and then put the book down and leave.' And when I went up to the room, the book on the top was *Between the Acts*, Woolf's last book. So, I started reading it aloud. I got exhausted after an hour or two, and I left. Over the course of the first two or three days, I read the whole of *Between the Acts*. Before we did anything else, I read a book aloud to Anne. At that point, we didn't even have the script from Jocelyn yet.
>
> It was important to Anne that we not make any assumptions that we knew who Woolf was. We knew she had a very particular physique, long, lanky, elegant, even regal. It was her idea that we begin to build the piece

physically based on the photographs we were gathering. So, one of my assignments was to learn twenty-six photographs of Virginia Woolf from the books that we had. I began to memorize her body and imprint it on my body. I learned twenty-six containers or physical positions, and we gave each one a number. Eventually Anne said, 'Are you ready? Here we go!' and I would go into the room and she would call out the number of a photograph – '19! … 9! … 22!' – and I would strike the pose and speak the text at that point and we would see how one thing would lead into another.

Over the course of rehearsals, we cut more and more of this 'alphabet' until we ended up with nine iconic postures, which became a kind of sign language that echoed through the piece. Anne's driving interest was to capture how someone named Virginia Woolf created, the artistic, expressive state that she was able to get into, the feeling of that in the room, the spirit of it in the atmosphere. We were also going after the question, 'Can we capture the sensation of reading, that particular kind of private dream state, for an audience in the theatre?'

Jocelyn sent us the script about six days into this process and soon we moved to working in Anne's barn. We cleaned it out and then one morning Anne went up to the hayloft. There was a small red chair there, a ladder-backed, Shaker chair with arms and a woven seat and legs that were sawed off so it was low to the ground. And it was angled towards a little window high in the barn wall, and she said, 'All right, this is our room'. And so, from then on, she would go up to the loft and wait, and I would climb up the ladder and walk to the centre, turn and say, 'Good evening' and begin to speak the text that I had learned for that day. When I was done, I would say 'Thank you', and go back down. That first day working in the barn – and every day forward – she would come down and sit on the steps with me. We opened the big sliding barn doors and didn't say anything, just stared out at the fields and listened to the birds until she said, 'OK, ready?' And she opened up her script and said, 'This is what you did. You moved your left hand on this word. You turned here. You looked up at the window here …' She had been transcribing everything I did.

I was astonished. She had never moved her gaze; she never looked down or away. She watched me with such care that I learned to listen more closely to how the text was lining up with my body. I began to investigate how one position moved to another, and how to speak Woolf's long lines of thought taking fewer breaths. I was learning when something needed to change physically by listening to Anne's instincts. She'd continue to call out numbers, her impulses sometimes calculated, sometimes intuitive. We were both working in such a pure way. All the barriers of insecurity and ego and hesitation fell away between us. In the afternoon, we'd make gallons of coffee and sit and 'iron' the text, as we called it. I would speak and Anne would stop me for every misplaced comma, every misspoken word. For example, Woolf uses the words 'think' and 'feel' in her syntax very specifically, and I was always switching them.

There were times when I wanted to strangle Anne for stopping me every other word, but it led to an incredible meditation on the language. I will treasure those hours all my life. The math of it worked out that we were staging three pages a day. And it worked out perfect that on the last day of that phase of the work we could do a run-through. Anne made a video so we could remember what we had done. You have to understand, this was unprecedented for SITI at that time. We were working, just the two of us alone, in her barn in the country. No other SITI members were around. People weren't happy about Anne and I going off on our own like that. I wouldn't have been either.

Later in the autumn, the time came to show the company what we'd come up with. We pushed aside furniture in Anne's apartment in New York. I was terrified and I think Anne was, too. Even now, seventeen years later, I can honestly say that this was the toughest audience I have ever faced with the piece. I wanted the Company to embrace what we'd done, even in this raw unfinished state. Everyone was packed into Anne's living room, and I was sitting there with them looking at the empty dining room. I stood suddenly, walked to the centre of that space, turned on my shaking legs, took a breath, and said, 'Good evening'. At that moment, a little clock on Anne's mantle chimed its hour. Darron West, our extraordinary sound designer, stood and whispered, 'I'm in …'. I don't remember the eighty minutes after that very well, but I remember the feeling in the room of my colleagues being engaged, rooting for me, for Anne. I remember leaning into the physical score we made as if pressing against an actual tangible surface. I remember them standing at the end and clapping and the excitement in the room afterwards that a new SITI piece, however it had been rehearsed, was born.

Even as the SITI design team joined the collaboration and other company members sat in on rehearsals and offered input, Room *retained the tremendous intimacy that marked its initial phase of its creation. The piece premiered at the Wexner Center in Columbus, Ohio, in November 2000 and continued with a four-week run at City Theatre in Pittsburgh in January 2001. It toured off and on for years and was seen in New York in runs at Classic Stage Company in 2002 and the Women's Project in 2011. Then, after a five-year hiatus,* Room *was revived in 2017 for a brief New England tour to Connecticut College and the Pinkerton Academy in New Hampshire. Coming back to the piece after such a long time had its challenges.*

A lot of questions were in the air, like the level of fitness that I would need to do the show. On some level, I am more efficient and thus in better shape than when I was in my forties. Certainly, I know how to delegate my concentration and budget my energy. And going through that massive experience with *Electra* was a help in reminding me where my breathing can go and what strength I can summon if I am dogged about it. The Suzuki training is designed for material like Woolf, where the thoughts are long and labyrinthine.

When we went back to work on *Room*, I went to my cupboard and pulled out a red plastic-covered script in which I had tried to record as much as I could as it morphed over the years. I opened it and had this 'Oh, no!' sensation. I did not understand my personal hieroglyphics, the numbers, slash marks, circles and arrows. But the minute I started to speak it, I remembered the gestures and poses and sensations. And when I went back to the resource books we used, some still had sticky notes with numbers by a photograph we took a pose from. It was like opening up a photo album or a diary from your high school days and re-living all of those feelings, all the victories and defeats and humiliations and recognizing how you are not that person anymore, happily, and feeling excited to have the gift of coming back to it and starting a new chapter with it, as in 'How am I going to do it now? What is it now?' As an artist of a certain age, what more do you want?

* * * * * * * * *

SCOT's Electra *and SITI's* Room *were well-established pieces in each company's repertoire when Lauren worked on them around the time of our conversations. In 2017, SITI Company created its first new piece in two years,* Chess Match No. 5, *a two-hander for Lauren and Will Bond based on the public conversations of composer John Cage. Once again, Bogart compiled an almanac of raw material which was arranged by Jocelyn Clarke and then staged in a hurried three-week rehearsal process. Conceived as the centrepiece of an eventual large-scale, interdisciplinary Cage project to be titled* Theater Piece #1, Chess Match No. 5 *premiered in March 2017 at the Abingdon Theatre Company in New York. Making the piece, a matter of creating gestural, movement, dance, sound, lighting, music and design scores to accompany and surround the speaking of the Cage texts, was in keeping with SITI's tried-and-true methods.*

> We had some givens: a toaster, a coffeemaker, a utility table up right, a radio down left, two doors, some stage directions in Jocelyn's text, Darron's soundscape, and the idea of a series of chess games. That was it. There was no road map or particular strategy for how we were going to build the piece other than the one we always begin with: the combined vocabularies of the Viewpoints and the Suzuki training as it lives in our bodies. This leads us into realms of creativity and expressiveness that we probably would not find if we approached the text conventionally in terms of character and situation. Anne's premise was that it is a concert really. So, every prop we touched, every bite of toast or brush of my skirt or adjustment of a chair was scored and timed. We memorized the text, started at the beginning, and made really quick decisions.
>
>   That is the way the SITI Company works. You make a choice – I'm going to pick up a coffee cup, I'm going to open the door slowly, I'm going to take my coat off – and as you execute your choice, you're getting feedback at an incredibly fast rate and you filter this feedback through the aesthetic net of what seems necessary for me, for Bondo, for Anne, for the designers. We had a lot of cooks in the kitchen for this one, happily. Still, a lot of it came down to Bondo and me figuring out something real but mysterious between us that threaded through the piece. We quickly understood that the thread was our thirty-year friendship. One of the benefits of working together for so many years is that we have a short-hand. We don't need to talk a lot. We make a choice and that choice is either an anchor and we hold onto it or it is a diving board and it launches us into something else.

Chess Match No. 5 *is presented as a series of exchanges, verbal and physical, between two figures identified only as He (Bond) and She (Lauren). Over the course of the ninety-minute action, they come and go, make toast or coffee, listen to a radio, don silly pointed party hats, line up for a couple of whimsical soft-shoe dances, and sit down again and again at a small table centre stage and play chess. All the while, He and She exchange Cage quotes in the manner of light-hearted, well-mannered conversation.*

Everything in the production is geared towards heightening the audience's attention to Cage's favourite subject: the sound of silence. Microphones hanging down close to the work table make sure that incidental, everyday sounds – toast popping up, the clinking of a spoon, water boiling – are conspicuous and resonant. In the moments of prolonged silence and stillness as He and She stare at the chessboard, the tap of a foot or the slow slide of a coffee mug across the top of table becomes music. Spectators who are comfortable with the lack of narrative and give over to the piece are rewarded with a charming tune-up of the senses.

People ask us how *Chess Match No. 5* is different from other shows we have done [See Figure 10.2]. It's not different. Acting is acting. If I am working for Suzuki or for Anne, I am calling on different skill sets, but it is all acting. Acting is sensation. Just because you don't have a narrative or an Aristotelian sequence of causally related events does not mean you are not getting sensation. That's what acting is: generating and experiencing sensation, and sensation is located in the body. It originates with you. You are receiving the world. Or, as John Cage would say, you are noticing the world. Good acting depends on how expert you can become at noticing sensations, cultivating them, using them to your advantage, and getting the audience to experience sensation because you are.

Because of who Cage is, this piece focuses on the sensation of sound, so the act of hearing becomes the subject between us and the audience. Not only the sounds we are making onstage, but the audience's sounds, too. People rustling their programmes or talking to their neighbour, somebody dropping their phone, clapping. The audience is creating sensations with a force equal to the actor. It is not a conscious thing on their part, whereas it is a conscious thing on our part. They often do not realize how much they are imprinting their existence on us, not just by moving around in their seats or making other sounds, but by their presence. That presence is a tangible thing, hard to point out, hard to talk about, but the quality of their attention or lack of it, someone's disgust or approval or boredom, exists in the room. It is tangible. We have to notice all that and incorporate it, literally take it into our bodies.

Figure 10.2 Ellen Lauren as She and Will Bond as He in the SITI Company production of *Chess Match No. 5* directed by Anne Bogart
Photographer: Maria Baranova

Contemplation is a sensation, too. That's what chess is – the sensation of contemplation – and we try to put that sensation into the room in a way that the audience can access it, even if they don't play chess. What is it like to meditate over a chess move? The classic example is Rodin's famous statue of *The Thinker*. Nobody really sits and thinks like that: bent over, elbow on knee, chin on the back of the hand. But the shape that Rodin chose for that sculpture generates the sensation of contemplation, just the way that the score of Beethoven's 'Ode to Joy' creates the sensation of elation in another human being. Nobody would say that joy sounds just like that. Actors do the same thing. We try to create the vessel or structure or shape of the sensation that we want to make happen in the room. We are not imitating characters or daily life, at least that's not the goal, even if at moments we have to appear as if we are.

In theatre, we tend to think that a character means a person. It does not. A character is simply a composite of certain human qualities that you have and I have and the guy across the street has. Character for me is showing those different qualities back to back to back really fast as organized by the playwright's text. And the great texts do it in a way that makes you think, for example, that Amanda Wingfield is a real human being. But Tennessee Williams is doing the exact same thing as Euripides. He is picking a sequence of words to represent something of the invisible world that we all contain. A human being's consciousness, what is actually going on inside of us – Virginia Woolf was dealing with this and so was John Cage – is complex, multitudinous and rapidly changing. The words the playwright writes are just the jagged tip of that iceberg. To get at that, I have to work with my personal and professional field of reference, my own memories and habits, and my understanding of what I am able to do with the sound and range of my voice, how deep my breathing is, my sense of timing. If I can line all that up right as an actor, I can be the conduit for the audience not only to objectify something called Clytemnestra or Virginia Woolf and watch her as a form of entertainment but also to recognize subjectively what it means to feel like that. And that is what I mean when I say there is no such thing as character.

As of 2017, Ellen Lauren had been working with Tadashi Suzuki for nearly thirty-five years and with Anne Bogart for more than twenty-five years. In addition to her extensive teaching through SCOT and SITI, she has been on the faculty of the Juilliard School of Drama for more than eighteen years.

If there is one thing that I try to teach to young artists about the Suzuki work it is that wrestling with difficulty can be productive, fruitful and ultimately joyful. Sometimes it is hard to understand why you should do something that requires such a fight and will never really be finished or good enough. As a teacher, I'm only going to give you the problem, not the solution. Each artist has to figure out how to solve it in their own way and even why they are doing it at all. The Viewpoints, the Suzuki training are ways to articulate the problem, not the solution. And then, as in life, you are on your own.

Still, I always have been and always will be an actor dedicated to being part of a company. It is the only life that makes sense to me. SITI and SCOT have been my greenhouse. In the end, we are the sum of our friends and our teachers. Suzuki and Anne have given me two different languages to bridge the distance between us and what we are each trying to say to the world. They threw me into the deep end of these problems and then allowed me the space and time to swim to a place where I can rely on my own taste, talent, discipline, physical instrument and expanding field of awareness. These kinds of relationships between a director and an actor are few and far between. They only come over time. The work has been difficult, and it remains so, but I am aware of just how lucky I have been.

Discussion Questions

1. What does Lauren suggest was the greatest challenge working with Bogart? Suzuki?
2. What was Lauren's experience of being in Japan?
3. How did Lauren prepare the role for the character of Electra? Virginia Wolf?
4. Are there aspects of Lauren's performance preparation that you believe you could incorporate in your performance style?

Websites

Bogart and Suzuki in joint symposium: https://www.youtube.com/watch?v=DGtCo9MQMUU
Anne Bogart:
   https://video.search.yahoo.com/search/video?fr=mcafee&p=ann+bogart+youtube#id=2&vid=5b90011b2a5fd8317f30e41d7e1cd9a0&action=click
   https://www.youtube.com/watch?v=SpPPGXPQ7TU
Tadashi Suzuki:
   https://www.youtube.com/watch?v=n3xO6MG1d9c

Resource material

Allain, P. (2003) *The Art of Stillness: The Theater Practice of Tadashi Suzuki* (London: St. Martin's Griffin).

_____. (2011) *The Theatre Practice of Tadashi Suzuki: A Critical Study with DVD Examples* (New York: Methuen).

Bogart, A. (2003) *A Director Prepares: Seven Essays on Art and Theatre* (London: Routledge).

_____. (2007) *And Then, You Act: Making Art in an Unpredictable World* (London: Routledge).

Bogart, A. and T. Landau (2004) *The Viewpoints Book: A Practical Guide to Viewpoints and Composition* (New York: Theatre Communications Group).

Suzuki, T. (1993) *The Way of Acting: The Theatre Writings of Tadashi Suzuki*. Trans. T. Rimmer (New York: Theatre Communications Group).

_____. (2015) *Culture is the Body: The Theatre Writings of Tadashi Suzuki*. Trans. K. Steele (New York: Theatre Communications Group).

11

People Like Us
Revolutions in Australian Theatre

Julie-Anne Long

There are two factors that lead me to write this chapter on narrative and performance in an Australian context.[1] Firstly, limited attention has been given to the alternative histories of innovative artists working in the largely under-recognized dance theatre genre in multicultural Australia. Secondly, in 1985 I joined the One Extra Company as a performer and resident choreographer and worked with Kai Ta Chan on a number of seminal works, including performing in his swansong work *People Like Us* (1991).[2] I was drawn to the unique ways in which Kai Tai challenged understandings of what could be conveyed through dance in both form and content. As Kai Tai himself puts it:

> For me dance is a form in which you can tackle a wide range of subject matters. It is basically communication of the human experience. It can be pure form, but I see it as something beyond that. I approach it from a controlled state, a realistic angle into an abstracted form. Hopefully the audience will link to the honesty and truth of what we are saying, and that is when it has great power.
>
> (Landman, cited in Lester, 2000: 223)

Kai Tai's desire to connect to an audience, to speak about things that might matter and mean something in relation to the social and real world is also shared by Kate Champion, another major influence on Australian performance, and as she stated in a 2017 interview: 'it's always mattered to me that we somehow reflect the people that are in the audience' (Champion, 2017).

Since 2002 I have regularly witnessed, as an audience member, the work of Kate Champion as artistic director of Force Majeure. Throughout the development and presentation of six major full-length works, Kate's commitment to interrogating universal themes in contemporary culture has always been present:[3]

> If you are looking at a social, political, contemporary issue all I've ever wanted to do is to try looking at it from a different angle, to try to shift people's perspectives about something. If anything, to raise more questions than they had thought previously about it, so they try to answer them themselves. But never to be didactic and say this is what you should think this is how it should be.
>
> (Champion, 2017)

Both Kate and Kai Tai[4] consider the frames of reference the audience brings to the performance work and understand the potential for dialogue between their audiences and their respective artistic visions. Abstract and conceptual dance performance is often criticized as difficult to understand and only for the initiated. In the dance theatre works of both Kate Champion and Kai Tai Chan, an explicit consideration to entertain and stimulate their audiences, emotionally and intellectually through the use of narrative, is primary.

Kai Tai Chan and One Extra

Kai Tai Chan arrived in Sydney in the 1960s from Penang, Malaysia, as a young architecture student. While undertaking his university studies he discovered dance, attending classes with Margaret Barr[5] and going on to perform with her Sydney Dance Drama Group. As he became increasingly involved with dance he discovered an ambition to create his own performances, eventually abandoning architecture and forming his own dance theatre company, One Extra, in 1976.

As the number one son born to Chinese parents many of his cultural traditions and family expectations were challenged in Australia. For Kai Tai, this fluid identification of his Chinese heritage and cultural values, along with his everyday life in Australia, became a distinctive characteristic of his identity as an artist. His complex identity provided a constructive tension and unique point of difference through all of his work as artistic director of One Extra. In relation to the English, European and American dance influences prevalent in Australia at the time One Extra provided an alternative 'dance experience' to the mainstream. While drawing on his dance-drama experiences with Barr, Kai Tai was also exploring influences from Asian dance-drama, reflected in theatrical form, thematic content and his approach to interdisciplinary collaborations and the creative processes.

One Extra became known for its 'Australian-ness' developed from Kai Tai's experiences as an Asian migrant observing and immersed in a multicultural Australia. In an interview with his long-time associate Garry Lester, Kai Tai explained:

> My work is the expression of the human condition as I experience it. It is from the perspective of someone from a minority community within a dominant culture – a migrant from a non-English speaking background, Asian and gay, who has great empathy with other minorities including different races such as Aborigines, and different cultural expressions manifest through dance and art and explorations across different art forms ... I have a commitment for the concerns of minority groups and a belief that we have important things to say to the mainstream or dominant culture. There is great strength in diversity and understanding of each other's backgrounds and lifestyles. My work is about Australia and its search for national cultural identity and not a ghetto mentality.
>
> (Lester, 2000: 119)

In a cultural survey on East-West, Asian and Australian hybridity in the arts, Alison Broinowski remarked: 'Australia offered Kai Tai things to say and permission to say them' (1996: 154). *People Like Us* (1991), his final full-length work before his resignation from One Extra, was a work that provided Kai Tai with an opportunity to bring together many of these key concerns and themes.

People Like Us: Narrative and Narration

People Like Us was a large ensemble piece that consisted of a culturally diverse cast of seventeen Asian, Aboriginal and Anglo dancers, actors and singers, who ranged in age from early twenties through to artists in their fifties (including a young child, Kai Tai's nephew). In collaboration with theatre director, Peter Kingston, Kai Tai created an insightful depiction of an Australian identity inclusive of difference utilizing the diverse skills of his cast.

> Look, one of the things I want to portray, and it's hinted at in the title of my work, *People Like Us*, is the commonality of people and their life experiences. What better place than Australia can we be examining this theme?
>
> (Lester, 2000: 147)

People Like Us was structured in three acts with Act One defined by 'the mother's story' and Act Two by Kai Tai's own life experience. The final act, the most abstract of the three, brought together intersecting storylines from the previous acts to reveal connections between the stories, all clearly located in contemporary Australian society. The complex composition of this work incorporated a range of theatrical performance modes: delivering emotion and character through narration of personal stories; creating three distinct 'worlds' onstage through the underlying evocative sound and musical score; choreographing stage action and tableaux with physical impact; and generating imagery through the relationship between all the theatrical elements, to create a cohesive theatrical narrative from the three acts. This approach to dance theatre enabled shifts in narrative mode – in time and space, and from literal to abstract.

Act 1: The Mother's Story

The first act was developed from a series of in-depth interviews with an Australian woman about her family life in a country town. The verbatim interview transcript was crafted into a monologue for the actress who played the mother. While utilizing the actual spoken words of the interviewee, the final script was edited and crafted to tell the mother's story with dramatic cohesion for a live audience. The focus on constructing the mother's script was to retain a sense of authenticity, especially with the Australian accent and laconic, self-deprecating, often humorous tone and rhythms of speech carefully memorized by the actress, who spoke directly to the audience, as well as to and with the other characters onstage.

The mother's story unfolded primarily through spoken narration directly addressed to the audience. The mother also moved in and out of the stage action. Her role provided a point of identification for the audience between the action and images created as her narrative intercepted the movement. *People Like Us* was primarily not text-driven as many of the images dealing with often ordinary, easily identifiable events in a family history such as births and family celebrations were expressed through a collage of physical images. The first act clearly established the dance theatre performative mode of *People Like Us*, moving from the literal, theatre world of stories as exemplified by the mother's narration, to an abstract, more suggestive world of dance, supported by the live music, which ranged from medieval madrigals, to gospel songs, to contemporary world music.

The use of minimal props, sparse set elements and simple costumes was supported by powerful, embodied, often metaphorical images that were driven by the movement. For example, the narrative between the mother and her heroin-addicted son was represented by a highly physical duet between the two characters, connected by a bungy rope (umbilical cord), which generated an emotional, conflicted push-pull dynamic, strongly suggesting his decline and her frustration and despair when she finally relinquished the connection.

Act 2: The Migrant's Story

The second act was Kai Tai's story. As he cooked onstage – a traditional Malaysian meal with the aromatic smells filtering throughout the theatre – he recollected fragments of stories about his family and upbringing and examined his identity as 'other': his 'Chinese-ness' and his identity as a gay male, in the dominant Anglo-Celtic, heterosexual society of Australia, the country where he now lived. In this way Kai Tai's story was unmistakeably manifest in the work through the information and experiences he shared with the audience about his personal life.

Like the mother's story, the autobiographical content of the second act was crafted from a series of interviews with Kai Tai, who used the structure of his script as an improvisational score. Like the mother, he spoke directly to the audience, with many audience members knowing that this was his final work for One Extra, and as such, the story took on poignancy beyond purely the theatrical construct. Kai Tai's narration was littered with grammatical idiosyncrasies and delivered in a natural, albeit slightly halting way, unlike the memorized script faithfully delivered by the actress in the first act. As with the mother, Kai Tai was also integrated into movement sequences and staged tableaux and at times was represented by and shadowed an indigenous actor/dancer as his younger self.

Act 3: A Metaphorical Metaphysical Portrait

With its white costumes and stark staging, Act Three was a more abstract, ethereal world – a 'white ballet'.[6] The final act brought together characters and narrative threads from the previous two acts when Kai Tai's lover, the mother's eldest son, is discovered to have AIDS. Here the narrative mode shifts from the specific story of an Australian family, who the audience have come to know over the previous hour, to a universal story reflecting on human relationships and ultimately death.

Throughout *People Like Us* the verbal narration and text was at all times in considered dialogue with the movement, the soundscape and the visual images. The balance of what the audience saw and what they heard created a theatrical narrative: Kai Tai revealing his emotional reaction to the 1989 massacre in Tiananmen Square; a sound collage of news items referencing the destruction of AIDS in the gay community and homophobic bashings in Sydney; a Bondi Beach life saver heading an immigration line, set against the musical dramaturgy of uplifting gospel songs, sung by the five singers moving back and forth on large swings. Interspersed with a mix of religious references, including a young female Asian dancer, performing a delicate lyrical dance with small golden Christian angels, a tall Greek male dancer methodically moving with lit candles in graceful circles of his arms. In addition to these powerful images the family members from the first and second acts reappeared. Repetition of earlier scenes, such as a family gathering, conveyed a different and new reading with the knowledge of the eldest son's death from AIDS.

Several large-scale meditative scenes created a potently reflective atmosphere for Act Three. The cast performed a slow motion stylized tai chi sequence and the final image was a line-up of the entire cast walking slowly towards the audience, allowing time for the audience to reflect on and identify with the diverse characters and their various storylines, and 'the people' in the cast and their real-world identities.

Multiple Perspectives

Scene content, led by Kai Tai's vision that was often motivated by his personal experience, was generated from an improvisational creative process that acknowledged the multiple perspectives of the diverse cast. The various experiences and skills of the highly trained dancers, actors and singers contributed to the devised material and content of the work. The ideas were carefully considered, reworked and often transformed in recognition of a universal resonance before being adopted into the interdisciplinary framework.

Additionally, culturally specific dances or dance motifs were often referenced and assimilated into the work. In Act Two a 'Woman Warrior' burst onto the stage, riding a shiny red Vespa motorcycle, circling through the scene with flags flying from the back of her traditional Chinese Opera costume. Her movements intercepted the stage action: East meets West and traditional meets contemporary. As theatre and dance reviewer Matheson wrote:

> In this way, a Chinese Australian grieving for the massacre at Tiananmen Square and a country mother who has decided to cut ties with her heroin-addicted son embrace in the dance as friends. It is a sophisticated and visionary work. It probes our understanding of culture by presenting issues from multiple points of view and forms. Chan's generous vision of humanity works to combine the different forms of dance, theatre and music with apparent effortlessness.
>
> (Matheson, cited in Lester, 2000: 151)

Kate Champion and Force Majeure

Kate Champion first danced professionally as a teenager in Germany before returning to Australia where she joined the One Extra Company under the artistic direction of Kai Tai Chan in 1981. Kate was also a founding member of Dance North in Townsville before moving to Adelaide to dance with Australian Dance Theatre.[7] In 1992 Kate travelled to London, where she worked as a performer and rehearsal director with Australian-born Lloyd Newson, artistic director of DV8 Physical Theatre, working intermittently with the company over the next eight years.[8]

It was Lloyd Newson's approach to dance theatre that significantly influenced Kate's methods and philosophy when creating work for her own company Force Majeure, formed in 2002. Both Kate and Lloyd Newson share a commitment to making dance about real-world issues and communicating directly with an audience. As Newson puts it:

> To me, what is wrong with a lot of contemporary dance is that it is a licence to indulge, to be unclear in what you might be saying. What concerns me is that the elitism of dance not only removes choreographers and dancers from talking about the real world, about the particular experience, but it also distances some of the critics from the particular.
>
> (Sykes, 1996)

As in Kai Tai's work, the intention of a scene and the particular motivations of each performer were of utmost importance for Newson when devising the dance movement.

Kate Champion was interested in creating identifiable experiences and characters for her audiences and engaged with themes that were not necessarily her direct experience of the world. Unlike the direct connection of Kai Tai's personal life to understanding his work, Kate's personal life is not manifest directly in her work and not necessary for an understanding of her work. Kate noted that reporters and interviewers often assumed the work would be or should be autobiographical and was somehow less authentic if it was not 'her personal story'. For example, *Never Did Me Any Harm* (2012) explored contemporary attitudes to raising children, despite not having any children of her own. One interviewer referred 'to the fact that I didn't have any children, with the subtext suggesting that I wasn't as qualified to make a work with this subject matter' (Champion, 2017).

Nothing to Lose: Dramaturgical Decisions and an Emerging Narrative

Reviewers' responses is one of the reasons, with her 2015 work *Nothing to Lose*, and its cast of big-bodied dancers, Kate invited artist and fat activist Kelli Jean Drinkwater to be artistic associate. Kelli Jean's lived experience as a big-bodied, plus-sized person provided the insider information for Kate, who is not large herself. Kate often received questions about her own motives for the work, given that it was not her direct experience. Even the director of the Sydney Festival, who commissioned the work, asked Kate if she was prepared to put on weight. With a cast of big-bodied performers not usually seen in conventional dance companies, Kate decided to be explicit about her position in relation to the context and content of the work: 'I asked them "how do you feel about a slim-ish, white, heterosexual, blonde, blue eyed, Northern beaches brought-up choreographer asking you to do these things?" I had to put that out there at the beginning' (Champion, 2017).

Nothing to Lose was not Kate's story and the cast teased her endlessly, calling her a 'chubby collector'.

Kate was interested in the bigger body in a choreographic sense, as she had not previously worked with larger dancers. She was not interested in 'making steps' but was curious as to how the performers moved and what it means to move in certain ways in a body of size. Ultimately for Kate it was as simple as 'I haven't seen this – I would love to see this, I think this would be a fantastic thing to see on stage!' (Champion, 2017). This approach was a continuation of exposing the audience to new ways of viewing their community. For her, being an artist is about creating a resonance for an audience, if it's not their own experience then at least something they can relate to. Previous themes explored in her work include living in an age of anxiety post-September 11, *Already Elsewhere* (2005), different stages of life and the aging process, *The Age I'm In* (2008), and *Not In A Million Years* (2010), which was inspired by true stories of people who had endured extreme circumstances.

The generating and devising process for *Nothing to Lose* produced individual responses to tasks set by Kate, which she then structured into the final non-linear narrative. American choreographer Lliane Loots describes her working process in a way that is instructive for and similar to the creative process that Kate engages with:

> Working with guided improvisation and guided physical dance play in the studio, I ask the dancers to take verbal or physical ideas which I give them and ask them to generate dance material on their own bodies – material that is both personal and 'fits' the idiosyncrasies of their own individual body movement patterns. In this way the dance material becomes deeply personal and is physically resolved on the body doing it. I then use the dance material and cut, edit, re-arrange, re-shape, create duets, and sometimes choreograph in a manner that suits my vision of the whole. The dancers thus present me, their choreographer, with the stories they write on their own bodies. As a choreographer, I thus begin to think of myself as a type of 'collector of stories' – some are my own, but others come from the dancers I am working with.
>
> (2016: 383)

Making devised dance theatre is a communal act; however, it was Kate's directorial vision, in consultation with Kelli Jean and the performers,

People Like Us: Revolutions in Australian Theatre

Figure 11.1 *Nothing to Lose* by Kate Champion, produced by Force Majeur
Photographer: Toby Burrows

individually and collectively, contributing their stories and their moves, that made decisions about what made it in and what got cut in *Nothing to Lose* (see Figure 11.1). This is not a cause and effect movement-based process, but rather a theatrical non-linear narrative that is particular to performance work that deals with the body.

Personal Stories and Powerful Emotions

In *Nothing to Lose* the body is central – subject and object. The work is written on and by the body. In this regard, it is a work full of autobiographical material where the starting point is 'the self'. *Nothing to Lose* drew on the personal stories, lived experiences, histories and memories of the cast, five women and two men, all large-bodied performers. A driving force that was always present and amplified for this dance theatre work was these particular bodies.

Stories told through the body in *Nothing to Lose* were about physical difference; fat-shaming and prejudice; notions of slimness reflecting goodness, beauty, success and fashion; reclaiming the word 'fat' that is used to abuse and hurt; this was a world where fat was beautiful, interesting, strong, funny and deserved to take up space. The obvious visual nature of fatness can never be hidden and these performers and this work unashamedly claimed fat, which elicited powerful emotions.

Between Disturbing and Delightful

Emerging from a prop-based improvisation the performers tied up body parts – binding their fleshy stomachs, buttocks, thighs, breasts and arms, to create irregular shapes and silhouettes. The body was treated in a sculptural way with a focus on form, shape and size of the performers' bodies, with possible connotations of bondage creating additional impact. This imposing, powerful movement section wouldn't have been possible with smaller bodies. Some of the audience appeared to find it enticing, while others averted their gazes, tangibly disturbed by the flesh in front of them. The intention of this section was not to purposely shock or dictate a particular view but rather provoke questions, which for me included: Why are we so scared of flesh? And, what is our conditioning that makes us respond in these ways?

From Anger Comes Fierceness

Anger was a powerful emotion evident throughout *Nothing to Lose*, specifically, anger and fury transformed by the performers into a quality that Kate calls 'fierce'. This was a fierceness fuelled by anger from the abuse and hurt experienced over years of being fat-shamed, fierceness from lived experience of the challenges of overcoming discrimination and claiming their own identity as a fat person. In the solo by Scarlett, she threw her strong, compact body down onto the ground repeatedly and quite forcibly. Although she didn't hurt herself, for many of the audience members it created a visceral reaction of shock and dismay. Even Kelli Jean found it confronting and wasn't sure it should be included in the final performance, but for Kate it was essential to push those watching to a point of uneasiness. Anger repels and Scarlett's solo diffused that extreme emotion and expressed it through the physical intensity and concentration of this repetitive action of falling and getting up again, to highlight the strength and power of the performer.

Relax and Laugh with Me

Often victims of discrimination bypass humiliation and anger, and, as a way of dealing with it, turn the negative emotions into humour by laughing at themselves. A group dance, 'jiggling piece', demonstrates this familiar trope through a lighter change of tone. The performers appeared to enjoy shimmying and shaking different parts of their bodies, relishing the display of holding their stomach rolls, gleefully feeling the texture and weight in their hands. In performing what could be construed as a subversive act they claimed power.

Sculptural Beauty and Joy

Adonis (Anastasia Zaravinos) is a veteran of the queer, underground performance scene and is clearly comfortable in her own skin. While the politics of *Nothing to Lose* were not as explicit as her own artistic practice, the solo performed by Adonis made the private public. Only her body could perform the solo, on the cusp of gender definitions. It was sculptural, beautiful, lyrical and sensuous as she moved slowly to an operatic aria. It was brutally confident as the movement, derived from hip-hop moves, revealed itself to be fiercer than first impressions suggested. This was, as with all the solos in *Nothing to Lose*, an autobiographical story: their bodies, their personalities, and their experiences. Stories of each performer, that spoke of the moment and of the time. Stories that came out of the zeitgeist, bringing fat politics and fat dancers centre stage.

Ultimately, *Nothing to Lose* makes four moves between the performers and audience: one, I'll show you (the audience) how you look at me (the performer); two, I'll invite you to get to know me more deeply; three, I'll try to help you to know what it is like to be me; four, I'll encourage you to try on my skin. The dancer/performer accomplishes this by inviting some of the audience onto the stage, so they can touch and talk to the performers, reversing the gaze, to see that the performers are not 'other'. So, the narrative could be described as: looking outside, to inside, to looking back through me and then in the end now look at me do what I'm doing with skill.

Conclusion

Both works discussed in this chapter were made at particular times in Sydney and engaged with themes that communicated to their contemporary Australian audiences. Coincidentally, both works, by directors Kai Tai Chan and Kate Champion,[9] were the final works as artistic directors of their respective companies. The narrative structure of *People Like Us* was supported by the direct narration of two autobiographical stories, the mother's story (Act One) and Kai Tai's story (Act Two). These personal stories intersected in the third act representing universal themes in an image-based theatrical narrative. Narrative in *Nothing to Lose* was created through the dramaturgy of a non-linear collage of scenes, generated from the performers' individual lived experiences.

Storytelling in dance theatre in Sydney continues today, represented in the work of two companies who tell stories through dance: Shaun Parker & Company and Bangarra Dance Theatre. Shaun Parker & Company premiered its first show *This Show is About People* (2008) at the Sydney Festival and was immediately acclaimed for its Tanz theatre lineage, evident in its diverse, easily relatable characters located in an undisclosed waiting room. Kristy Edmunds, artistic director of the 2008 Melbourne International Festival, recognized 'from the reaction of the audience I would say they certainly felt it was for them' (Shaun Parker & Company, 2017). Over the following decade Parker has continued to make works about identity, where audiences recognize themselves in the themes and community of characters presented onstage.

Bangarra Dance Theatre is Australia's major Aboriginal and Torres Strait Islander dance company. Based in Sydney, since its inauguration in 1989 by artistic director Stephen Page, Bangarra has been bringing indigenous 'authentic stories' to the stage through 'a unique Australian dance language' combining traditional Aboriginal, Torres Strait Island and contemporary dance. Bangarra collaborates closely with artists in dance, music and sound, set and costume design, actors and writers. Bangarra's repertoire includes dance works that explore themes of identity, inequality, climate change and sustainability with a hopeful and positive outlook for the future.[10] Bangarra's world premiere of *Bennelong* (2017) with choreography credited to Stephen Page and the Bangarra dancers, tells the story of the important historical figure of Aboriginal leader Woollarawarre Bennelong and is described as: '[a]n extraordinarily powerful work, a benchmark in Australian dance creativity. It sums up yesterday, today and perhaps tomorrow in a swirling series of storytelling episodes that explore Indigenous lives in an Australia colonised by Europeans' (Sykes, 2017). The historical and cultural construction of Bangarra's dance theatre establishes political provocations of indigenous heritage and cultural identity that demand urgent attention in Australia today. Much like Kai Tai Chan's explicit engagement with multicultural Australia of the 1970s and 1980s and his search for a national cultural identity inclusive of difference and Kate Champion's challenge to an audience regarding physical difference, the larger body and preconceptions of the dancing body, dance theatre in Sydney continues to be peopled with identifiable characters, connections to real-life issues and social, cultural and political meanings relevant to the directors and their audiences.

Discussion Questions

1. What role does autobiography play in the works discussed?
2. Neither Kai Tai or Kate were interested in dance steps and technique for their own sake. Their interests were on embodied presence and using whatever movement style or choreographic approach best communicated the idea or the issue. How is this attitude similar or different from other directors and choreographers?
3. Thinking about your own cultural context and the place and time you live in, if you were to devise a dance theatre work about 'identity', what aspects of your own identity would you explore? For example: race, sexuality, body image, etc.?

Websites

ABC 7.30 Report (Monday 29 December 2014) *Dancers with 'Nothing to lose' challenge body image ideas*: http://www.abc.net.au/7.30/dancers-with-nothing-to-lose-challenge-body-image/5992124

Force Majeure (2014) *Nothing to Lose*, Promotional Video: https://vimeo.com/110962808

Force Majeure (2015) *Kate + Kelli Jean on 'Nothing to Lose'*, Sydney Festival: https://vimeo.com/104987653

One Extra Dance (1978–2006) (2009) Trove, accessed 15 March 2018: https://nla.gov.au/nla.party-726053

Notes

1. The author wishes to thank Garry Lester who worked closely with Kai Tai and One Extra from 1976 to 1991. His unpublished PhD 'Kai Tai Chan: A Different Path' provided an invaluable and unique insight into Kai Tai Chan, his philosophies, his challenges and ultimately his decision to leave the artistic world in 1991. Thanks also to Kate Champion for taking time to talk to me about *Nothing to Lose*.
2. Malaysian-born architect and dancer Kai Tai Chan formed the One Extra Company in 1976 as a vehicle for his eclectic experimental multicultural dance work. In 1985, I joined the company when it became fully professional maintaining a full-time ensemble for five consecutive years by means of regular public arts funding. Based in Sydney, the company toured extensively in Australia and overseas.
3. *Same, Same But Different* (2002) blurred boundaries of dance and theatre; *Already Elsewhere* (2005) created an atmosphere post-September 11 of living life in fear; *The Age I'm In* (2008) expressed the complexity of human relationships and the aging process; *Not In A Million Years* (2010) was inspired by true stories of people who had endured extreme circumstances; *Never Did Me Any Harm* (2012) explored contemporary attitudes to raising children; *Nothing to Lose* (2015) challenged expectations of the fat body in performance.
4. In this chapter, I refer to Kai Tai and Kate by their first names. I write of them in relation to my relationship, having worked with both of these artists. They are as subjects not objects of study.

5. Margaret Barr (1904–91) was known for her dance-drama works, which were 'theatrical with overt political messages about contemporary economic and social conditions' (Lester, 2014) and her innovative approach to movement, outside the confines of classical ballet and traditional expressive dance styles.
6. Romantic era, classical ballets have a tradition of the 'white ballet' where the location is often a metaphysical world, populated by ghosts and supernatural creatures. Examples include: *La Sylphide* (1832) and Act 2 from *Giselle* (1841) set in the supernatural world of the Wilis.
7. Kate Champion has also created and performed solo works *Face Value* (1995) and *About Face* (2001), and worked in theatre and opera as choreographer, notably with director Neil Armfield on *Cloudstreet* (1997) and Wagner's *Ring Cycle* directed by Armfield for Opera Australia (2016), as well as being choreographer on musical *Dirty Dancing* (2004).
8. Lloyd Newson travelled as a dancer with One Extra to England in 1980. He stayed to study at London Contemporary Dance School and danced and choreographed with companies such as Extemporary Dance Theatre (UK) before forming his own company, DV8 Physical Theatre, in 1986. DV8 has been acclaimed for its interdisciplinary approach working with dance, text, theatre and film. Since 2007 Newson's works have been described as documentary-style dance theatre utilizing verbatim theatre processes and archive footage: *John* (2015), male sexuality and love; *Can We Talk About This?* (2011–12), freedom of speech, censorship and Islam; *To Be Straight With You* (2007–09) on issues of religion and sexuality from multi-ethnic perspectives.
9. Kate Champion continues to work as a creative artist in opera, theatre and on a range of other creative projects. Following Kate's resignation in 2015, Danielle Micich was appointed artistic director to Force Majeure and the company continues to develop dance theatre that examines contemporary culture in Australia.
10. The first full-length work created by Stephen Page for Bangarra Dance Theatre was *Praying Mantis Dreaming* (1992). This story of a young Aboriginal girl, on a quest to reconcile her traditional homelands with the city, was told in what has become Bangarra's distinctive combination of traditional and contemporary dance styles. Other works followed that brought together dancers, actors and singers, *NINNI* (1994) exploring Aboriginal identity in urban and traditional contexts. Abstract dance works in the repertoire include *Ochres* (1994) with choreography by Stephen Page, Bernadette Walong-Sene and Djakapurra Munyarryun, and *Fish* (1997). Both tell stories about the earth and the sea, portraying the spiritual meaning of the elements for Aboriginal identity.

Works Cited and Resource Material

Bangarra (2017) Website. https://www.bangarra.com.au/, accessed 16 August 2017.
Broinowski, A. (1996) *The Yellow Lady – Australian Impressions of Asia*, 2nd edition (Australia: Oxford University Press).
Champion, K. (2017) Interview with author, Sydney NSW, 14 July.
Force Majeure Website. http://www.forcemajeure.com.au, accessed 20 July 2017.
Lester, G. (2000) Kai Tai Chan: A Different Path, Unpublished Doctoral Dissertation, School of Contemporary Arts (Melbourne: Deakin University).
_____. (2014) Barr, Margaret (1904–1991), *Australian Dictionary of Biography*, National Centre of Biography, Australian National University, http://adb.anu.edu.au/biography/barr-margaret-14855, accessed 10 August 2017.
Loots, L. (2016) The Autoethnographic Act of Choreography: Considering the Creative Process of Storytelling with and on the Performative Dancing Body and the Use of Verbatim Theatre Methods, *Critical Arts*, 30(3), pp. 376–91.
Shaun Parker & Company (2017) Website. http://www.shaunparkercompany.com, accessed 22 August 2017.
Sykes, J. (1996) DV8 to Men's Emotional Needs, *Sydney Morning Herald*, 11 March, https://www.newspapers.com/newspage/120396223, accessed 20 August 2017.
_____. (2017) Bennelong Review: Bangarra Dance Theatre Have Produced an Exceptional Work, *Sydney Morning Herald*, 30 June, http://www.smh.com.au/entertainment/dance/bennelong-review-bangarra-dance-theatre-have-produced-an-exceptional-work-20170630-gx1u5m.html, accessed 22 August 2017.

12

Jacques Lecoq and This Theatre Called My Body

Nikole Pascetta

Twenty-five years ago, on the heels of graduating from the Jacques Lecoq Theatre School (Paris, France), I joined the cast of a new French play called *Croquis Marrant d'une Vie Redoutée*. In English, the title literally translates as Funny Sketches of a Formidable Life. This essay is a narrative account of my experience as the lone North American in the *Croquis* ensemble.[1] I address the subtle nuances language and cultural communication played throughout the collaborative working process. This is not limited to words for the making of verbal meaning, but also reflects the enacted embodied language rooted in the lived experiences of our meaning making (Johnson, 2007; Van Manen, 1989). In the fields of cognitive science and applied linguistics this is sometimes referred to as 'languaging' or language as whole-body sense-making where movement is a way of knowing (Sheets-Johnstone, 2013).

Backstory

Funny Sketches of a Formidable Life is a collectively devised performance piece that examines disparities of social power and wealth. Created by the France-based physical theatre company Théâtre de la Jacquerie, the piece questions the authority of the corporate elite, called *les Gris* (the Greys), whose angular movements and monochromatic wardrobe reflect their social control over less privileged workers. Using body-based devising techniques informed by Lecoq's pedagogy, the piece compiles thematic sketches that satirically buffoon structural power and the hierarchy of intra-organizational decision-making. As a member of the ensemble, the experience brought to light a shared physical capital[2] of the widening global gap vis-à-vis imbalance and systemic inequality.

I will begin by offering some information that speaks to the inception of the material and how it informed both the ensemble and the many elements that came together in the rehearsal process. Next, with the assistance of former company members,[3] I will describe the method of devising and the role of the exchange of cultural knowledge played in influencing the embodied storytelling of social capital and mobility in the making of this piece. I include some thoughts on laughter and humour and the approach taken by the collective to 'put funny on its feet'. The sections that follow outline a few of the specific impulses that lead to character and plot development, concluding with final reflections on embodied epistemology and this theatre called the body.

In large part, the thematic narrative for *Croquis* was inspired by Franz Kafka's 1926 novel, *The Castle* (*Das Schloss*) – its reading and discussion became part of our rehearsal process. In Kafka's narrative, the castle plays a central, menacing character, representative of power, authority and inaccessibility. It towers over a surrounding village inhabited by commoners. Alain Mollot, director of Théâtre de la Jacquerie, was drawn to the space between the castle and the villagers as a dichotomous tension between two opposing extremes: the haves and the have-nots. Kafka's castle and the rawness of its characters would reflect the contemporary concerns of social order and inequality the company sought to explore through this piece. The tone of the story would provide a foundation for *Croquis*.

In the novel, the protagonist is a stranger only known by his letter initial 'K' who wanders into the village. He claims he is a land surveyor, although several critics of the piece have challenged this fact, as he never really demonstrates any kind of land surveying knowledge or skill. The LEC collective found the ambiguities of Kafka's *The Castle* and the dilemmas of resistance 'K' encounters throughout very enticing. The idea of a main character, who is foreign to the ways of a new community, would become the method or narrative technique and subsequently provide the way in for the audience.

Little by little, we began to scaffold scenes, looking for a thread or through line (*fil conducteur*). No one in the company had actually ever worked in the corporate world and none of us were driven by the lure of big money. Yet, as young middle-class actors, we were familiar with the grimmer realities of when things in life go wrong. Spanish cast member Antonio Gil-Martinez shared how, irrespective of our cultural differences, many fundamental, dark aspects of urban life and living we sought to explore were universal themes that exceeded gender, class and race. Our goal as Lecoqian trained actors was to find the poetic comedy within the darkness. Collectively we compiled a list of potential scenarios taken from our individual life experiences. Some of the rehearsal ideas explored were as follows:

- the dread of the future
- human failure
- miscommunication
- egocentrism
- love/marriage/divorce
- the exacerbated materialization of human relationships
- the impossibility of love in a society where everyone seems to want more, something else
- the overuse and presence of mass media
- media's catastrophizing view of the world
- the absurdity of bureaucracy and the corporate world
- living paycheque to paycheque and the daunting menace of homelessness.

One of the original core members of the group, French-Israeli born actor Ami Hattab, created a character who, similar to Kafka's 'K', would be known by the monosyllabic noun of 'the man' (*l'homme*). Yet, contrary to Kafka's story and clever protagonist 'K', 'the man' would become the 'Jacques', or everyday man. The man epitomized humaneness in every sense of the word: caring, hard-working, honest, kind, optimistic, and so forth. The man was the labourer who works but never gets ahead. He was the voice of the masses. Physically Ami developed heavy grounded movements for the character, earthy with a tinge of clunky. Together with an unkempt appearance, he exuded a rather boring invisibleness to him. He was the 'wallflower', easily overlooked and forgettable.

With suitcase in hand, the man, rather unexpectedly, arrives at the City of Grey. Once we had this part of the narrative in place, the man would become the travelling lens of the naïve perspective. Everything he encountered throughout his journey in the City of Grey would be antithetical to his understanding of the world. The trajectory of the man's character development throughout the arc of the show, as outsider, a foreigner, begins to disrupt the spaces of ambition, power and pride in the City of Grey. He would become the revolution personified.

Collective Creation, Social Awareness and Thematic Narrative

The performance premise of *Croquis* emerged out of two basic questions: What makes us laugh today? And can we revolutionize a new form of contemporary comedy? Working in the Lecoq physical theatre style, under the direction of artistic director Alain Mollot, the objective was to explore comedic styles anchored in contemporary concerns of the early 1990s (see Figure 12.1). With a new millennium and new century on the horizon, the history-making events of the times could be felt worldwide: the economic crisis resulting from a stock collapse and ensuing recession, the mounting Iraqi tensions that led to the Gulf War, the fall of (the Wall) communism in Eastern Europe that ended the almost forty-five-year Cold War.

The material is a compilation of satirical sketches that poke and prod at the complexities (*vie redoutée*) of urban living in postmodern times. Specifically, the piece examines social order and inequality to, in turn, buffoon the hierarchal power structures that enable them. At first blush, the intersection of humour[4] and hegemony may seem an unlikely pairing. Let me back up a bit to offer some of the personal, social and contextual factors that led to the convergence of these two thematic topics and the movement-based collective approach taken to build the piece.

Founded in 1974, the 'Jacquerie' company namesake typifies its mandate in the creation of this piece. La Jacquerie is essentially two ideas.

Jacques Lecoq and This Theatre Called My Body

Figure 12.1 The *Croquis* ensemble, Théâtre de la Jacquerie
Photographer: Claude Gugny

First, it is a group of actors, collectively drawing on the strengths of their combined skills to develop a piece. Second, it is the search for a universal theatre – an artistic medium that crosses cultural, linguistic and socioeconomic borders and boundaries. 'Jacquerie' is a historical term that comes from an actual revolt that took place between nobles and peasants in fourteenth-century northern France. To call someone 'Jacques' has a double purpose and meaning. At that time, the name 'Jacques' was equivalent to the use of 'Joe' in English as in 'Joe Blow', the everyday ordinary guy on the street. It was also used as a less than complimentary commentary on the combative jacket, a padded surplice called a *jacque* worn by the commoners in battle (Tuchman, 1978).[5]

A graduate of the Lecoq School, Mollot founded Théâtre de la Jacquerie shortly after graduating. Years later, he would go on to become a cherished faculty member at the Lecoq School teaching scene-study to the second-year cohort. It was during his tenure *chez* Lecoq that Mollot began working with a group of former students with the objective to create a collaborative theatre piece that would be anchored in, and give voice to, current social, political and cultural issues. The twist: using humour to locate the laughter of a rapidly changing social world.

The original *Croquis* ensemble had been formed a year prior to my joining. They were graduates who had completed the Lecoq training the year before. That core group consisted of eight cast members, who came from France (two), Israel, New Zealand, Spain (three) and the United Kingdom. Over the course of their two years at the school, they had become exceptionally skilled collaborators, whose bond would further strengthen throughout the *Croquis* devising process. I, a Canadian of Italian heritage, would replace the actor who had returned home to London. I would also add (or rather bring) another continent and multicultural identity to what had been, up to this point, an exchange of Euro-Middle Eastern-South Pacific perspectives. We were high-spirited 'Gen Xers' full of ideas and very prolific about using theatre to create social change. In hindsight, I am not sure we were aware of how the integration of our diverse sociocultural life experiences contributed to the discovery and development of the shared embodied vocabulary and experience.

You Say You Want a Revolution?

Prior to my joining the Jacquerie, the ensemble had begun to discuss and analyse the narrative style of comedic forms in an effort to examine situations which create laughter. Initially the vast range and scope of comedic methods, genres and techniques raised questions as to the necessary criterion or parameters in which laughter occurs. This task was further challenged by the fact that we had narrowed the scope to what makes us laugh in troubling times.

Some significant topics discussed considered how 'funny' was dependent on place. How much of what makes us laugh relies on the set-up and execution of the delivery and/or presentation of the deliverer? Is humour, as the saying goes, 'all in the timing'? Finally, how much is laughter influenced by others? Is it socially imposed, or a subjective experience?

Then there was the concern of ethical narrative humour and the fine line between moral and immoral content material.[6] Present-day politics have (more than) demonstrated how easy it is to poke fun at the prevailing systemic power (world leaders) and im/balance (the 99 per cent versus the top 1 per cent of income earners), over tragic events or taboo subjects. Apropos to these situations, what is it about the tension, discomfort or dread (foreboding) that could transform the direction of their demise towards humour? In the attempt to revolutionize comedy, the company was looking for what makes 'funny' so funny.

A phenomenon of particular interest was the advent of 'canned laughter' or artificial laughter brought to us courtesy of the Golden Age of Television. Here, recorded laughter takes on a Pavlovian dimension informing the audience where the comic relief occurs and when to respond accordingly. Originally created by CBS sound engineer Charley Douglass, fake laughter was used to manipulate where the laughs occurred in relation to the text (typically recorded during dialogue-free sequences in variety programming). It allowed the creative team to insert or remove the live audience reactions, often unreliable (laughing too loudly or for too long) or insufficient reactions (laughing at the wrong time) (Armstrong, 2016). Mollot felt that laugh track laughter helped inform the degree to which the mindless consumption of parodic narratives can influence our perceptions of socially shared humour. He had us question the imposed laughter of television comedy, to instead search for 'a noble style of comedy'. Here, noble is intended in the (adjective) sense of virtuous or ethical and not that of (noun) aristocratic social prestige.

By this time, the ensemble had acquired the name le LEC, short for the Laboratoire Ecriture Comique or 'Comic Writing Lab' in English. Inclusion of an embodied dimension called for a review into the varied types of humour, the most obvious divided into two categories of lexical/verbal and visual/physical. Within these divisions existed many more genres (dry/witty/cheesy/absurd – clowning/shtick/slapstick) that provided a broad foundation in which to demystify the moments that lead up to and provoke laughter (Nichol, 2015). The challenge was in the exploration of these forms both with and without the use of verbal language. In other words, setting the scene for the comedy to occur before or regardless of the verbal text.

As the old adage 'get back to basics' goes, the LEC collective considered those aspects of life and humour that get us through the difficulties of living. Drawing from simple, ordinary and even unfunny scenarios, we began to improvise around the common banalities of the mundane. True to Lecoq's pedagogy, our improvs began with the body and not with the text. Jos Houben, a current teacher at the Lecoq School, explains:

> The precondition for [Lecoq's] theatre is that someone will come in, and then he can stumble, or he can all of a sudden make a dance movement, or all of sudden in front of our eyes he can take some clay and make a sculpture.
>
> (Barker, 2012)

In this regard, 'theatre is taken as, here's a space, and here's an actor, now what can you do. And not, here is a text, already a written material, or already a created piece and how would you interpret that' (Barker, 2012)? With this very basic premise as the objective, Mollot wanted to explore what it is about a rupture in the quotidian that makes us chuckle.

In an applied context, Mollot had us begin improvising very basic scenarios. These took the shape of thematically driven situations, where we isolated words and phrases that represented ideas of *une vie redoutée* (a redoubtable life). Take for example the quintessential situation of the neighbour innocently asking to borrow a cup of sugar from the house next door. Titled *The Unexpected* (*L'Inattendu*) the twist in this improv is what the neighbour does not know – she has accidentally interrupted the couple in the middle of an argument. Suddenly, the neighbour becomes involved. Our question was: Is there humour in this situation?

Leah Fletcher shared her example of an improv she was given based on the word 'Misery' (*La Misère*). Here, a young couple learns they are going to be first-time parents. In discovering that they are pregnant, each actor in the improvisation is given the direction to push the themes of innocence and naïveté – both verbally and physically vis-à-vis text and character development. Raising the stakes, the actors must reduce their play (*le jeu*), as a result of space constraints in their tiny studio apartment. The tension between the enormity of the situation and the restraint of the living quarters begins to lay the groundwork for funny to happen.

'Comedy is Tragedy + Time'[7]

In addition to the spatial restrictions in the performance of 'play', Mollot further framed the situation in the improv game of 'Love/Hate'. Here, Leah and her scene partner, Jean-Phillipe Buzaud, alternate between loving statements about one another to hateful ones. What was discovered through the improv process was the more poetic their words, 'You are like a flame that burns tenderly in my heart' combined with balletic nuanced movements (*relever*, *brisé*, *cou-de-pied*, etc.), the funnier (in a farcical sense) the scene became, whereas the more emotionally realistic delivery of deadpan insults such as 'You stink!' were less funny. Mollot would explain that distancing oneself from typical emotional responses and behaviour freed up more space for funny to occur, which in turn enabled a larger range of acting play (*jeu*).

Other theme words and situational improvisations included:

- 'Unemployment' (*Le Chômage*). Here two stay-at-home dads find themselves in a park squabbling under the watchful eye of their young children who, in a reversal of roles, monitor them apologizing to one another for their misbehaviour.
- 'Violence' (*La Violence*). A young uneducated and inexperienced thug attempts to mug a man in a parking lot. The victim happens to be an academic philosopher.
- 'Madness' (*La Folie*). A woman goes to see a doctor for her family who, she explains, are all sick. The doctor motions to invite the family into his office. The woman explains they are in her purse. She proceeds to present her husband (a water bottle), her children (wallet, comb), and the dog (a fork). The examination begins.

These scenes would not become part of the final performance but fleshing them out allowed us to start searching for a sort of artistic universe or theatrical style unique to the telling of the story. We imagined each sketch as a rough line that would eventually connect to other lines. The combination of interconnected lines would eventually lay the groundwork for the sequencing of the narrative.

The Grey People

In one Jacquerie rehearsal session, Mollot raised the issue of the image we have of people in positions of enormous power, those people we frequently see on television, politicians, executives, CEOs and so forth. Paraphrasing Mollot, he explained how, often, these people are portrayed as serious and important. Accordingly, there is an assumption that they are responsibly looking after important issues very conscientiously. But, what if it wasn't true? What if they were like everyone else, as lost and capable of going off the edge as ordinary folk? Would we perhaps be closer to a truer reality (of life)? Moreover, what if we were to dig a little deeper to explore a sort of fundamental madness at all levels of power; only to find, at the root of power, lies a dangerous madness? What if, as ordinary citizens in the hands of these people who have power, there is realization of the enormous means they possess in pulling us all into the abyss?

This was the beginning of our research into the citizens of the City of Grey. Eventually they would be simply referred to as the greys (*les gris*). Notice Mollot chose the noun 'image' and not 'idea' in his explanation. He wanted the company to begin to explore their world through movement. We looked at how they were portrayed in the media and how these images contribute to the illusion of their importance. Often, they are photographed or recorded in professional attire, clean-shaven, hair neatly coiffed, impeccably mannered all the while speaking about important things set in important locations.

It was decided that the citizens in the City of Grey would have a distinctly different physical disposition from the everyday 'man' of Hattab's character. We worked extensively on the movements of insects, molluscs and other forms of exotic animals to create bodies and idiosyncrasies that were peculiar, almost unrealistic. These movements were then costumed in severely tailored grey suits, which further contributed to the tension and restriction of motion. As actors, we were trying to maintain a form that was further impeded by the boundedness we felt in our monochromatic, slightly tighter than tight, custom fit suits. No piece of garment was out of place, no action or gesture superfluous. The greys' movements, similar to their wardrobe, were highly efficient. In the end, we scaffolded thirty scenes together to create a thirty-scene narrative that included:

1. Entrance/Introduction to the City of Grey (*Passage et Présentation des Hommes Gris*)
2. Arrival of 'the man' to the City of Grey (*Arrivée du Petit Homme dans la Ville Grise*)
3. In Search of his Lost Suitcase – The man encounters a citizen of Grey (*Il Cherche a Retrouver sa Valise*)
4. No Touching 500 E fine (*Vous m'avez touché c'est 500*)
5. Outsider Perspective (*Jugement du Petit Homme*)
6. Man's Stolen Suitcase (*Vol de la Valise – du petit homme*)
7. The Neverending Corridors (*Les Couloirs*)
8. Looking for Assistance (*Cherche de L'aide*)
9. The Rat Race – Women in the City of Grey (*La Course des 3 Femmes, le travail*)
10. Love Triangle: A City of Grey Love Affair (*Le Trio Amoureux*)
11. First Date, Love, Abortion, Divorce (*Rencontre, Amour, Avortement, Divorce*)
12. Bar Fight: The Disco (*La Discothèque: le petit homme se fait harceler par une femme*)
13. The Distressed (*Les Angoissées*)
14. TV (*La Télé*)
15. Ballet of Work Dossiers (*Le Ballet des Papiers*)
16. The Amnesiac Company President (*Le Président Amnésique*)
17. Homeless Person, Cigarette Butt and the Grey Man (*Clochard, Mégot, Citoyen Gris*)
18. Gigolo, Grey Style (*Le Draguer*)
19. Restructuring North District: CEO & Staff Inspection (*Restructuration du Nord: le PDG et les 2 cadres*)
20. President's Ballet (*Ballet du Nouveau PDG*)
21. At Work: The Grey's Regress (*Au Travail: Les Hommes Gris Retombent en Enfance*)
22. The Company Meeting (*La Réunion*)

23. You're Fired! (*Petit Homme est Licencié par le PDG*)
24. Couples Who Swing (*Le Couple Échangiste*)
25. Grey Men's Brawl (*Bagarre des Hommes Gris*)
26. Queuing up for Food Bank Soup (*La File D'attente pour la Soupe Populaire*)
27. Homeless Grey Speaks to his Bench (*Clochard Parle à son Banc*)
28. New Order: Adapt, Integrate, Resist, Reformat (*Adapter, Intégrér, Résister, Reformater*)
29. Eff-off! (« *Fais chier* »)
30. Black Out (*Noir*).

From a sociological perspective, it would not be much of a stretch to parallel the man's arrival to the City of Grey with that of an immigrant's journey to a new country. Twenty-five years ago, when we were developing *Croquis*, the current political climate and rising neo-nationalist populism around globalization, transnationalism and interculturality had not yet reached the fever pitch it has today. Throughout the introductory scenes (1–8) outlined above, the character of the man encounters many common forms of dislocation and discrimination faced by new immigrants (Nangia, 2013). In his attempt to integrate, he is tokenized for his (cultural) difference. He is the 'other' in the eyes of the citizens of Grey. This angle was not a conscious part of the narrative process; however, in hindsight, I cannot help but marvel at how our individual experiences as cast members and non-citizen residents of France subconsciously resonated with the building of this collective creation.

Theatre of the Body

> Any living space has 'dramatic possibilities' that influences the behaviour of the people who enter it or the characters who perform in it. A change of place modifies all our attitudes and behaviour, down to the pace at which we walk ... Before constructing a habitable space, whether in real-life dramas or for those off the stage, it is important to work out in advance the life, which will exist in the space.
>
> (Lecoq, 2000: 155)

As the above extract demonstrates, a critical part of the collective training at the Lecoq School was spatial awareness of the body. Over the course of the first year in the programme, students become aware of how they uniquely occupy physical space, as they naturally project (stand, move and extend our limbs) and move their bodies into the three dimensions of space (height, width and depth) (Goldman, 1999: 1). How our bodies make patterns through our use of space in a repetition of physical dimensions, restrictions and perimetric (associated to vision) boundaries help define who we are to ourselves and to others.

Lecoq often correlated certain movements to gender and culture. Although many rebelled against the implied stereotypes, there was truth to the particular lines and movements unique to the various cultures that had travelled to work under Lecoq over a fifty year period. This became obvious to me in the *Croquis* rehearsal hall. For example, I remembered Lecoq saying that North Americans and Australians take more space than those from other countries. This was attributable to many social factors. Compared to Europe, Canada, Australia and the United States have more space. This directly reflected how individuals take or impose themselves in their surroundings – both physically and verbally (expanse = amplifying sound).

Two key areas discovered in the cross-cultural devising exchange of the LEC ensemble boiled down to the intimate and immediate relationship of the body with regards to space and language (Tuan, 1997; Lefebvre, 1991). This was encountered through: (1) the difficulties in translating humour across language; and (2) language and its reliance on context. To the first point, in France and in French, humour is heavily reliant on wordplay (Bell, 2017). I recall an improv with Jean Phillipe, a native of Paris. During our scene he said, in his rapid mother tongue, the words *entre guillemets* – which means 'in quotes', as in quotation marks. French being my fourth language, I thought he said *entre Guillaume*, which means 'William enters' (the name Guillaume is equivalent to William in English). As scene partners, both our timing and our *jeu* (play) were off as I sat waiting for a character who I thought would enter and Jean Phi's character continued to question why I lingered. All the while Jean Phi (the actor) knew full well that I (Nikki the actor) had misunderstood him.

Transcending Culture: Embodied Epistemology

The company's primary concern was in the movement of humour and not solely on the (risible) words necessary to create laughter. Representing five different countries on four different continents, what became immediately clear was the need to map out the underlying commonalities of our movements. Widely recognized as body language or the shared physical expressions of an embodied vocabulary, these, for the most part, are foundational verbal borrowings that transfer across modalities (Wohlgemuth, 2009).

Lecoq believed the actors' language *is* the body (Lecoq, 2000). During training, students learn about performance barriers in the form of the spoken word, culture, class, customs, gender and so forth. Hence, the first-year curriculum focuses heavily on a 'process of demystification' where students are invited to examine 'enculturated habits of socialized movement' played out in the theatre of the body (Chamberlain and Yarrow, 2002: 2; Damasio, 1999: 8). This is not to be confused with forgetting or erasing of one's prior knowledge. Instead, the training pursues the awakening of expression through corporeal forms to develop visual literacy that intentionally transcends the limits of spoken language (Storr, 2008: 23).

Bodies, as basic structures of culture, are visible definitions of social class and thus social formation, imprinted and embodied in our physical being. So, bodies 'as bearers of symbolic value' are organisms in perpetual development, affected by social influences and location, where forces at play become a form of physical capital (Shilling, 2003: 111). Societally influenced cultural schemas develop out of a collective group experience as individuals acquire similar forms of expression in the shared environment.

What was discovered throughout the LEC devising process was the degree to which an epistemological foundation bound our idiosyncratic movements. Maxine Sheets-Johnstone (1999) describes this best through her theory on movement epistemology as the work of a 'symbol-making' body, where animated physical gestures complement or imitate thought and language (490). In this instance, the same laws of movement apply to those found in language. Random and/or abstract movement are equal to the nonsense speech of gibberish; an unintelligible production of verbal sounds (Jaffe-Berg, 2008). I would go so far as to say that the pragmatic aspects of verbal language competence share a corporeal equivalent (Felner, 1985: 150). Just as speaking does not of itself constitute communication, neither do idiosyncratic gestures of body language (Celce-Murcia, 1991; Wagner, 2002). That is to say, the critical semiotic mechanisms of meaning-making context, content and sense (syntax) as inextricable features of kinaesthetic consciousness ('thinking movement') replicate themselves in Lecoq's physical theatre training, except here the discourse is visible (Sheets-Johnstone, 1999).

Re-evolution/Re-revə'luːʃən/[8]

My six years with the Jacquerie Company, and ten years living in France, was life altering. The process of learning to devise a narrative performance with such a highly skilled group of international actors helped me transition from student to professional in the development of my voice and identity as both a socially conscious actor and a social actor.

Beyond my initial experience as a student of Lecoq and the foreign language/culture displacements of studying, working and living abroad, the time also emphasized my social position as a first generation Canadian, daughter of immigrant parents. It would seem that a trip back to Europe, land of my people, would align my first language (Italian) and the body. This proved otherwise. My parent's postwar relocation to Canada altered the authenticity of my cultural roots, in some ways even severed them. On my return to the land my parents emigrated from, I became aware of the 'neither here nor there' in-between-ness of my hyphenated cultural identity. Paradoxically, the process of learning to create theatre in the absence of verbal language at Lecoq and La Jacquerie both freed and confused how I knew to be, in my body and through my languages. I began to see that the 'me' in my body and what I communicated through language(s) were not one and the same. The most obvious reveal uncovered a conflicted space between the spoken language of my maternal/home-life and the English of my educated/social-life. Of greater interest, and consequently what surfaced through the years with La Jacquerie, lay in recognizing how linguistic tensions were all contained within the biology of my body. I became aware of how as a young person alternating between the rural dialect (Abruzzese) of my parent's ancestral region and the required dominant social/school language contributed to an invisible friction demarcating an incompetency in my body-of-origin compared to the more competent 'educated body' costumed by the English language (Carozzi, 2005: 32). Much like the trajectory of the man travelling through the City of Grey, it revealed an othering of self to self.

Discussion Questions

1. What are the primary social/cultural communities that have influenced your verbal and gestural language?
2. What are your experiences in communication outside the community you reside in?
3. What are some of the important Lecoq principles of devising a narrative?
4. What makes you laugh? Is it the situation? The text? The characterization?
5. Do you remember a specific time when you said or did something that made people laugh?
6. Can humour reveal social politics?

Website

The Jacques Lecoq School: http://www.ecole-jacqueslecoq.com/en

Notes

1. This chapter is dedicated to Alain Mollot and his creative presence.
2. Pierre Bourdieu's physical capital or 'habitus'. Bourdieu sees power as culturally and symbolically created, and constantly re-legitimized through an interplay of agency and structure. Habitus is 'the way society becomes deposited in persons in the form of lasting dispositions, or trained capacities and structured propensities to think, feel and act in determinant ways, which then guide them' (see Wacquant, 2005: 316, cited in Navarro, 2006: 16). See Bourdieu, 1986.

3. It is with great thanks that I acknowledge fellow cast members, Jean-Phillipe Buzaud, Leah Fletcher, Ami Hattab, Antonio Gil-Martinez and Maria Victoria Monedero for their help in recalling specifics of the *Croquis* devising process.
4. Throughout this text I use the Canadian spelling of particular words: 'humour', 'analyse' and 'grey'. This too is intended to reflect the subtle *complexities* of our cultural relationships with language development and the formation of *identity*.
5. See Tuchman (1978), especially Chapter 7, entitled 'Decapitated France: The Bourgeois Rising and the Jacquerie', for further insightful analysis.
6. Humor Research Lab combines a 'humor code' with 'Benign Violation Theory'. The theory builds on work by a linguist, Tom Veatch, and integrates existing humour theories to propose when humour occurs. See McGraw and Warren, 2010.
7. Based on the famous Mark Twain quote 'Humor is tragedy plus time'.
8. The word 'revolution' has an interesting etymology. When asked by Soviet sociologists what it meant to them, Russian peasants responded '*samovol'shchina*' or, roughly, 'doing what you want'. In modern advertising, 'revolutionary' has come to mean 'radically new', and hence, by implication, 'improved'. When used in everyday speech, it is another way of saying 'drastically different'. See Richard Pipes, 1990.

Works Cited and Resource Material

Armstrong, J. K. (2016) Where Does Canned Laughter Come From – and Where Did It Go?, BBC Culture, 26 September, www.bbc.com/culture/story/20160926-where-does-canned-laughter-come-from-and-where-did-it-go, accessed 25 July 2017.

Barker, J. M. (2012) Jos Houben Talks About Lecoq, Complicité, Beckett & Working with Peter Brook, Culturebot Maximum Performance, 25 October, www.culturebot.org/2012/10/11643/jos-houben-talks-about-lecoq-complicite-beckett-working-with-peter-brook/, accessed 10 June 2017.

Bell, N. D. (2017) Failed Humor, in S. Attardo (Ed.) *The Routledge Handbook of Language and Humor* (New York: Routledge).

Bourdieu, P. (1986) The Forms of Capital, in J. Richardson (Ed.) *Handbook of Theory and Research for the Sociology of Capital* (New York: Greenwood Press) pp. 241–58.

Gaventa, J. and J. Pettit (2011) Bourdieu and 'Habitus', *Powercube*, University of Sussex: Institute of Development Studies, www.powercube.net/other-forms-of-power/bourdieu-and-habitus/, accessed 2 July 2015.

Carozzi, M. J. (2005) Talking Minds: The Scholastic Construction of Incorporeal Discourse, *Body and Society*, 11(2), pp. 25–39.

Celce-Murcia, M. (1991) *Teaching English as a Second or Foreign Language* (Boston: Heinle & Heinle).

Chamberlain, F. and R. Yarrow (Eds) (2002) *Jacques Lecoq and the British Theatre* (London: Routledge).

Damasio, A. (1999) *The Feeling of What Happens: Body and Emotion in the Making of Consciousness* (San Diego and New York: A Harvest Book, Harcourt).

Davila, M. R., M. J. Owren and E. Zimmermann (2009) Reconstructing the Evolution of Laughter in Great Apes and Humans, *Current Biology*, 19(13) pp. 1001–111.

Felner, M. (1985) *Apostles of Silence* (Toronto and London: Associated University Presses).

Girdwain, J. (2013) What Your Sweet Tooth Really Means, *Men's Health*, 16 July, www.menshealth.com/health/what-your-sweet-tooth-really-means, accessed 5 June 2017.

Goel, V. and R. J. Dolan (2001) The Functional Anatomy of Humor: Segregating Cognitive and Affective Components, *Nature Neuroscience*, 4, pp. 237–8.

Goldman, E. (1999) *The Geometry of Movement: A Study in the Structure of Communication*. © Copyright Ellen Goldman.

Hurley, M. M., D. C. Dennett and R. B. Adams (2011) *Inside Jokes: Using Humor to Reverse-Engineer the Mind* (Cambridge, MA: MIT Press).

Jaffe-Berg, E. J. (2008) *Multilingual Art of Commedia Dell'arte* (Ottawa: Legas Publishing).

Johnson, M. (2007) *The Meaning of the Body: Aesthetics of Human Understanding* (Chicago and London: University of Chicago Press).

Kafka, F. (1926) *The Castle* (London: Minerva).

Korn, C. W. (2012) The Neuroscience of Looking on the Bright Side, *Scientific American*, 10 January, www.scientificamerican.com/article/neuroscience-looking-bright-side/, accessed 20 May 2017.

Lecoq, J. (2000) *The Moving Body* (London: Methuen).

Lefebvre, H. (1991) *The Production of Space* (Oxford: Blackwell Publishing).

McGraw, A. P. and C. Warren (2010) Benign Violations: Making Immoral Behavior Funny, *Psychological Science*, 21(8), pp. 1141–9, http://leeds-faculty.colorado.edu/mcgrawp/pdf/mcgraw.warren.2010.pdf, accessed 4 May 2017.

Maréchal, G. (2009) Autoethnography, in A. J. Mills, G. Durepos and E. Wiebe (Eds) *Encyclopedia of Case Study Research* (Thousand Oaks, CA: Sage) pp. 43–5.

Nangia, P. (2013) Discrimination Experienced by Landed Immigrants in Canada, RCIS Working Paper No. 2013/7, November, http://www.ryerson.ca/content/dam/rcis/documents/RCIS_WP_Parveen_Nangia_No_2013_7.pdf, accessed 25 July 2017.

Navarro, Z. (2006) In Search of a Cultural Interpretation of Power: The Contribution of Pierre Bourdieu, *IDS Bulletin*, 37(6), pp 11–22.

Nichol, M. (2015) 20 Types and Forms of Humor, *Daily Writing Tips*, 12 June, https://www.dailywritingtips.com/20-types-and-forms-of-humor/, accessed 30 April 2017.

Pipes, R. (1990) *The Russian Revolution* (New York: Alfred A. Knopf).

Provine, R. (2000) The Science of Laughter, *Psychology Today*, 1 November, https://www.psychologytoday.com/articles/200011/the-science-laughter, accessed 11 June 2017.

Redgrave, P. and A. Redden. (2011) Neuroscience: What Makes Us Laugh, *Nature International Weekly Journal of Science*, 473, published online 25 May 2011 Doi: 10.1038/473450a.

Reed-Danahay, D. (1997) *Auto/ethnography: Rewriting the Self and the Social* (Oxford: Berg).

Sample, I. (2009) Our Primate Ancestors Have Been Laughing for 10m Years, *The Guardian*, 4 June, www.theguardian.com/science/2009/jun/04/laughter-primates-apes-evolution-tickling, accessed 12 July 2017.

Sheets-Johnstone, M. (1999) *The Primacy of Movement* (Amsterdam: John Benjamins).

_____. (2013) Movement as a Way of Knowing, *Scholarpedia*, 8(6), p. 30375, http://www.scholarpedia.org/article/Movement_as_a_Way_of_Knowing.

Shilling, C. (2003) *The Body and Social Theory* (2nd edition) (London: Sage).

Storr, R. (2008) Show and Tell, in P. Marincola (Ed.) *What Makes a Great Exhibition?*, pp. 14–31.

Teodorescu, A. M. (2012) Language Ambiguity in Translation, PhD Dissertation, Babeş-Bolyai University of Cluj-Napoca, 193.231.20.119/doctorat/teza/fisier/223.

Tuan, Y. (1977) *Space and Place: The Perspective of Experience* (Minneapolis: University of Minnesota Press).

Tuchman, B. W. (1978) *A Distant Mirror: The Calamitous 14th Century* (New York: Ballantine Books).

Van Manen, M. (1990) *Researching Lived Experience: Human Science for an Action Sensitive Pedagogy* (London and Ontario: The Althouse Press).

Wagner, B. J. (2002) Understanding Drama-Based Education, in G. Brauer (Ed.) *Body and Language: Intercultural Learning Through Drama* (Westport, CT: Ablex) pp. 3–18.

Wohlgemuth, J. (2009) *A Typology of Verbal Borrowings* (Berlin: Mouton de Gruyter) pp. 72–4.

13

Pina Bausch
Narrative, Gender, Reception

Jade Rosina McCutcheon

Pina Bausch, as a dancer and choreographer, created and refined the genre of Tanztheater (Dancetheatre) in Wuppertal, Germany, from 1973 until her death in 2009. In Pina Bausch's own words, dance theatre was not about mere 'provocation', but rather about establishing 'a space where we can encounter each other' (Aylmer, 2016). This chapter will consider two of Bausch's pieces (from a portfolio of over forty original works), *Kontakthof* (1978) and *Café Müller* (1978), focusing on Bausch's methods in constructing narrative and the role that gender plays in narrative and performance.[1]

As Peggy Phelan notes in her book *Unmarked*, live performance cannot be repeated exactly, every performance is different despite the text, choreography and direction, which are all designed to create a map for live performance rather than a captured 'replica'; Phelan notes, 'Performance's only life is in the present' (Phelan, 2001: 146). The interaction between the audience and the performance is also unique to every performance and cannot be repeated. The narrative of live performance is an engagement between the audience and the performer, the only story that 'matters' is the one taken home by an audience member.

Phelan also describes performance as 'moving from the grammar of words to the grammar of the body, one moves from the realm of the metaphor to the realm of the metonym' (Phelan, 2001: 150). Phelan is suggesting that the body in live performance acts as a container for the unspoken text of the body, as opposed to the spoken word representing subtext or what is not spoken. The power of Bausch's work lies in its visceral approach to narrative in that it not only breaks boundaries and challenges norms but also highlights the pathos of human behaviour as it is exhibited by women and men.

Pina Bausch defied the ethos of the traditional ballet company when she took over as artistic director of the Wuppertal Opera Ballet in 1973. Her unusual methods and style pushed against the more traditional approach to opera-ballet, creating friction among the regular opera-ballet audience. She never used leotards, preferring formal wear costumes, often from the 1920s and 1930s, in strong pastel colours for the women, and grey or black suits for the men. The dresses were often satin and the suits very formal. This change of ballet attire in itself was immediately confronting to the traditional ballet opera audience in Wuppertal, with spectators leaving, slamming the doors, booing and calling out during the performances.

Ultimately, Bausch created an entirely new language, transcending traditional forms of dance and theatre and their individual reliance on movement and text. The use of the spoken word in dance began with Mary Wigman's *Totenmal (Call of the Dead)* (1930) and was used by Martha Graham in *Deaths and Entrances* (1943). However, as well as using spoken word, Bausch's dancers directly addressed the audience and each other, sometimes using the dancer's real name and sometimes using that of a character; confusing the lines between dancer, character and audience. Much of the material used for each piece was drawn from the dancers themselves, evolving from questions Bausch would ask: 'Who are you? What do you love? What is love? How do you feel when you lose love?'

Chantal Akerman, in her film *One Day Pina Asked* (1983), notes that Bausch constructs her pieces from collages which consist often of personal biographic detail about the dancers themselves. 'They are little films to which she adds dance' (Akerman, cited in Lucca, 2014). These collages are made up of repeated gestures that come from the dancer's interpretation of their response to Pina's questions. Royd Climenhaga writes about the creation of *Kontakthof* in his book *Pina Bausch*: 'In the first weeks of rehearsal, the company simply starts with a vague collection of ideas about desire and connection' (Climenhaga, 2009: 72), and goes on to describe how Bausch drew the material from her dancers using the same method of asking such intimate questions such as 'What part of their body do they like or not like?' John O'Mahony of *The Guardian* writes, 'Bausch's themes are positively Strindbergian: loss, loneliness, grief, death, leave-taking and the tortuous relations between the sexes. But there is also wicked humour too' (O'Mahony, 2002).

Bausch's work focuses on the potent dynamics of gender, sexuality and power, exposing cultural expectations of gender roles and performance. Although clearly influenced by her own German life experience, Bausch's choreography still speaks to us across the Western world today, to all ages, religions, backgrounds and gender. In 1990, Judith Butler wrote a seminal book, *Gender Trouble: Feminism and the Subversion of Identity*, in which she argues that gender is 'performed' and not a genetic behaviour or a scientific fact-that gender roles are often power based and influenced by such factors as sexuality, class and ethnicity.

Gender is not such an easy and clear category these days and so a brief discussion on some clarification around these terms is necessary. The sex of a person is a biological fact at birth, but gender is not; according to Butler, it is a learned behaviour (see Judith Butler, 1990, for more a more comprehensive discussion around this), and therefore can be assumed to be a more fluid aspect of identity. Today, the possibilities of gender have morphed into a wide spectrum of categories, including androsexual (being primarily attracted sexually, romantically, emotionally, to men/males/masculinity), bicurious, pansexual (a person who experiences sexual, romantic, physical, and/or spiritual attraction for members of all gender identities) and a recent category 'third gender' for those who do not identify with either male or female. There are many terms listed on various websites and one article published on the UK's *The Telegraph* website, 27 June 2014, cites Facebook's possible seventy-one gender options for users.[2] Following on from this transformation of how we see gender, the ideas of masculine and feminine could well be understood differently; for example, if an image is 'masculinized', what do we expect to see? Do we assume a performative notion of how males were/are expected to behave traditionally, or do we imagine a female body dressed as a soldier, a male flexing muscles, smoking a pipe or what? Similarly, with a 'feminized' image, are we expecting fragility, sensuality, passivity in a male or female body; or can either body assume muscularity, strength (inner or outer) and agency and still be feminine?

Through psychoanalysis we know that behaviours and attitudes are developed in subtle ways from images, language and systems of control at an early age. These attitudes and behaviours form a part of our identity and 'suture' themselves to our very personality. They become manufactured fabrications created by public and social discourse. '[A]cts, gestures and desire produce the effect of an internal core or substance ... produce this on the surface of the body, through the play of signifying absences that suggest, but never reveal, the organizing principle of identity as a cause' (Butler, 1990: 136).

Importantly, the relationship between culture and art is also a key factor in the analysis of the construction of gender roles via narrative. Griselda Pollock, in her book *Vision and Difference: Femininity, Feminism and Histories of Art* (1988), points out that art must be considered as product and therefore as influenced by the strictures of production, elements of consumerism, aesthetic values and purposes of the work. We are all aware of the power and influence social constructions of male and female genders via mediatized images have on our identity, power relations and behaviours. 'The making of masculine and feminine subjects crucially involves the manufacture and regulation of sexualities, radically different and hardly complementary let alone compatible, between those designated men and women' (Pollock, 1988: 13). From the early 1900s until the 1960s, dance halls provided a site for not only dancing, but for meeting potential partners. Ballroom dancing might be considered a precursor to the dance hall, with the nightclub then replacing the dance hall in the 1960s and 1970s. Certainly these 'meetings' occurred between both same sex and heterosexual couples, and although *Kontakthof* focuses clearly on heterosexual couples and behaviours, interactions between male and female bodies, sexuality and the power relations that evolve from these can be understood by all genders.

Kontakthof (1978)

In *Kontakthof*, painful explorations of gender and identity are performed to a musical score played on old 78 records and tape players, resulting in a 'time warp' depicting women and men painfully reaching out to each other in a local town hall dance scenario. An empty stage, chairs, a microphone and a mechanical riding horse act as components of the narrative set into motion by bodies, music and occasional text. As the dancers attempt to find a rhythm together, interruptions, often violent, throw the performance into a painfully close reflection of our own lives. Bausch was interested in creating a representation of a 'meeting place' where people search for contact, exposing fears, desires and disappointments experienced around reaching out and searching for love.

Men, sitting in chairs, move awkwardly across the stage towards the women leaning against the wall on the other side. They reach out towards the women with what could be seen as 'groping' and 'grabbing' movements, supposedly expressing their desire for the women. The women perform exact, precise gestures, flinching, scratching, rubbing, gyrating and jerking their bodies in states of both desire and agitation. When the men finally reach the women, the meeting is more than uncomfortable, although they are both moving, they are unable to connect. Physical prodding, slapping and pushing occurs as the dance hall inhabitants attempt to 'connect'. Tenderness; 'what is it? How does one do it? Where does it go? When isn't it tenderness anymore' (Hoghe, cited in Climenhaga, 2009: 72)? The men eventually move to centre stage and dance their own more stylish dance while the women move separately around them. Bausch reaches her audience by removing the 'outer skin' of the dancers, exposing the nervous anticipation, raw animal desire and frightening inability to connect meaningfully with each other:

> According to Climenhaga (2009), Bausch devised the sequence by asking her dancers to present the parts of their bodies they most disliked; hair is scraped back from their faces, and each individual stands facing the audience with teeth bared in an emotionless grimace.
>
> (Weir, 2014: 24)

The dancers often return to the front of the stage where they position the audience as a mirror, performing daily gestures such as checking their hair, teeth and face. These gestures are precise and repeated daily movements that any of us might engage with in private. Bausch confronts us with these gestures, breaking the 'fourth wall', engaging the audience in both reflection and reception. When the fourth wall is removed, the audience is suddenly reminded they are no longer just an 'observer', they are being addressed, spoken to, reminded that this performance is a two-way interaction, reducing the audience's potential to silently observe and increasing their potential to engage with the narrative as they are now part of it. 'Bausch's approach is unique in its array of potential meanings; it transgresses the concept of audience immersion, blurring the boundaries of narrative theatre and personal interaction between performer and spectator' (Weir, 2014: 18).[3]

Elisabeth Grosz, in her book *Volatile Bodies* (1994), offers a consideration of the body as a 'shadow' or 'interior' of the physical, another dimension entailing receptors and processes, linkages and assemblages existing in the same space as the physical body, intellectual body and the emotional body. 'The body can be understood as the site of the intermingling of mind and culture' (Grosz, 1994: 116). Viewing the body as a symptom 'of a hidden interior or depth' (116) is worth consideration, as the body does not exist in isolation; it is indeed a product of the time, culture, politics and economy of the moment in which it exists. Therefore, a performance work created in different cultures and times will bring a framework of 'difference' that could at once be alienating, inspiring and confronting. It is the universal aspect of the work communicating through choreography and text that becomes a *currency of transaction* for the spectator, through which she or he 'connects' to the work. 'Seeing the other is a social form of self-reproduction' (Phelan, 2001: 21).

Vivian Sobchack, in her book *Carnal Thoughts* (2004), uses Merleau-Ponty's framework of existential phenomenology and guides us towards the notion that our lived body 'entails both the body and consciousness, objectivity and subjectivity, in an *irreducible ensemble*' (4, emphasis in original). Her writing persuades us to consider spectatorship as far more than just visual, but rather as a multi-layered body of 'unruly responsive flesh and sensorium' (59). Sobchack's work assists the journey into receptivity of the performance image as a contemporary interpretation of Merleau-Ponty's phenomenology and as understanding the lived body as far more than flesh and far more than subject. Suggesting that in the interaction between the 'seer' (spectator) and the 'visible' (the performer), the idea of 'self' becomes blurred, Sobchack's closing paragraph cites Merleau-Ponty in *The Visible and the Invisible* (1968: 139): 'Since the seer is caught up with what he sees, it is still himself he sees ... so that the seer and the visible reciprocate one another and we no longer know which sees and which is seen' (Merleau-Ponty, cited in Sobchack, 2004: 317).

Sobchack interprets this 'seeing' as an ecstasy of reciprocity, a 'condition of a deep and passionate recognition of ourselves' (2004: 318) wherein the subject is transcended. These ideas of seeing ourselves through the other onstage invite us to consider the nature of this effect, on both the performer and the spectator. During *Kontakthof*, one woman, Ophelia Young, sits on a mechanical horse in a rigid position, only her hips move suggestively in rhythm with the movement of the horse – a line soon forms behind her of dancers drawn (supposedly) by the continuous thrusting movement of the hips. This image alone underlines Bausch's deeper, darker and more playful nature, portraying an otherwise immobile figure, unable to express emotions, such as desire, doomed to live out her sexual fantasy on a mechanical horse. Is it a gender specific spectator experience? By this I mean that if you are male watching, for example, Ophelia Young ride the mechanical horse, would you take a position of desire towards Ophelia? Identify with Ophelia's female sexuality? See yourself as the mechanical horse? Imagine your own sexual desire in relationship to Ophelia's suggestive hip thrusts on the horse? I suggest there is no clear answer for any of us in this regard as our identity, sexuality and gender are so complex that we would find markers for both genders, varied sexual responses and such a mixture of identity frameworks that we could be capable of many varied responses to the one movement. We learn through awareness of our responses to performance, noting, through reflection, our most potent reactions, then deconstructing with great honesty what those moments mean to us.

The dancers in *Kontakthof* exhibit passive aggression towards each other, both female to male, male to female, female to female and male to male. Little gestures of hostility, dislike and anxiety appear in the forms of pinches, slaps, pushes, jerking of arms and fingers backwards and flicking the other's body. All of this is carried out as the perpetrator of the

Figure 13.1 Meryl Tankard in *Kontakthof* (1984) surrounded by male dancers of the Pina Bausch Company including Dominique Mercy, Jean Laurent Sasportes, Arthur Rosenfeld and Hans Po. Stockholm, Sweden
Photographer: Regis Lansac

gesture looks directly at the audience as though 'displaying' their negative behaviour for the audience's benefit, inviting the audience to become an accomplice to the act. In perhaps the most confronting scene (for women particularly) in *Kontakthof*, one woman (played by Meryl Tankard and later Nazareth Panadero) (see Figure 13.1) is repeatedly scratched, tickled, poked, pushed, jabbed, lifted up and pinched by a group of men. Neither the men nor the woman shows any emotion, although Tankard admits she broke into tears on some occasions and claimed that it 'felt like being raped' (in Weir, 2014: 26).

Gia Kourlas describes this scene in her review for the *New York Times*: 'And when Nazareth Panadero[4] is left standing alone onstage, like the ultimate wallflower, a man appears, seemingly to comfort her. Soon she is surrounded by a swarm of others who poke and prod at her — rubbing her nose, her hair, a knee — with nasty aggression' (Kourlas, 2014).

Kontakthof was developed into two other versions after the 1978 original, one using teens and the other using over-65s which is still touring today. Watching the first version and the over-65s, it is hard not to assume that gender behaviour is the same throughout our life, almost like a tired old mating ritual. However, this is also the perspective, dreams, memories of the choreography of one artist. The interpretation of gender behaviour, which, according to Judith Butler, is a learned, performed behaviour, not innate, nor in our genetic makeup, can be seen as a response to the time, the culture, the social formulas for establishing a basic blueprint for establishing 'acceptable' gender roles and behaviours.

In all three versions, females and males flirt, preen, exhibit and move suggestively in the hope of finding a partner. Is it more shocking to see elderly women and men engaged in such tactics? Do we assume that (in Judith Butler's terms) the body is not sexed[5] beyond its reproductive age? To watch older women and men engage in the same flirtatious, anxious and desperate searches for intimacy brings Bausch's work to a place where the audience can no longer dismiss such behaviours as products of a desire to reproduce, but as behaviours springing from a desperate desire for closeness, intimacy and communion. The power of these repeated desperate gestures and movements as performed by older dancers confronts us with the fact that older bodies are as 'sexed' as younger bodies and the vulnerability of this need for union is, at times, terrifying.

The narrative of *Kontakthof* is not a 'beginning, middle and end' structure, nor is it a logical plot point through line; Bausch's stories are full of gestural metaphors, interrupted by 'direct to audience' speeches and music on scratchy 78 records and cassettes as well as atypical lighting. The narrative is constructed by the viewer as much as it is created by Bausch, by the dancers and the set. As such, the narrative received by the audience is a collaboration between the audience and performers, involving the designed narrative by Bausch, the performance of it by the dancers and the audience members' own configuration of 'self' with all that it entails. 'Watching such discomfort never becomes comfortable, but in *Kontakthof*, as Bausch glides from light to dark and back again, she brings us closer to humanity. Even in her absence, she makes us see ourselves for what we are' (Kourlas, 2014).

Café Müller (1978)

'The space has its limits: like the perimeters of a prison. The body has its limits: its eternal need for contact and love' (Bentivoglio, 2010: 81). *Café Müller* reveals an almost desperate hopelessness of the human condition as dancers collide, sleepwalk and haunt this café. *Café Müller* speaks to Bausch's own experience as a child watching life in her parents' restaurant/café during the war and postwar periods. The set is all black consisting of many chairs in various forms: fallen over, upside down, sitting upright, jumbled on top of one another with two large glass doors stage right rear. We see the dancers enter and exit through these doors; the chairs form the backdrop, set and props, as six dancers move through them, dream-like, to female arias from Purcell's *Fairy Queen* and *Dido and Aeneas*. The arias are described by Norbert Servos in his chapter, 'Café Müller', (2010) as 'laments, revolving around the subjects of unrequited love, separation, grief and despair' (Servos, 2010: 72). Servos suggests the 'chairs become symbols and substitutes for human absence, signifying the void, the impossibility of making contact' (72).

A lone dancer in a light satiny slip wanders into the café, as though blind, in a trance, or in a daze; this dancer is Pina Bausch, who dances almost as though she is reconstructing her childhood in the restaurant/café. Another woman in the same satiny slip continually falls against a wall and down onto the floor, yet another woman, with curly bright red hair, in a coat, saunters in to the café in high heels, seemingly oblivious to what is happening around her. A man furtively moves chairs out of the path of the dancing women, another man tries to dance with the woman from the wall – he holds her, drops her, pulls her to her feet, holds her in his arms, drops her, over and over. This set of movements is like watching a disastrous act of abuse, with no 'off' button; the movements are precise, exact, emotionless, and yet they foster an emotional reaction in the viewer. Arlene Croce from *The New Yorker* (1984) writes: 'The café – apparently meant to resemble a real place – seems to be the canteen of a mental hospital. A small cast of inmates gives us intermittent doses of violent/apathetic behavior.'[6] Although the title suggests the setting is a café, yet another reviewer, Donna Perlmutter (1984), notes: 'Obsessive, mindless self-flagellation takes over in this psychiatric back ward.'⁷ Chaotic behaviours, longing, grief, paranoia, fear and cruelty instil this work with a sense of both nightmare and dream, place and loss, co-dependency and dysfunction.

For a period of forty-five minutes, dancers fall, stumble, sleepwalk and run chaotically through this dark, basement-like set. Purcell's arias add to the pathos of the dancers and their anguished attempts to reach each other. A solo dancer, Bausch, appears to be in a state of desperate longing to reach either herself or a lost love, dancing to her own inner rhythm, oblivious to what is going on around her. Towards the end of the piece, the woman with red curly hair and fur coat transfers the coat and red wig to Bausch as though trading identities. One might wonder what significance this has and who the two dancers are representing in Bausch's early childhood memories. Born in 1940, Pina Bausch's most formative years were during World War II when her parents owned a café/restaurant in Solingen. While Bausch learned to perform for the guests here she would also have witnessed the tragedies, hardships and grief of war during that time. Servos points out about *Café Müller* that 'The inability to communicate, estrangement between couples and the undaunted quest for intimacy and security are once more the basic themes' (Servos, 2010: 73). One imagines it is impossible to separate the influence of a childhood during war time and the choreography of *Café Müller*. 'As she grew up in that post-war season that the French call *l'après-guerre*, with an early childhood submitted to the rhythms of bombings and destructions, she carried her fears, melancholy and pessimism throughout her life, and mostly throughout her creations' (Adnan, 2010: 83). Bausch steered away from using traditional narrative form, choosing to create collages, collections of moments that had been rehearsed and rehearsed. Refining gestures that came instinctively from the dancers in response to questions about love, loss, fear, loneliness or tenderness, Bausch added music and sparse sets, and costumes that her audience would wear at functions or in daily life. Her processes produced raw, honest, confronting material that was not bound by the parameters of traditional storytelling, yet a 'narrative' existed and a story was told. I suggest that it is the spectator who plays the role of the storyteller, selecting moments, images, sounds and words to create their own 'montage' of narrative.

Theresa de Lauretis, in her book *Alice Doesn't* (1984), argues that 'narrativity, because of its inscription of the movement and positionality of desire, is what mediates the relation of image and language' (1984: 79). Here the term 'desire' arrives as a blueprint threaded throughout image, as the driver behind the way we receive image and the narrative embedded within. According to de Lauretis, the spectator's *movement* is the movement of the narrative, 'the very work of narrativity is the engagement of the subject in certain positionalities of meaning and desire' (106). In other words, a narrative is implicated with the viewer's association with the image. As audience, we merge with the performance, projecting, transferring and imagining ourselves as any one of the characters onstage, and in so doing, we create the possibility of memory, of identification and of experience. Clearly, the gender, ethnicity, age and physicality of the performer will also inform our engagement with that body.

Judith Butler suggests that we learn how to behave like a 'man' or a 'woman' from birth and because gender is performative, 'it produces a series of effects, we act and talk and speak and walk in ways that we consolidate an impression of being a man or being a woman'.[8] Butler claims that rather than being an innate part of our biological nature, gender is a phenomenon that has been 'produced' and 'reproduced' over time to the point where we are not aware of gender as performance. Butler separates the performativity of gender from biological sexual reproduction and asks whether it is possible to perceive what she calls the 'sexed body' outside the framework of reproduction. By asking this question, Butler invites us to consider the performance of mating, for example, as a learned behaviour that potentially has very little to do with biological sexual reproduction. In this, she claims, we are ruling out the possibility of sexual behaviours that have nothing to do with sexual reproduction, pointing out that a good part of the population is unable to reproduce due to age, biology or choice.

Bausch's choreography in both *Kontakthof* and *Café Müller* creates an atmosphere of desire between men and women while demonstrating the utter dysfunction, clumsiness and failure of these learned behaviours towards each other. What we are left with are compelling images of desire thwarted by our own human flaws. Notions of love, tenderness and communion all arise as aspects of the questions Bausch asks her dancers to think about, answer and respond to, with text as well as movement. Every response to Bausch's work is legitimate, unique and personal, whether the spectator 'sees' heterosexual couples trying to connect with each other, or a group of human beings of different sexualities and genders stumbling around in the dark trying to reach each other. The work of Pina Bausch invites us into a shared encounter where we, as audience, are provided with an opportunity to re-consider our daily roles in relation to power, gender, sexuality and desire in our own continually evolving identities.

Questions for Discussion

1. If the dancers were all male or all female, how would it affect the meaning of either *Kontakthof* or *Café Müller*?
2. What significance is gender to Bausch's work? How do you as an audience member experience her representation of gender? Do you recognize the gendered elements in her dances as similar to what you normally see?
3. In what ways are *Kontakthof* and *Café Müller* relevant to audiences today?

Websites

Pina Bausch company website: http://www.pina-bausch.de/en/
The Rite of Spring: https://www.youtube.com/watch?v=2w8ww_BfQBY
Pina Bausch on receiving the Kyoto Prize: https://www.youtube.com/watch?v=WSvqC3oKiq8

Notes

1. Pina Bausch's works include: 1968 *Fragment*; 1969 *Im Wind der Zeit*; 1970 *Nachnul*; 1971 *Aktionen für Tänzer*; 1974 *Fritz*; *Iphigenie auf Tauris*; *Ich Bring Dich Um Die Ecke*; 1975 *Orpheus und Eurydike*; *Frühlingsopfer*; 1976 *The Seven Deadly Sins*; 1977 *Bluebeard*; *Come, Dance With Me*; *Renate wandert aus*; 1978 *Takes Her By The Hand And Leads Her Into The Castle*, *The Others Follow*; *Café Müller*; *Kontakthof*; 1979 *Arien*; *Legend Of Chastity*; 1980 *A Piece By Pina Bausch*; *Bandoneon*; 1982 *Walzer*; *Carnations*; 1985 *Two Cigarettes In*

The Dark; 1986 *Viktor*; 1987 *Ahnen*; 1989 *Palermo, Palermo*; 1995 *Danzon*; 1998 *Masurca Fogo*; 2000 *Wiesenland*.
2. https://www.telegraph.co.uk/technology/facebook/10930654/Facebooks-71-gender-options-come-to-UK-users.html, accessed 14 May 2018.
3. Lucy Weir, Audience Manipulation? Subverting the Fourth Wall in Pina Bausch's *Kontakthof* (1978) and *Nelken* (1982), *Scottish Journal of Performance*, 1(2) (2014), pp. 17–36.
4. Kourlas had seen a later production where Nazareth Panadero played the woman previously played by Meryl Tankard shown in Figure 13.1.
5. For further information on the sexed body, see Butler (2014) *Bodies That Matter: On the Discursive Limits of 'Sex'*, Routledge.
6. 'Dancing: Bad Smells', *The New Yorker*, 16 July 1984.
7. Donna Perlmutter, 'Reviews', *Dance Magazine* 58(9) (1984), pp. 28, 34–5.
8. J. Butler on YouTube, Big Think, published 6 June 6 2011, https://www.youtube.com/watch?v=Bo7o2LYATDc, accessed 6 July 2018.

Works Cited and Resource Material

Adnan, E. (2016) A Revolution Named Pina Bausch, in *Café Müller: A Piece by Pina Bausch*, P. Bausch (Paris: L'ARCHE).
Akerman, C. (1983) film, *One Day Pina Asked* (Brooklyn, NY: Icarus Films).
Aylmer, O. (2016) The Aesthetic Language of Choreographer Pina Bausch, *AnOther*, http://www.anothermag.com/fashion-beauty/9028/the-aesthetic-language-of-pina-bausch, accessed 18 July 2017.
Bentivoglio, L. (2010) The Impossibility of Really Seeing Each Other', in *Café Müller: A Piece by Pina Bausch*, P. Bausch (Paris, L'ARCHE).
Butler, J. (1990) *Gender Trouble: Feminism and the Subversion of Identity* (New York: Routledge).
_____. (2014) *Bodies That Matter: On the Discursive Limits of 'Sex'* (London and New York: Routledge).
Climenhaga, R. (2009) *Pina Bausch* (New York: Routledge).
Croce, A. (1984) Dancing: Bad Smells, *The New Yorker*, 16 July.
De Lauretis, T. (1984) *Alice Doesn't: Feminism, Semiotics, Cinema* (Bloomington, IN: Indiana University Press).
Grosz, E. (1994) *Volatile Bodies: Towards a Corporeal Feminism* (Bloomington, IN: Indiana University Press).

Hoghe, R. (2016) *Bandoneon: Working with Pina Bausch* (London: Oberon Books).
Kourlas, G. (2014) Wallflowers and Lotharios in an Age-Old Courtship Ritual, *New York Times*, 28 October, https://www.nytimes.com/2014/10/29/arts/dance/kontakthof-by-tanztheater-wuppertal-pina-bausch-at-bam.html#story-continues-2, accessed 15 July 2017.
Lucca, V. (2104) Review: One Day Pina Asked, https://www.filmcomment.com/blog/review-one-day-pina-asked-chantal-akerman/, accessed 9 July 2018.
Merleau-Ponty, M. (1968) *Visible and the Invisible* (Evanston, IL: Northwestern University Press).
NYC Dance Stuff (2014) https://nycdancestuff.wordpress.com/2014/11/09/tanztheater-wuppertal-pina-bausch-kontakthof-a-piece-by-pina-bausch-at-bams-2014-next-wave-festival/, accessed 12 July 2017.
O'Mahony, J. (2002) Dancing in the Dark, *The Guardian*, 26 January, https://www.theguardian.com/books/2002/jan/26/books.guardianreview4, accessed 6 July 2018.
Perlmutter, D. (1984) Reviews, *Dance Magazine*, 58(9), pp. 28, 34–5.
Phelan, P. ([1993] 2001) *Unmarked* (New York: Routledge).
Pollock, G. (1988) *Vision and Difference* (New York: Routledge).
Servos, N. (2010) Café Müller, in the booklet accompanying the DVD *Café Müller: A Piece by Pina Bausch* (Paris: L'Arche).
Sobchack, V. (2004) *Carnal Thoughts* (Berkeley, CA: University of California Press).
Weir, L. (2014) Audience Manipulation? Subverting the Fourth Wall in Pina Bausch's *Kontakthof* (1978) and *Nelken* (1982), *Scottish Journal of Performance*, 1(2), pp. 17–36.
Williams, R. (2014) Facebook's 71 Gender Options Come to UK Users, *The Telegraph*, 27 June, https://www.telegraph.co.uk/technology/facebook/10930654/Facebooks-71-gender-options-come-to-UK-users.html, accessed 14 May 2018.

14

Narrative Pivots
Text and Movement in Crystal Pite's Dance-Theatre[1]

Peter Dickinson

According to Vancouver-based choreographer Crystal Pite:

> A pivot ... allows for another point of view. It is a turning point, something of crucial importance. It is a repeatable, refinable action that extends our perspective of the possible. The accuracy and focus, in combination with the instinctual, chaotic, and risky nature of improvisation, define both the process and the result.
>
> (cited in Shaw, 2006: 14)

As scholars attuned to the institutional and ideological genealogies of our respective disciplines, we have become increasingly adept at the discourse of 'turns': we have learned to talk, for example, of the 'turn to performance' in theatre studies; or the 'turn to critical theory' in dance studies; or the 'turn to affect, cognition and the senses' in both. But we don't spend much time talking about our own individual research and teaching pivots, the small, accretive changes in direction we have made either in sympathetic (perhaps even fatalistic) response to those bigger disciplinary turns or, more provocatively, that collectively may have enabled them in the first place. Nor do we, as critics sensitive to charges of dilettantism when we risk venturing outside our fields of specialty, often discuss the role played by instinct, improvisation and sheer pleasure in prompting such pivots.

This is all by way of accounting for how and why I, a literary critic by training, have gradually come to shift the main focus of my research and writing over the past fifteen years to an exploration of the historical, dramaturgical and material relationships between dance and theatre. The short answer to that question is that the trajectory of my scholarly career – which has always pivoted around performance, broadly defined – has tended to mirror my progressive immersion, as a spectator, teacher, critic, creator and volunteer board member, in the local live arts scene in Vancouver. Then, too, it seems important to acknowledge the very strong, almost instinctually kinaesthetic, response I have always felt toward dance-theatre as a form, one whose various elements and sensory stimuli come closest, for me, to an Artaudian total theatrical experience. But old habits die hard, and while my own aesthetic tastes skew far more towards contemporary dance than classical story ballet, I find that I am often unable – and perhaps also unwilling – to resist reading much of this work within an expressive, and overtly narrative, representational frame. Prompted, in turn, by a renewed attention to language, text and storytelling in theatre, including physical and dance-theatre, this has led me to rethink some of the scholarly criticism on the intertwined histories of postdramatic theatre and postmodern dance. As Maiya Murphy (2015) has recently noted, physical theatre and postmodern dance in North America, Western Europe and Australia have evolved in response to many shared points of reference from the mid-twentieth century onwards. One of those shared points is an apparent rejection of the central importance of narrative and story to traditional scripted drama and classical ballet, with the devised theatre and improvised dance training that flourished from the 1960s onwards instead emphasizing the role of the performer as co-creator of the work (Murphy, 2015; see also Banes, 1993; Murray and Keefe, 2007). And yet, while physical theatre and postmodern dance might in this respect seem to constitute a single unified field of performance via their *separate* body-based disavowals of the hegemony of language, parallel to these disciplinary experiments there evolved a hybrid genre of dance-theatre that distinguished itself precisely through its combining of text and movement, speaking and dancing.

By now audiences are fairly used to dancers talking onstage. But – and this is no doubt the residual literary critic in me speaking – it seems to me

Narrative Pivots: Text and Movement in Crystal Pite's Dance-Theatre

that dance and theatre scholars have yet to adequately explain the central historical, political and affective importance of text as one of the indicative signs of dance-theatre as a form. Nor is there much discussion across both disciplines of why, as dramatic text generation came to be regarded as antithetical to the devising practices and communicative goals of theatre post-Artaud, scripted and improvised speech became increasingly integrated with movement and dramaturgy in the rehearsal, performance and documentation processes of many contemporary dance artists. Among the most influential of these artists is, of course, Pina Bausch; however, as Ramsay Burt has usefully reminded us, the 'discursivity' of the Judson Church performer-choreographers was just one of the 'theatrical' affinities they shared with their European contemporaries (2006: 18–21).[2] In the ongoing project of which this chapter is a part, my aim is to examine text development, adaptation and incorporation in the movement work of a generation of artists working in the wake of both Judson Church and Bausch and who, in the words of Meg Stuart, have not felt compelled to choose between the 'conceptual ideas' or the 'theatrical concerns' of either (2010: 174). In so doing, I wish to contest some of the received disciplinary accounts of postdramatic theatre's *non-representational* debts to postmodern dance (see Bogart and Landau, 2005; Overlie, 2006), suggesting instead that contemporary dance artists have long borrowed from the *representational* conventions of the theatre – not least those surrounding language – often to produce a discourse on the very institution of dance itself.[3] Indeed, in overcoming her own initial suspicion of language – in part via the collaborations between her company, Damaged Goods, and Forced Entertainment's Tim Etchells – Stuart has steadily expanded the list of words she 'is not afraid of when [thinking] about dance', including 'emotions, excess and narrative' (2010: 193, 175).

Though their choreography could not be more different, such descriptors apply equally well to the dance creations of Pite, who has always been as concerned with – and 'challenged by' – the 'theatrical side of making work' as with 'the actual making of the movement' (Pite, 2012b), and who has consistently pushed against what she has called the 'taboo around narrative' in contemporary dance (Pite, 2012a). In seeking to account for my own emotionally excessive responses to the pieces Pite has made with her company Kidd Pivot over the past fifteen years, I find that on both a proprioceptive and a cognitive level I am unable to disjoin the ways I have learned to anticipate, in performance, her signature movement patterns from my perceptual processing and interpretation, post-performance, of her source texts. If, as Teresa Brennan has written, feelings are 'sensations that have found the right match in words' (2004: 5), then to what extent do words, when linked to choreographed dance, facilitate – or even govern – the conditions under which social empathy might take place, our bodily claims, as Susan Leigh Foster has so compellingly put it, 'to feel what another body is feeling' (2011: 174–5)? How do textual address and theatricality in dance, more generally, help to hail audience members whose engagements with dance are deeply felt, but who may not be able to articulate precisely what about the movement they have watched has so transported (or alienated) them? In posing these questions, I am suggesting that words, in dance-theatre, function as a medium of communication, but in ways that sometimes exceed 'the lexical confines of [their] enunciation as text' (Welton, 2007: 153). Indeed, when considered as but one element within the total sensory environment of the performance, rather than as that which exists externally and a priori to make sense of this environment, then text starts to take on added texture; it begins to matter not just indexically or symbolically, but also acoustically, visually, somatically. 'Textscape' is the term Hans-Thies Lehmann uses to describe this characteristic feature of postdramatic theatre-making, with an emphasis on the text's phonetic materiality, auditory decomposition, temporal diffusion and spatial dispersion signalling a move '*[f]rom sense to sensuality*' (2006: 148). I am suggesting that, as mutually constitutive elements of the textscape of dance-theatre, speech and movement become sensorially interpolated and, in fighting for our perceptual attention, mutually interpellating of the spectating subject, each working to influence how we apprehend a given performance work, how, in the words of Martin Welton, we 'get a feel for how it goes' (2012: 3).

Recent cognitive approaches to theatre spectatorship confirm Foster's neuro-physiological investigations into the kinaesthetic responses of dance audiences, suggesting that 'when they pay attention to intentional human action (in a performance or anywhere else), spectators mirror the actions of social others', and that this 'interactional simulation' precedes, and is even primary to, the interpretation of spoken language (McConachie, 2008: 79). Yet, most spectators have more training in the semiological interpretation of words. Moreover, that training has usually come at the expense of refining our ability to register and synthesize what Patrice Pavis has identified as performance's myriad other, mostly non-representable, 'body-to-body ... sensory-motor perceptions' (2003: 24). As such, words may be what resonate with us most after a performance is over, or what we first recall when thinking about that performance days later. In this regard, I find particularly useful Carl Lavery's understanding of the dramatic text less as a blueprint to be actualized onstage than as what he calls a 'postscript' of the performance, a spectral artefact that allows for multiple rereadings and re-experiencings of a performance that has passed, what he calls a 'post-evental' 'critical phenomenology' (Lavery, 2009: 40). Focusing on his experience of Lone Theatre's 2005 devised theatre piece, *Alice Bell*, Lavery notes that in his reading of the rough and unpublished script provided to him by company members a year later, what was initially triggered was an aural rather than a visual memory – in particular the voice of lead actress Molly Haslund during her opening poetic speech. The 'grain' of Haslund's voice animates, in turn, the printed text's graphic signs, enabling a post-evental aesthetic encounter that seeks neither to supersede in authenticity the subjective experience of the original performance, nor to 'impose a fixed [literary] meaning that would disavow the ontological contingency and partiality' of the rest of the performance's *mise en scène*' (44). Rather, the text, for Lavery, is a 'fleshy ghost': it at once haunts and provides an additional means through which to analyse 'the lived phenomenology of the work itself' (45).

I am similarly interested in how text re-embodies, and theatrically remediates, movement (and vice versa), how it might linger as a ghostly reminder and affective remainder in an audience member's consciousness *and* a company member's repertoire – the line of remembered prose, or the page of reread poetry, that might trigger a felt, kinaesthetic response in either's body. As Deidre Sklar has persuasively argued, in making a case for kinaesthesia's inclusion in the wider sensorium: 'Words in the intimate space of sensual aliveness reverberate with somatic memory. One feels their meaning as rhythm, texture, shape, and vitality as well as symbol' (2007: 44). And so, it is for me that as I sit at my desk and type into the computer the words 'fate' and 'fake', 'falling' and 'flying', I cannot help shifting slightly in my chair, responding to their alliterative sonorousness, their balanced syllabic metre, but also accommodating their material substance, their directional weight, in relation to my cumulative sense memories of the works by Pite in which the words appear. Each of these words I experienced – and continue to re-experience – twice: once at the level of linguistic sign, whether the words were narrated in voice-over, written on a sign, projected on a screen or spoken orally; the other as a danced enunciation, the movement-based activation of an additional haptic register to these words prompting, in the influential framework outlined by perceptual psychologist James Gibson, a bodily experience of the sensory environment adjacent my own body (1983: 97). That I cannot any longer disentangle the message consciously received in the first instance from my non-conscious, affective response to the bodily source of that message in the second is part of what I wish to explore in what follows. In pivoting between Pite's use of text and movement, I mean to make each matter equally, to take on substance in both a physical and an ideational sense. In this way I am following from Rebecca Schneider in suggesting that Pite's textual postscripts 'remain' not just as constitutive repertory elements in her company's subsequent live performances, but also as an archival record of those performances that can prompt additional 'flesh memories' at odds neither with performance's disappearance, nor its re-citation' (Schneider, 2011: 104).[4] Indeed, as a dance artist keenly interested in engaging with storytelling as a live – and living – event, it would seem that the textual document becomes a way for Pite of extending (backwards and forwards) the temporal and narrative duration of that event: backwards to the literary and narrative sources that figure so prominently as part of Pite's composition process; and forwards to the embodied artefacts those sources inevitably become.

Dark Matters

Born in Victoria, British Columbia, Crystal Pite began her career as a classically trained dancer with Vancouver's Ballet BC, before going on to join Ballett Frankfurt. There she assimilated William Forsythe's approach to structured improvisation (she is a featured performer in the CD-ROM accompanying his *Improvisation Technologies* [2003]), collaborative choreography and deconstructive theatricality. Having debuted as a choreographer in 1990, while still a company member at Ballet BC, Pite has gone on to create works for such acclaimed international companies as Nederlands Dans Theater (NDT), Cullberg Ballet, Ballett Frankfurt, The National Ballet of Canada, Les Ballets Jazz de Montréal (where she was choreographer-in-residence from 2001 to 2004), Cedar Lake Contemporary Ballet, Ballet Jorgen, the Paris Opéra Ballet and the Royal Ballet, where her *Flight Pattern* (2017), a moving meditation on the global refugee crisis set on thirty-six dancers, was that institution's first new work commissioned by a female choreographer in eighteen years. Pite is currently associate choreographer at NDT, associate dance artist at Canada's National Arts Centre in Ottawa, and associate artist at London's Sadler's Wells, where her works have twice won Olivier Awards for outstanding achievement in dance: in 2015 for *Polaris*, a work for sixty-four dancers set to the music of Thomas Adès; and in 2017 for *Betroffenheit*, about which I will have more to say at the end of this chapter. The winner of numerous choreographic prizes in Canada, in 2011 Pite was also awarded the fifth annual Jacob's Pillow Dance Award. In 2002 she formed her own company, Kidd Pivot, as a way of creating her signature performances, which, in the words of her website, integrate 'movement, original music, text, and rich visual design', and which are 'marked by a strong theatrical sensibility and a keen sense of wit and invention' (Kidd Pivot, 2012). *Lost Action* (2006), an award-winning work for seven dancers that played on themes of love and war, firmly established Kidd Pivot on the international scene, with critics especially noting Pite's facility for orchestrating the bodies of her dancers in the large group massings and accordion-like chains that have since become her trademark (see Mackrell, 2009); it was also the Vancouver premiere of this piece that first prompted me to write about the company (see Dickinson, 2010). From 2010 to 2012, Kidd Pivot was resident company at Künstlerhaus Mousonturm in Frankfurt, which provided Pite with the means to employ her dancers fulltime as they created and toured *The You Show* (2010) and *The Tempest Replica* (2011), both also discussed below. Having settled back in Vancouver in 2012, Pite has striven to balance her increasingly busy calendar of international commissions with the creation of new work for Kidd Pivot.

Even since the early days of the company, when Pite was creating smaller scale duets for herself and collaborators Cori Caulfield and Richard Siegel, most of that work has been self-consciously, even obsessively, concerned with the creative process, and as a dance artist Pite has repeatedly turned to literature and the theatre as pivot points through which to explore some of the paradoxes of choreographic inspiration. Thus, in the first part of the evening-length *Uncollected Work* (2003), 'Farther Out', Pite explicitly references the genre of science fiction as a way to thematize the 'uncharted territory' (both the limitless possibilities and the potential black holes) that marks the threshold of artistic invention. In the second part, 'Field: Fiction', she finds herself on the other side of this threshold, using the writings of Annie Dillard to explore what it means to edit, and even destroy, one's own work. Likewise, the very title of *Double Story* (2004), created in collaboration with Siegel, hints at the necessarily plural and revisionist nature of narrative. *Dark Matters* (2009) combines elements from these first two works: it expands on *Double Story*'s use of text and puppetry; and, as in *Uncollected Work*, it sees Pite drawing from science as a point of departure. Specifically, *Dark Matters* tropes on the strange astronomical energy that, though undetectable to the human eye and emitting no electromagnetic radiation, still somehow exerts a gravitational pull on visible matter and that, according to experts on the Big Bang, is believed to make up the vast majority of our universe. In Pite's hands, dark matter becomes a metaphor for the unconscious, for both the wellsprings and the recesses of the imagination. As Pite and her dancers demonstrate in this piece – and as she herself has talked about in print in relation to her own uncertainty about where and when ideas will come to her for new work (Smith, 2010) – bursts of inspirational energy can just as quickly turn to a paralysing abyss. Creation is often followed (sometimes inexplicably and tragically, sometimes necessarily) by destruction. And once again it is text that provides our entrée into this paradox.

Dark Matters is structured in two parts, with the first operating as a quasi-theatrical dumb show (and, in fact, a stage dummy does make a crucial appearance) to the more 'pure dance' explorations of the second. To this end, in the opening minutes a single follow spot moves restlessly

Narrative Pivots: Text and Movement in Crystal Pite's Dance-Theatre

about the stage, revealing glimpses of a clearly makeshift set (designed by Pite's partner, Jay Gower Taylor, himself a former dancer); we see flimsy paper walls, a table filled with cardboard and various outsized props, a cheap tin ceiling lamp. An amplified male voice (Vancouver actor and director Christopher Gaze), rich and sonorous, starts to intone with oracular emphasis excerpts from Voltaire's 'Poem on the Lisbon Disaster', which is subtitled 'Or an Examination of the Axiom, "All is Well"', and which, needless to say, does not portend at all well for our own story:

> What is the verdict of the vastest mind?
> Silence: the book of fate is closed to us.
> Man is a stranger to his own research;
> He knows not whence he comes, nor whither goes.
> Tormented atoms in a bed of mud,
> Devoured by death, a mockery of fate.
> But thinking atoms, whose far-seeing eyes,
> Guided by thought, have measured the faint stars,
> Our being mingles with the infinite;
> Ourselves we never see, or come to know.
> This world, this theatre of pride and wrong,
> …
> This frail construction of quick nerves and bones
> Cannot sustain the shock of elements;
> This temporary blend of blood and dust
> Was put together only to dissolve.
>
> ([1755] 1912: 261–2)[5]

Thus, cognitively cued by the words being spoken, and affectively cued by the tone in which they are spoken, we are primed for something bad to happen. What we do not yet know is the way in which movement figures into the equation. Retrospectively, Voltaire's poem offers some clues.

A reflection on the massive 1755 earthquake and resulting tsunami and fires that devastated the Portuguese capital (a subject the writer would later explore at greater length in *Candide*), 'Poem on the Lisbon Disaster' is also a philosophical treatise on the nature of evil and the existence and providential power of God. Taking on both Leibniz and Alexander Pope (the axiom in the poem's subtitle refers to Pope's *Essay on Man*), Voltaire desists from their view that: 'in the best of all possible worlds' (wherein human suffering is unavoidable), we should place both our reason and our faith in a mostly benevolent God – summed up most famously in Pope's line 'All partial evil, universal good' ([1733–4] 2009: 280; see also Leibniz, [1709] 1952). If this were true, Voltaire argues in his preface to the poem, then it 'follows that human nature is not fallen' and not in need of salvation ([1756] 2000: 97). Moreover, according to Voltaire ([1755] 1912: 256), the idea of an all-powerful God looking after the best interests of human beings is not just impossible to defend rationally, but – in the face of a calamity such as the Lisbon earthquake – also morally, requiring one to resort to a sordid cultural relativism: 'Did fallen Lisbon deeper drink of vice, Than London, Paris, or sunlit Madrid?' With human existence all that is verifiable, and much of that existence bleak and painful, the best we can do is accept our lot and muddle on with our lives – a sentiment that would earn Voltaire the ire of his compatriot, Jean-Jacques Rousseau.

Upon reading this text post-performance, one notices several interesting aspects to Pite's use of it in *Dark Matters*: that she has been drawn more to Voltaire's empiricist than his anti-theodic argument; that in the temporal illusion through which Voltaire sees us navigating our empirical world (the impossible distance between its mud and its stars, summed up in his later maxim 'All will be well one day—so runs our hope./ All *now* is well, is but an idle dream' [1912: 262]) she sees a synecdoche of performance; that of the fifteen lines Pite quotes from the 244-line poem, the last four of them have been transposed from an earlier part of the stanza; that those lines are given sinewy substance via fleshly nouns like 'nerves and bones', the organic matter of 'blood and dust'. Indeed, hearing those words repeated in the dark as the voiceover loops and the follow spot sweeps across the stage is to begin the process of embodying and animating what we have assumed to be an empty and unpersoned space. Martin Welton has argued that words, when spoken in the dark, shift 'participants' focus from interpretation to the immediacy of sensation' (2007: 153). Likewise, Lehmann claims that postdramatic theatre's 'decomposition' of the voice from the presence of the speaking actor 'recomposes' itself in new perceptual modes of '*sono-analysis*' (2006: 149). I would argue that it allows for a new kind of *soma*-analysis as well, one that in the case of *Dark Matters* originates in the audience. Nervously stimulated and synaptically triggered by the sound and tone and rhythm of the voiceover, and by the anxiously roving follow spot, we respond with a kind of kinaesthetic anticipation of what's coming next; that is, we begin to move before we see any movement onstage.

To be sure, as the opening voiceover begins to fade, the follow spot does eventually come to rest on a man (Peter Chu), now sitting at the table filled with paper, cloth, scissors, thread; he seems to be experiencing some sort of blockage. Out of this pile he pulls two marionette legs, crafting a little dance with them centre stage. Suddenly the creative juices are flowing again and over the course of a few quick blackouts (which are used most effectively throughout the first half) we are eventually introduced to his creation, a benign-looking puppet attached to wires manipulated by the rest of the Kidd Pivot company, clad all in black like the traditional puppeteers in Bunraku theatre. However, in *Dark Matters* it turns out our puppet is very far from benign, and combining verbally unspoken but clearly recognizable intertextual references to *Frankenstein*, *Pinocchio*, *Pétrouchka*, *Coppélia* (the story by Hoffman and the ballet by Saint-Léon), *The Wizard of Oz* and Freud's *Ego and the Id*, among other texts (including B-grade movies like *Chucky* and its sequels/imitators), Pite tells the familiar story of creature rising up against creator (as in the best of Chekhov's plays, those scissors are onstage for a reason).

Except, wily creative artist that she herself is, Pite renders the familiar strange once the inevitable climax has occurred and the puppet, having stabbed his creator/amanuensis, and with nowhere left to channel his energy, himself expires. It is at this point that the black clad supernumeraries – the literal dark matter in this show – take centre stage. Their previously discrete yet no less precise manipulations of the restless puppet (and it is revelatory to see how Pite transposes her choreographic vocabulary onto the startlingly lifelike movements of the puppet) are now unleashed in a riot of acrobatic and martial-arts-like movements as they rush about like would-be ninja-assassins, clearly emboldened by the acts they just witnessed *and* abetted. Pite is having fun here, and her cultural touchstones during these sequences are as much *Spider-Man* and *Crouching Tiger, Hidden Dragon* as they are the high art works of Shelley and Stravinsky. All of this energy culminates in an inexorable gravitational pull being exerted on the visible matter before us onstage, i.e. the set, and when this comes crashing down – as, of course, it must – Pite literally reveals to us, in the form of the stage's back safety wall, the 'invisible' scaffolding of the theatrical *deus ex machina*: what we take to be *fate* is in fact just *fake*. We have, of course, been primed for all of this via the quoted lines from Voltaire; however, having initially received those lines less as signs for sense-making than as a species of extrasensory stimulation, we now require an actual sign, held aloft by one of the supernumeraries, to let us in on the ruse. But even here there is a productive sense of confusion, a kinaesthetic tension, between the word and its material referent: in both the choreographic and what, after Julia Kristeva, Lehmann has called the 'chora-graphic' spaces of the body–text relationship in performance (2006, 144), the word 'fake' refers at once to the entire collapsed *mise en scène* and, metonymically, to the swaying dancer brandishing the sign within that space.

Coincidentally, it is at this point that both the follow spot and the voiceover from the opening return, the former eventually picking out of the detritus the half-buried arm of our protagonist-creator as the latter repeats, in a loop, the same lines from Voltaire. Once again, the text, in this instance, functions less as a prophecy to be confirmed through our visual interpretation of the scene before us than as a sonic score. It is the basso-continuo that through its repetition becomes a kind of gestural noise and that, in my post-event recollection of the performance *and* repeated recitation aloud of the quoted text, provides an additional modal frequency through which to register – to feel – the otherwise noiseless entrance from the wings of one lonely supernumerary. Her hands and feet skirt the edge of the follow spot as she approaches the apparently dead creator. Tugging at his arm, the supernumerary eventually frees his entire body, props him up like a dummy, and begins to help him to walk. And then, because we are still quite clearly in the world of the theatre – no matter, in Voltaire's words, that this world is filled with 'pride and wrong' – something magical happens: the creator, his feet at first unsteady, his knees occasionally buckling, begins to walk on his own, exiting stage right. Lest we think this trick repeatable, however, the supernumerary is not about to let us forget what we have just learned: that the slippage between fate and fake is but one transposed letter. Having picked up what appears to be another one of her confrères from the wreckage onstage, she walks with the body to centre stage and promptly tosses it on the pile of debris in front of us, where it lands with a definitive thud.

The remaindering of this 'real' dummy at the end of the first act provides the visual segue to the start of the second, as the lights come up on the body of our super-supernumerary splayed on the bare stage. Slowly she raises the bottom half of one leg, flexes her foot, and then drops it to the floor. Eventually she lifts her pelvis and raises herself onto her elbows, testing limbs and joints in a rehearsal for ambulation – much like our creator teaching his puppet to walk at the beginning of act one, and then himself being taught by the character we now see before us at its end. In the production I saw in Vancouver in February 2010, Pite played this latter role herself, at once half-heartedly attempting to disguise *and* make manifestly visible her own creative energies as an artist. That is, in the fifty-five minutes that follow, we witness the rest of the company (Chu, joined by Eric Beauchesne, Yannick Matthon, Cindy Salgado and Jermaine Spivey), now all in regular street clothes, 'animate' her emblematic choreography – which tends to burst forth in rippling eddies from the body's core, limbs buckling or departing in waves in response rather than arriving neatly at an end point of vertical alignment, arms and legs extended as if on strings. But we are also witnessing (although not without careful concentration) the black-clad Pite rushing about the stage moving lights, doing things behind scrims, popping up in unexpected places (including emerging from the orchestra pit at the very lip of the stage). Finally, she inserts herself within the other dancers' bodily chains to provide them with an added force, or a change of direction. She, quite materially, becomes the 'pivot' between their deliberately uncertain movements.

In so doing, she likewise makes manifest another way in which this work pivots, for me, between text and movement, allowing me to 'get a feel' for each. By that I mean that as choreographer and as the literal dark matter between her dancers onstage, Pite is in a very real sense making their bodies speak. We saw a version of this at the end of act one when, having guided Chu's creator to an unsupported standing position, Pite uses unison movement as a means of modelling actual locomotion. Even more interesting in act two is the way in which Pite positions her own body as a ballast between the balance and imbalance of her dancers, whose various choreographic structures of support – the weight each bears and transfers, the bodily shape one might assume or the surface offer – owes much to release technique generally. More specifically, however, it is of a piece with the contact-improv-inspired partnering and group work that Pite began incorporating into her movement vocabulary beginning with *Lost Action*, and that Nancy Shaw has described, with specific reference to that work, as a 'kinesthetics of rescue' (Shaw, 2006: 10). As chief rescuer, Pite's super-supernumerary provides the second half of *Dark Matters* with much of its energy, flow and momentum, 'invisibly' helping Salgado, for example, to walk on and with the upturned palms of Matthon's outstretched hands, or else steering all five dancers in various massed tableaux across the stage. Read in the context of the first half's more overtly theatrical exploration of the consequences of training a body to move to a set of authorial conventions or codes, to in effect perform according to a script, I am reminded of Michel de Certeau's assertion that walking is an enunciatively equivalent to speech (1984: xiii, 91–110). But I am also reminded of Susan Foster's claim, in adapting de Certeau to the specific performance tactics of contact improvisation, that non-narrative and 'non-message oriented' movement is not so much anti-theatrical as constitutive of an 'alternative theatricality', using the choreographic score in place of the script to alter the sense relationship between body and/as text (2002: 136, 135).

In this regard, it is worth noting that, in my initial post-eventual use of Voltaire's text to re-experience on a somatic and kinaesthetic level the live experience of *Dark Matters*, I had forgotten the final return of the piece's voiceover, a lapse in sense memory that was only remedied by subsequently viewing a video recording of the work. It was then that I rediscovered that the voiceover recurs just prior to the piece's coda, a very moving duet between Chu-as-creator and the now disrobed super-supernumerary (performed by new company member Sandra Marín Garcia in the video), in which they reciprocally exchange the roles of choreographer/dancer, puppeteer/puppet, creator/doll. So effective is this danced postscript to the dialectic of creation and destruction at the heart of the piece as a whole, it is perhaps understandable that I would have dismissed as insignificant the re-verbalization of this dialectic via voiceover in the solo by Jermaine Spivey that precedes it. Which is also to say that by then I was no longer attuned to speech solely at the level of linguistic sign. Rather, what de Certeau refers to as the 'performance' of speech – including the sound and rhythm and tempo and breath accompanying its enunciation – had been 're-appropriated' by Pite's dancing bodies, literally incorporated into the general habit of motion. This perhaps explains why the super-supernumerary, hitherto the invisible animating force behind Spivey and the other dancers' movement, is now stilled, watching from upstage as the looping voiceover does the work of animation for her. And, sticking with the terms supplied by de Certeau, I want to suggest that this in turn posits a new '*contract with the other*' (1984: xiii) – in this case the spectator – one in which the uttering of words like 'nerves' and 'bones' and 'blood' and 'dust' alongside their physical manifestation and excitation transforms information into sensation.

The Tempest Replica

On this last point, it also bears mentioning that one other thing that dissolved amid the blood and dust of the postscript to *Dark Matters* was Pite's professional identity as a dancer-choreographer. In 2010, pregnant with her first child, she ceded her role in the piece to Marín Garcia. Since then, she has not danced in any of Kidd Pivot's performances, though she has continued to travel with the company. One cannot help but wonder if this move from creator-performer to creator-director influenced the choice of source material and the style of presentation for *The Tempest Replica* (2011), which at that point was Pite's most explicit engagement with narrative in dance, and the result of her first time working so comprehensively with a pre-existing script. The work premiered in Frankfurt in the autumn of 2011; however, Pite remained dissatisfied with several aspects of the performance, and so she continued to fine-tune them with the aid of a residency at Simon Fraser University's Goldcorp Centre for the Arts in Vancouver in the summer of 2012, before sending a retooled version on a four-month North American tour that doubled as a farewell of sorts for the company, which was to take an indefinite hiatus following the end of its residency in Vancouver. Coincidentally, between the 2011 premiere and 2012 remount of Pite's dance-theatre take on Shakespeare's *The Tempest*, she was approached by the Québec theatre and opera director Robert Lepage to choreograph his production of the recent Thomas Adès opera, thus cementing her artistic association with a text she initially felt incapable of adapting (Lepage and Pite, 2012).

Perhaps even more pertinent to the present analysis is the fact that Pite's adaptation actually shares many affinities with Lepage's own theatrical aesthetic. This is most apparent in the production's juxtaposition of bravura and technically sophisticated moments of design magic (described at more length below) with simpler bits of imagistic minimalism. To that end, the action of *The Tempest Replica* begins even before the house lights dim. As audience members file into the theatre and begin taking their seats they glimpse Eric Beauchesne, dressed in street clothes, kneeling downstage right, in front of a large shimmery and billowing silver cloth that stretches the length of the stage. He is intently folding sheet after sheet of white paper into perfect origami sailboats, which he promptly lines up in neat rows. Thus, are we introduced to Prospero, and to another kind of kinaesthetic labour that, precisely because it eschews overt pantomime, approaches the precision and virtuosity of classical ballet. To be sure, the scene does serve to telegraph for those in the audience unfamiliar with Shakespeare's play (or who haven't bothered to read Pite's careful synopsis of the action in the programme) the famous opening high seas storm. But in the number and colour and scale of the boats' replication, it also recalls one of Pite's explanations for the faceless, all-white fencing-style costumes we will soon see worn by the other dancers in the first part of her work: they are meant to recall the scale human figures used in architectural models (Pite, 2012a).

Manipulating one of the boats in the same way that he will soon manipulate the bodily figures occupying his island, Prospero speaks aloud the word 'shipwreck', and then promptly calls the spirit Ariel (Marín Garcia), the real architect of his designs. Ariel, also dressed in street clothes, does not look particularly pleased by the summons, a reminder that she has not chosen to do Prospero's bidding, something captured in two simple movements introduced here that will be repeated by her throughout the work: a fluttering of her hands over her heart; and an elbow thrust akimbo out from her side, a reflex response perhaps to a phantom wing that has been clipped or tamped down by her master. Taking the paper boat from Prospero, Ariel places it in her mouth and starts to chew. This is the signal for the storm to begin. But also condensed in this image is Pite's choreographic challenge in taking on a sacred cultural text like *The Tempest*: how, precisely, to make the words have flesh? In considering this question post-performance, my trusty *Norton Shakespeare* close to hand for reference, I find I am far less concerned with what Pite has left out or telescoped in the story than with how she has translated into movement the smaller, more intimate emotional arcs of select characters, a relationship of scale between bodies and text she in turn maps onto the two mirror halves of the work as a whole.

Thus, in the first half, Pite uses an arsenal of effects to 'storyboard' for the audience major plot points in a succession of bodily tableaux, a style of physical and gestural exposition she first started exploring in narrative-based commissions for Nederlands Dans Theater (*Plot Point*, 2010) and Cedar Lake Contemporary Ballet (*Grace Engine*, 2010) that were inspired by film production techniques (Pepper, 2012). For example, in the storm conjured by Ariel we witness pre-recorded digital images of a flailing Ferdinand (Jermaine Spivey), in casual rehearsal sweats, projected onto the stage left portion of the billowing curtain; these are then overlain with projected droplets of pelting rain. Behind the curtain, a live 'replica' Ferdinand, all in white, his face masked, struggles to maintain his balance in response to the lashings of the storm – or is it in response to his 'real' digital image? Rolling back and forth on the floor upstage right are the similarly clad bodies of Prospero's sworn enemies, Alonso (Bryan Arias) and Sebastian (Jiří Pokorný) and Antonio (Yannick Matthon), chalk outlines at a crime scene but for the fact that they refuse to stay still. In calling for a furious unleashing of thunder and lightning in his opening stage direction, Shakespeare issues a virtually impossible challenge to any director: create an opening sound and light show equivalent to and representationally illustrative of the powerful magic of Prospero. Pite does not shy away from enjoining technology to aid in this task; but in rereading the poor Boatswain's calls for the masts to be lowered and to lay into the wind as he deals with an interfering Alonso and Sebastian, I was reminded of how Pite simultaneously uses technologies of the body to heighten our kinaesthetic response to the storm. Indeed, one of the more surprising things about the projections in *The Tempest Replica* is the sheer amount of movement contained within them, and the extent to which that recorded movement merges with and in effect hypermediates the shadow outline of live movement onstage via lighting effects in front of and behind the piece's two cloth scrims (the first downstage one is pulled down after the storm by Prospero, to reveal a second upstage one).

In an essay partially focused on the Toronto company bluemouth inc.'s *Dance Marathon* (2009), a site-specific and durational work of physical theatre that doubles as a kind of movement-based study in relational aesthetics, Bruce Barton argues that intermedial performance technologies frequently produce feelings of 'pronounced anxiety' in both spectators and performers. At the same time, he notes, intermediality can heighten the possibilities for 'interactive intimacy', an 'openness to physical contact and connection' leading to a 'vicarious identification' that is at one and the same time a 'self-reflection' (2009: 280, 281). I want to argue that intermediality helps to facilitate a similar kind of intimacy, or kinaesthetic empathy, at the outset of *The Tempest Replica*. The digital projections create a visually immersive textscape in which an optical illusion of external movement at once amplifies the otherwise invisible kinetic forces buffeting the dancers onstage and, as result, the uncanny feelings of vertigo we experience in the audience. Which is also to say that Pite, in taking that word 'shipwreck' and planting it so firmly and forcibly inside our own bodies at the very start of this piece, is foregrounding the extent to which any empathetic impulse must first begin with an often-painful diagnosis of one's physical limits to feeling what another will feel.

Other projections, such as Prospero's explanation to Miranda (Cindy Salgado) following the shipwreck of how they came to find themselves on the island as a result of Antonio's usurpation of Prospero's dukedom in Milan, or the banquet conjured by Ariel – now dressed head to toe in a shimmery white body suit – for Alonso, Sebastian and Antonio, are more clearly cinematic (often expressionistically so). But if, after the philosophers Gilles Deleuze (1986) and Giorgio Agamben (2000: 55, 58–9), we understand the vocabulary of cinema, like that of dance, to be essentially gestural and movement-oriented, then we begin to see how the two forms combine in *The Tempest Replica* to create an intermedial language that does not so much supplant Shakespeare's source text as perceptually enrich and even 'enflesh' it. This occurs most successfully in the first half of the work in the sequence when we are first introduced to Caliban (Arias again), who slithers across the stage on all fours, led by Prospero and towards Miranda, seated stage left, as the projections economically telegraph (in the same direction) how the monster came to be enslaved by Prospero. Here, following from Deleuze's troika of movement-images, perception (the unidentified viewpoint of the camera that initially frames our own indeterminate registering of the scene) combines with action (the direction and duration of the interaction between the virtual and live bodies on screen and onstage) and affection (the interval/continuity between received and executed movement, associated by Deleuze with the face and/or, as with Caliban and Miranda, its obliteration) to produce a multi-sensory experience of kinaesthesia (1986: 64–6).[6]

This is just one example of how the 'plotting' of the first half of *The Tempest Replica* is not all in service of exposition. Indeed, to the extent that Pite employs her storyboard tableaux to distil the action of Shakespeare's play to its essence, she does so by locating that essence over and over again in gesture and movement: the fluttering of Ariel's hand over her heart, or the wild, apparently hipless careening and spinning of Ferdinand. Once again Lehmann is instructive here; he notes that the '*principle of exposition*', when 'applied to body, gesture and voice', foregrounds the materiality of language at the expense of its representational function. He writes: 'Instead of a linguistic *re*-presentation of facts, there is a "position" of tones, words, sentences, sounds that are hardly controlled by a "meaning" but instead by the scenic composition' (2006: 146; emphasis in original). In the scenic compositions that make up the first half of Pite's work, the positions of bodies, and the different tonal phrases they enact, are mostly controlled by Prospero. This is made clear via our introduction to Miranda, who first appears lying prone on the floor after her father tears down the front curtain following the storm. At first, I was confused by this image, and its suggestion that, in terms of the play's narrative, Miranda is the shipwreck's first victim. However, it made much more somatic sense when I returned to the text-as-postscript and recalled that in Shakespeare's play Miranda is the character distinguished by the depth of her feelings, and by a surfeit of empathy, in particular:

> O, I have sufferèd
> With those that I saw suffer! A brave vessel,
> Who had, no doubt, some noble creature in her,
> Dashed all to pieces! O, the cry did knock
> Against my very heart!
>
> (Shakespeare, [1611] 1997, I.ii.5–9)

In Pite's staging, this ghosted textual apostrophe (later to appear lexically as a projection in the piece's second half) is juxtaposed not just with Miranda's mannequin-like appearance, but also with her father's manipulations of her movements, pulling her up from the stage and then, as with the supernumerary's manoeuvring of Salgado across the body of Matthon in act two of *Dark Matters*, directing her to walk – and to look at the equally dark magic he has wrought. By contrast, when, later in the first half, Prospero finally releases Ferdinand from his Sisyphean labour of moving rocks and consents to letting he and Miranda wed, the young lovers break into an exuberant jive. What might at first appear to be another jarring misquotation, in this case of a social dance with roots in Jazz Age Harlem, takes on added resonance when we learn in the second half of the piece (or if we recall the projected images of him) that the dancer playing Ferdinand is African American. Read against an expressly postcolonial interpretation of the textual postscript, in which Prospero's enslavement of Caliban (here played by another dancer of colour) can be viewed in part as a defence against the possibility of miscegenation, Pite's choice of phrasing in this instance draws our kinaesthetic attention to the historically situated social and cultural forces Foster sees framing all empathetic responses (2011: 11) – and the choreographed movement that may have prompted them. In this scenario, as Sara Ahmed has persuasively argued, the experience of intersubjective feeling, of 'being moved' by an other, might actually work to fix and reify that other as an object of feeling '"having" certain characteristics' (2004: 11) – including a 'recognizable' or idiomatic style of dancing.

And on the subject of fixing meaning, I should be clear: there are certainly ways in which text operates logocentrically in *The Tempest Replica*. For example, in the first half surtitles provide act and scene numbers, and a brief, one-line synopsis of the corresponding action in Shakespeare's play. And in the second half actual lines from the play are projected on the screen, clearly meant to explicate the movement sequences we see taking shape before us. However, those lines also merge with the densely layered soundscape designed by Meg Roe and Alessandro Juliani to complement Owen Belton's electronic score, in which disembodied male and female voices fade in and out, whispering passages from the text, but often too rapidly and breathlessly to make any of it intelligible. Instead word, voice and body work discordantly to produce a new, environmental sense-logic out of the very incommensurability of each as an individual and self-contained sign system. Likewise, in the first part of the piece key words are projected onto unexpected surfaces, in the process giving otherwise abstract signifiers material weight and physical substance: 'daughter' appears on Miranda's raised skirt, for example, and 'doubt' on one of Prospero's unfurled paper boats, held up by an unidentified, white-cloaked avatar in the first half's final sequence. The latter word carries with it intertextual associations that extend beyond Shakespeare's play, as Pite had previously employed as an epigraph to her programme notes for *Dark Matters* an excerpt from John Patrick Shanley's introduction to his award-winning play *Doubt* (2005). In the void of belief, however, there is also the make-believe of theatre. Coincidentally, there is no textual synopsis to accompany the projected act five marker in this sequence, which also displaces the play's epilogue, cueing the transition into the second half of Pite's piece as Prospero, clearly in need of new magic, calls aloud for Ariel once again.

Her arrival, dressed in the clothes she was wearing at the piece's outset, begins the process of replaying in some more formally abstract way key scenes that were storyboarded for us in the first half. Now that we know who everyone is, and the nature of their relationships to one another, we can concentrate on how the movement intensifies the emotions behind those relationships. Although all the dancers get brief solo moments during these sequences – and none more stunning than Spivey's live recreation of the bodily shipwreck that we had previously witnessed digitally – Pite's basic architecture during the second half is the duet: between Prospero and Ariel; Prospero and Miranda; Antonio and Sebastian; Prospero and Caliban; and Miranda and Ferdinand. This is some of Pite's most complex and original partnering, giving a physical form to the degrees of indebtedness and obligation, choice and constraint, power and reciprocity that mark both the connection and the distance between different characters. Thus, for example, the opening duet between Prospero and Ariel is notable for its gorgeous lifts; but the striving for flight that we intuit in Ariel's impossibly fluid leg extensions especially is counterbalanced by arms that, though neither locked with nor pinned down by Prospero's, cannot seem to release her. Similarly, Caliban's head remains in a vice-grip for much of his duet with Prospero, and even when he does break free and stands up straight and smooths down the suit jacket he is wearing as a sop to his wounded dignity and pride, he is just as quickly forced back down to the ground by the unrelenting Prospero and must propel himself about the stage via his sit bones and knees. Caliban is the only dancer other than Prospero who speaks while moving, appropriate for the character who, having been taught Prospero's language, knows only 'how to curse'. The irony is that Shakespeare gives Caliban some of the most beautiful poetry in the play, a portion of which we hear in whispered voiceover. However, Pite largely confines Caliban's live enunciated speech – which Prospero seeks to stifle – to a single repeated utterance: 'This island's mine' (Shakespeare, 1997, I.ii.334). Here we have the flip-side of the scalar relationship between text and movement on offer in the first half of the piece; in this case, the simple linguistic declarative distils the intense, physical muscularity of Caliban's danced resistance to Prospero's dominance over him.

The Tempest Replica ends with the epilogue that was forestalled in the first half; Prospero, having given up magic, is shadowed and eventually overwhelmed by the four other male dancers, now back in their all-white costumes (see Figure 14.1). In the final tableau, Prospero is placed prone on the floor in a position akin to the one in which we first encounter Miranda at the start of the work; the other dancers stand over the stilled creator, silently clapping as the lights fade to black. The image alludes, of course, to Prospero's concluding speech, in which he asks to be released from his own creative bondage via the audience's applause, and which most critics read as a self-reflexive comment, in this his last major play,

Narrative Pivots: Text and Movement in Crystal Pite's Dance-Theatre

Figure 14.1 Eric Beauchesne (on floor) as Prospero and company in *The Tempest Replica* (2011)
Photographer: Jörg Baumann. Photograph courtesy of Kidd Pivot

on Shakespeare's setting aside of his writing quill. As a postscript to Pite's work, this scene has likewise come to overdetermine my post-eventual experience of *The Tempest Replica*. That is, given Pite's own longstanding concerns with the dialectic of creation and destruction, and taken together with her announcement at a pre-show artist's talk that following the conclusion of the 2012 tour of the piece she and Kidd Pivot would be taking at least a year's sabbatical (Pite, 2012a), I have on a very real and somatic level registered the performance as a wistful farewell from a choreographer who at the time did not know in what form, for how long, or even if her company would reconstitute itself.[7]

The You Show

That, in retrospect, I felt so keenly this perceived double ending to *The Tempest Replica* has much to do with the extended textual dialogue I have imagined myself to be conducting with the choreographer in this chapter.

Pite is herself exceedingly generous in talking about the work she creates: at open rehearsals; in public talks and pre- and post-performance conversations with audiences; in print and video interviews. Indeed, as my own consistent quotation of her words in these pages attests, the *matter* of dance's real and imagined interlocutors is clearly important to Pite. And it is one she addresses expressly in *The You Show* (2010), an evening of four shorter pieces whose genesis, again in her words, came from the idea of composing works of dance 'in the second person'. How might this in turn enable audience members to locate themselves in a dancer's movements, and see their own stories and conflicts and losses reflected in the physically embodied language onstage? As Pite explained at a talkback following the performance I saw in May 2011, when her dancers reach their arms behind them, or torque their bodies backward, or fall onto the floor, she is hypothesizing that, in witnessing those actions, we will feel something similar in our own bodies, whether as a result of our own storehouse of corporeal memories the dancers' movements trigger, or by virtue of imaginatively simulating, in direct motor response, those movements ourselves (Pite, 2011). Pite thus frames her impetus for the work in terms remarkably similar to Foster's and McConachie's applications of scientific theories of 'mirror neurons' to their respective conceptions of 'kinesthetic empathy' and 'social cognition' in dance and theatre performance (Foster, 2011: 165–73; McConachie, 2008: 70–9).[8]

However, what I find most interesting, and what I want to focus on in my discussion of *The You Show*, is that in the first and last pieces an active engine of Pite's experiments in second person sensory-motor response is textual address. At the same time, I must acknowledge that, unlike in my post-eventual phenomenological reflections on *Dark Matters* and *The Tempest Replica*, in this instance I am somewhat impoverished in terms of actual postscripts. The texts that accompany the opening and closing sections of *The You Show* were both written by Pite and have not, to my knowledge, been published. Indeed, as verbal prompts to my somatic memories of these works I have only their titles, a few lines from the former that I jotted down on my programme in the dark, and a very hazy purchase on the broad parameters of the story that takes shape from the words spoken in the latter. Supplementing this, however, is a much more acute sense of the *sound* of the recorded narration in the first piece and both the *sight* and *site* of its live enunciation in the second, a perceptual equivalence in the registering of and response to body, voice and text that has been my focus throughout this chapter.

Created between *Dark Matters* and *The Tempest Replica*, *The You Show* both draws from the movement vocabulary of the former and anticipates the partnering patterns of the latter. The work is made up of four duets, the first of which, 'A Picture of You Falling', was originally created as a one-off piece in 2008 for Peter Chu and Anne Plamondon, roughly coincident with Pite's preliminary work on *Dark Matters*. This helps to explain both works' shared fascination with the body's marionette-like qualities, the collapsings and strivings of which we are not always the agent. Indeed, the voiceover text (spoken by the actress Kate Strong) explicitly locates the impulse to move *outside* one's body, that is, in simultaneously fascinated and incredulous response to a *representation* of one's body moving: 'Is this your hand? Is this your back? Is this your hand *reaching* back?' Here, and elsewhere, the text at once describes and precipitates the movement. 'This is a picture of you *falling* – knees, hip, hands, elbows, head. This is the sound of your heart *hitting* the floor': as we hear these words intoned, with emphasis placed on the action verbs, Chu's liquid limbs begin to fold in turn as he crumples to the stage joint by joint. However, the effect is not purely mimetic. For one, there is Plamondon's own response to Chu's response to the text, which is primarily to seek to forestall the movement toward immobility, doubly represented in the live image of Chu's prone body onstage, and in the word-image being painted for us via the text. Then there is our own response, which I would argue is also double – textually and kinaesthetically. That is, to the extent that it might additionally feel like we are falling in response to or along with Chu falling, we cannot affectively and imitatively disjoin either response from the ambiguity of address embedded in that second person pronoun.

Who, in other words, is the 'you' who is falling? Answering this question in the context of Pite's stated aim of engaging feelings of kinaesthetic response in her audience requires shifting entrenched theories of mimeticism from the idea of performers imitating actions onstage to spectators mirroring those actions in the audience (McConachie, 2008: 71). What McConachie refers to as 'visuomotor observation' is, of course, the basis for training in all movement: from an infant learning to walk to the dancer learning new steps. But critics have not until recently paid close enough attention to how this principle operates for audiences watching movement-based work, despite the frequency with which we might find ourselves consciously or unconsciously mimicking that movement post-performance. The voiceover in 'A Picture of You Falling' commands us to pay attention. It opens with a deictic, 'this', which in my recollection of the stress placed upon it, and the slight pause that followed it, reads as the verbal equivalent of an extended index finger, locating us firmly inside the piece's scenic frame. Moreover, the rhythmic repetition of the two key phrases attached to 'this', and the play with pacing, tempo and emphasis therein, functions as a kind of aural entrainment, arguably helping to synchronize our internal sense of proprioception to the trajectory of downward movement we see represented externally in Chu's slowly buckling body: knees, hip, hands, elbows, head. Finally, there is what I can only describe as the sonic boom that accompanies Strong's richly textured and immensely seductive voice, one that, in concert with the movement, sets off a kind of haptic echo in our own bodies.

That echo reverberates with different degrees of intensity over the course of the next two pieces in the programme. Both use physical action and emotional reaction as structuring motifs. In 'The Other You' Pite pairs Beauchesne and Pokorný, dancers of similar height and build, and each sporting a shaved head and similar dark jacket. A study in increasingly high stakes brinksmanship and animal aggression, with each man's physical attempts at connection or dominance met by an equal and opposing force, the piece culminates in a surprisingly tender *pas de deux* to *Moonlight Sonata*. Here, in a consciously literary move, Pite uses a deliberately clichéd musical citation to throw into relief the darker archetypes explored in the first half of the piece, which by virtue of its contiguous relationship to the voiceover from the opening duet that lingers in our brains can certainly be read as taking up and extending the 'bad feelings' that underpin that text's images of romantic regret. By contrast, 'Das Glashaus', danced by Salgado and Matthon, and featuring a score by long-time collaborator Owen Belton composed of sounds of shattering glass, lacks similar dramatic tension. Arguably this has less to do with any inherent flaws in the movement's conceptual expression than with the distance of the piece – which follows an intermission – from the overall perceptual impression initially created by Strong's narration. Having been cued to listen, as well as to watch, the fact that we do not get any new textual input in this piece affects the way we process, store and respond to its physical language.

However, text returns in *The You Show*'s final piece, 'A Picture of You Flying', which in its title is quite clearly meant as a bookend to the opening number. But unlike in that piece, or any of her other works I have discussed up to this point, here Pite employs a new mode of narration: live speech. It begins with Spivey emerging from the wings and taking a seat on a simple wooden chair positioned downstage left. He begins to address the audience quietly, almost shyly. Notwithstanding the bold physical and scenographic uses to which chairs have been put in much contemporary dance – including now iconic works by Bausch (*Café Müller*) and Anne Teresa De Keersmaeker (*Rosas Danst Rosas*) – the image of Spivey sitting still on a chair, talking so conversationally, at first strikes me as completely incongruous. This undoubtedly has much to do with the fact that I have always identified with Spivey as among the most physically 'active' of Kidd Pivot's dancers when onstage. To see him suddenly not moving is strange. Contributing to one's sense of defamiliarization in this respect are the words coming out of Spivey's mouth, which actually draw added attention to his sedentariness by referencing things like sacrifice, strength, endurance, the body's armour, and the physical and mental toll exacted by his line of work.

At first, we are wont to think this is a bit of self-reflexive commentary on Spivey's profession as a dancer, especially when he mentions the drawbacks of wearing tights, lifting his pant leg to reveal a bit of red Lycra underneath. But before Spivey can continue further, he is interrupted by Marín Garcia, who enters speaking animatedly in Spanish – to our and Spivey's mutual confusion. At a workshop presentation of the piece in October 2010, Pite told the audience that she hadn't yet written the monologue planned for Marín Garcia, and so she had simply asked her to improvise for the time being in her native language (Pite, 2010). However, in the staged performance I saw the following spring, Marín Garcia's speech remained untranslated.[9] To be sure, we are able to discern from the intensely expressive delivery of her text, and via the hand waving and pacing that accompanies her speech, that the dancer is upset, and that the cause of this upset appears to be Spivey, who has arisen from his chair and now trails Marín Garcia, struggling like the non-Spanish speakers in the audience for an explanation of what's being said. However, taking Pite's own talk about what she had originally intended for this verbal exchange as one of the possible postscripts through which to re-experience the piece, I read her decision to leave Marín Garcia's speech untranslated, and thus its referential function inaccessible to many in the audience, as transferring emphasis not just to its expressive function, but also to its phatic function. That is, talk in this instance is at once task-oriented, in the sense that Bronislaw Malinowski originally gave to phatic as a term, and is being deployed, in Roman Jakobson's subsequent typology of speech functions, for interactive purposes, as a way of maintaining contact.[10] In this way, phatic speech more closely approximates the purely gestural, not least in how it draws attention to itself as a medium of (mis)communication – Spivey's own phatic declaration of 'I can't understand what you're saying' finding its gestural corollary in his upturned hands and shrugged shoulders. What I am trying to suggest, in other words, is that speech in this instance is operating like a movement phrase, which is why it should come as no surprise that Marín Garcia's explosive entrance and her plosive speech succeed not only in getting Spivey up off his chair, but also in propelling him across the stage. Whereupon we notice what has perhaps escaped our attention until now: a red towel lying on the floor. Marín Garcia picks it up and wraps it around Spivey's neck, like a cape. When Spivey mentions flying, the meaning of his earlier conversation to us from the chair becomes moderately clearer: that is, we are able to surmise that he was speaking to us not simply from his professional identity as a dancer, but also from the adopted theatrical persona of a superhero character. But then, as the movement-based elaboration of this text goes on to reveal, what precisely is the difference?

In this thirty-five-minute work, Pite quotes from some of the comic book and action movie imagery she played with in the supernumerary sequences of *Dark Matters*. This time, however, she deliberately slows down the motion, and the highlight is a Transformer-esque duet between Spivey and Marín Garcia, these two friend-foes and possible lovers raised aloft, their arms and legs and heads shielded and manipulated by other company members as they dance/fight to the death – or sheer exhaustion. As I have shown, Pite is a choreographer as obsessed with how the body is danced as with dancing bodies. The group scenes in 'A Picture of You Flying' operate in a manner equivalent to stop-motion animation, with Pite showing us frame-by-frame, or limb-by-limb, how these bodies can be made to soar through the air in the way that they do. Observing the preparation alongside the execution, we are able to intuit if not the actual sensation of flying in our own bodies, then at least the combined muscular effort that would be required to do so. And it is worth remembering, in this respect, that Spivey's talk has mostly been about the toil of and the toll on his body – and that he has delivered much of it while sitting in a chair, just like us. At the end of the evening, we, in the audience, certainly haven't done as much work as Pite's dancers. But the making human of what for most of us appears decidedly superhuman is one of the conceits of Spivey's opening conversation, which is as much about affective labour as it is about physical labour, and which acknowledges the work we in the audience are doing on both fronts via its second person address.

Betroffenheit

It is this intimate exchange of *e*-motional energy between performer and spectator that distinguishes Pite's dance-theatre as 'feeling' in the sense that Martin Welton employs the term to describe the perceptual ecology of performance more generally. That is, the works I am discussing in this chapter don't just transmit sensations or sense impressions to us, stimulating us aurally or visually or kinaesthetically; they also give us, as Welton states, 'the feel of feeling', providing instruction in how to attend or become newly attuned to a particular moment, or quality of feeling, to be more consciously open and receptive to a practice of spectating that for Welton perforce also 'includes haptic and locomotive capacities' (2012: 155). It is my argument that text is one of the pivotal means by which Pite helps us to experience her work more feelingly. And in the case of Kidd Pivot's most recent, and most self-consciously spectacular, work of dance-theatre, that text has its genesis in a real-life tragedy.

Betroffenheit, which premiered in Toronto in July 2015 as part of the Panamania Arts and Culture Festival that accompanied the Pan Am and Parapan Am Games, is actually a co-creation between Kidd Pivot and Vancouver's Electric Company Theatre (ECT), with whom Pite had collaborated in 2006 when she provided original choreography for their play *Studies in Motion*. Three years later, in the summer of 2009, two of the co-founders of ECT, actor and writer Jonathon Young and director Kim Collier, lost their 14-year-old daughter, Azra Young, when she perished along with two cousins, Fergus and Phoebe Conway, in a fire at the family's summer cabin in rural British Columbia. In the close-knit performance community of Vancouver, the news affected many, with Young and Collier, who were then in the midst of preparing for their company's most high-profile commission to date, having to work through their grief in the midst of some very intense public scrutiny. As Young noted in conversation with Pite at a public forum that preceded the Vancouver performance of *Betroffenheit* that I saw in February 2016, one mechanism he landed upon for coping with, and gaining a measure of control over, the traumatic loss of his daughter was to write compulsively (Young et al., 2016). Eventually he showed some of these pages to Pite, hoping that she might help him turn them into a stage narrative. At this point, neither collaborator was yet decided on whether that narrative would tilt more toward ECT's world of theatrical expression or Kidd Pivot's primary medium of dance. Nevertheless, Young knew he didn't just want Pite to choreograph the resulting performance; he wanted her to direct it as well. In making this request, Young was trusting Pite to constellate with her artistic intelligence and creative rigour the ideas and concepts and emotions in his writing so that they would become more than the sum of his and Collier's personal tragedy. In this regard, it bears commenting on the title of the work, which comes from Ann Bogart's *And Then, You Act*, and refers to a state of bewildered shock in the wake of a devastating event. Bogart, who discusses the term in the context of the imperative to keep making art post-9/11, claims that this 'stopped' or 'stuck' state exposes the limits of language to make sense of experience (including powerful aesthetic experiences); it is a space of 'profound and palpable silence' where, in Bogart's words, '[a]nything is possible' and 'everything is up for grabs' (2007: 2–3). A space, in other words, of theatrical imagination – one where social reality can be explored in another, more heightened register. And, indeed, it was only after the two artists had begun collaborating that they discovered that the story they were trying to tell was in fact about post-traumatic stress disorder (PTSD) and related issues of addiction (Young et al., 2016).

In *Betroffenheit* these issues are translated, initially, into the hollowed-out world of an empty sound stage that but for the electrical cables retreating like garden snakes before our eyes soon after the curtains part could double for the operations room of a nuclear bunker, or an antiseptic psych ward (the striking set is once again by Pite's partner, Jay Gower Taylor). Our protagonist, Young, cowers in a corner; soon we hear him having a conversation with himself about what he is *not* to do: that he shouldn't respond; that 'a system is in place'; that 'the user only gets used'. Importantly, this conversation alternates as a dialogue between the live instrument of Young's actorly voice and the mediated playback of his recorded voice. If, as Liz Mills has argued, 'the embodied sounding voice [in the theatre] is heard, first and foremost, as a signal of the phenomenological presence of the actor as a person as well as an acoustic image of the subjectivity who chooses to act or perform' (2009: 398), then in this instance the multiplication and diffracted distribution of that voice through additional electronic and digital technologies achieves two distinct, though I would argue not antithetical, goals. First, the mixing of live and recorded utterance offers, through self-consciously performative means, important clues about the apparently split subjectivity of Young's character within the narrative frames of his onstage world, where the choice to listen to or ignore the voices inside his head could have life and death consequences. At the same time, the orchestration of these voices into a kind of musical score invites us to attend to them as acoustically phenomenal in and of themselves, that is, to treat voice in *Betroffenheit*, like the voiceover in *Dark Matters*, first and foremost as sound – and thus, in Mills' words, to attempt a '"reading" [of] the text that is the sound of sound' (2009: 400).

That the sonifying of speech in *Betroffenheit* is expressly material can be seen (and heard) through the steady proliferation of Young's onstage interlocutors, his voice acousmatically distributed across various adjacent objects – including, most compellingly, a HAL-like amplifier whose algorithmically generated responses to Young's questions seem oddly reassuring, even comforting. Eventually, the narrative voice of Young's text gets distributed across other bodies as well, with Jermaine Spivey first showing up in a blue leisure suit, white eye makeup, and a beard snood to take over the amplifier's side of the conversation through the embodied technique of lip-synching, a choreographing of and to the voice that in Pite's hands is as precise and accomplished as the gestural phrasing of the dancer's limbs that accompanies it. As George Home-Cook has recently argued in an analysis of Robert Lepage's epic *Lipsynch*, the 'cut[ting] loose' of the 'phenomenal voice' from 'its corporeal and subjective origins' can, paradoxically, produce more attentive and 'playful' listening-spectating in an audience (2015: 85). For Home-Cook, looking 'always has a role to play in auditory perception', especially in the theatre, where the visual embodiment of sound emphasizes not just its temporal movement, but its physical movement (87, 86). This helps to explain our often viscerally embodied reactions of outrage when a pop star's vocal 'misstep' exposes that she has actually been lip-synching rather than singing live or, conversely, our physical delight at an especially virtuosic performance of mimed vibrato by a drag diva impersonating said pop star. In Pite's hands, the vocal virtuosity of her performers' lip-synching, which is often tied expressly to spectacular displays of dancerly skill (as when Spivey combines James Brown-style back bends with a quintuple pirouette), emphasizes the kinetic properties of sound, that it travels through time and space, and from body to body, actively moving us with its force and energy. In this way, the lip-synching also moves the text of Young's narrative from a singular authorial location in his character's body, apportioning some of its metaphorical and material weight to the other bodies onstage. This becomes especially important in the second half of *Betroffenheit*, when voice is replaced by touch, and the sharing of bodily weight enacts an ethic of collective care in response to an individual trauma.

For the moment, however, Spivey's presence onstage remains disconcerting. He seems to be playing a version of Young's alter ego; his, we might say, is the voice of Young's subconscious, or perhaps more properly, altered consciousness. For it is Spivey's role to lure Young, soon to don a matching blue suit, back to the razzmatazz world of 'showtime', the imagined variety show that is Young's drug of choice and out of

Narrative Pivots: Text and Movement in Crystal Pite's Dance-Theatre

which Pite conjures spectacular tap and salsa sequences. The first features David Raymond leading the rest of the ensemble, with members sporting matching bowler hats, in different variations of classic shuffle ball change footwork, the rhythmic syncopation of the tapping becoming a hypnotizing beat count with which Young, also donning a bowler, falls into lockstep. The second sequence showcases Bryan Arias and Cindy Salgado in a Vegas-style and salsa-tinged magic act that results in Young's character being made to disappear inside a wooden box. When he returns, summoned by Spivey – who now sports a wig and, having taken over as host, trails his own laugh track – it is as a hybrid or partially prosthetic version of himself, Pite's longstanding interest in both the theatricality and physicality of puppetry here manifested in the mini-marionette body that is now attached to Young's neck, and which is manipulated by the other dancers. Thus incongruously paired, Young and Spivey engage in a charming vaudeville-style double act, the patter of their simultaneously live and lip-synched conversation as benignly diverting and seemingly inconsequential as their accompanying soft-shoe routine: Young's character, desperate to be of use again as a guest star in the world of 'showtime', asks for 'an epiphany', to which Spivey, as host, inquires whether he wants 'some perspective with that'.

However, in her public conversation with Young that accompanied the 2016 Vancouver performances of *Betroffenheit*, Pite also commented that it was important for her to make this world of 'showtime' not just a pleasurable and joyful release – for us as much as for Young's character – but also dangerous (Young et al., 2016). To this end, we get Tiffany Tregarthen, who plays a devilish and (quite literally) explosive imp encountered by Young's character. It's not clear whether this creature is a magical being from another dimension or a product of Young's character's imagination; regardless, Young and Tregarthen appear to be simultaneously fascinated and repulsed by each other, and their duet unfolds as at once a solicitous sharing of each other's bodily proximity and weight and a desire to extricate themselves from a potentially threatening grip (see Figure 14.2). Thus, for example, Tregarthen at one point finds herself poised in the air over Young's prone body as she balances her knees on his raised hands and her own arms on his forehead. From this position she then somersaults backwards, while also managing to pull herself and

Figure 14.2 Tiffany Tregarthen and Jonathon Young in *Betroffenheit* (2015)
Photographer: Michael Slobodian. Photograph courtesy of Kidd Pivot.

Young up to sitting position, so that they are both facing each other with legs extended and intertwined. At an open rehearsal of *Betroffenheit* in the summer of 2015 I was able to observe Pite work this particular sequence a number of times with Tregarthen and Young, and the narrative of that experience has necessarily become part of my accumulated postscript of the actual performance. By that I mean that what I remember most about Pite's verbal instructions and responses to the performers were the slight physical adjustments she wished to test out in order to refine the overall timing of the movement (like having Tregarthen grab a bit of Young's shirt or getting Young to help out with momentum by giving Tregarthen a little shove). Young offered his own running commentary as all of this was going on, bringing to the immediate physical tasks he was being asked to execute and modify an actor's character-based 'motivation' for his actions (e.g. 'I have to get this thing off of me'). In other words, mapped onto my post-eventual recollection of the sensory experience of *Betroffenheit*, as *a performance*, is the text of this rehearsal conversation between Pite and Young (and also, it must be said, Tregarthen); much like their archived discussion (on ECT's YouTube channel) of the staging of PTSD to which I have returned in writing about the work, and once again (as with *The You Show*) in the absence of a published artefact of the actual written narrative from the show, these additional scripts have served as the primary – and textually uncanny – means by which I have been able to somatically re-experience the movement.

And so, it is perhaps no coincidence that what has registered most profoundly from *Betroffenheit*'s long and complicated first act is this intensely physical and entangled duet between Tregarthen and Young (who is revealed over the course of the entire piece to be an exemplary mover).[11] Their partnering eventually leads to what, in this 'disordered system' of the stage, is the equivalent of an overdose for Young. It takes all of the combined efforts of the other five performers to revive him for his climactic solo number, a moving lament sung into a microphone proffered by the group that is of course not a solo at all – because his amplified voice, at once within and without his own body, is here physically lifted by a chorus of other bodies, a corps, who in forming their chain of support illustrate through dance the network of sustaining relations in life that lets us know, no matter the claims we make upon them, that there are others who have our back, who will make sure we make it safely back down to the ground. This sequence also marks the return of Pite's choreographic signature: a penchant for tethering her group movement at the wrist. Whereas at times the accordion-like unfurling and contraction of bodily bellows in Pite's dances can seem like an exercise in momentum without direction, here the chains of movement hint both at sequentiality (events unfolding over time) and obligation (how we are fettered together by those events) – as when, for example, the group slumps in succession against the stage right set wall, a momentary, but by no means final, submission to the bewildering and disorienting effects of grief and trauma.

The second act of *Betroffenheit*, which begins after a brief intermission, follows the pattern Pite has established in previous works like *Dark Matters* and *The Tempest Replica*. The ensemble, having traded in their sparkly 'showtime' costumes for standard issue rehearsal sweats, deconstructs much of the action of the previous acts through an almost exclusively movement-based vocabulary. This includes a spectacular off-axis solo for Arias, in which he spins his body around violently, like he is trying to exorcise a demon. Later Arias and Salgado will partner in a ghostly echo of their 'showtime' salsa steps, only this time on their knees and in a desperately vertiginous bid to right themselves and prevent the other from falling over. Young, in his public dialogue with Pite, likened this section to the experience of withdrawal (Young et al., 2016), and Pite supplemented this idea by saying that she was interested in staging various micro-scenes of rescue (a favourite theme of hers).[12] To this end, I was most affected by the duet between Salgado and Tregarthen, who together helped convey a sense of shared pain through a simple bit of gestural unison, moving their hands from knees to hips to elbows to heads through a sequence of facings, but also interrupting the cycle at different moments to place a solicitous hand on the other's body. As compelling is when all five dancers find themselves on their hands and knees, their arms twitching uncontrollably – as if they are being collectively wracked by the DTs, or a horrible night sweat. The movement only stops when first one performer and then the next slides a hand across to the person adjacent them, applying a different kind of physical pressure to still the mental anguish. If one of Pite's greatest concerns was figuring out how to distribute the narrative voice of trauma across the piece's entire ensemble, a consequent result has been to show how the physical symptoms of trauma can likewise spread and be shared across different bodies.

And on this note, after a couple of chimeric glimpses of showtime's lingering traces (a curtain reproduction of the set and the mysterious reappearance of a self-ambulating version of Arias and Salgado's magician's box), the piece concludes with a reprise of Young and Spivey's act one duet. This time, however, it is Young who is mostly supporting Spivey. Having previously shared Young's narrative voice, Spivey now absorbs the material substance of that narrative into his body, his limbs crumpling and collapsing under the heavy burden of its assertive demands. If in dance the body is always the primary means of what André Lepecki has called the 'will to archive' (2010: 29), then in this movement-based replaying of Young's story we are witnessing the temporal transformation of Spivey's past, present and future dancing bodies into a single palimpsestic book of grief. But to echo both the voiceover (which has also returned) and the larger artistic and interpersonal conversation between Young and Pite, we are made to realize that from this text there will issue forth no epiphany. There can only be the slow and painful practice of learning how to re-engage with the world. As Spivey demonstrates for us, in another archival echo of Peter Chu's assisted walk at the end of the first act of *Dark Matters*, this re-engagement starts by standing up on one's own, finding one's legs, putting one of those legs in front of the other, and beginning to move uncertainly into the future – a future that doesn't try to leave behind the past, but that accepts (and not without a measure of comfort) that some felt sense of that past will always remain, will always be present.

The disappearing textual trace that is Spivey's body at the end of *Betroffenheit*, and its remaindering in my own sense-memories of the performance, thus serves as a metonym for how I have been trying to read the feeling incorporation of text into Kidd Pivot's dance-theatre more generally. On the one hand, Pite's use of text functions as a reassuring narrative anchor, helping to plant one cognitive foot firmly in the realm of the referential; at the same time, much of that text is often delivered by sensuous and often deeply kinaesthetic means: via bodies and voices and images moving through space. This suggests that our active response not just to a given work's message but also its (inter)mediality requires some improvisatory flexibility in shifting between what something might mean and how it actually works – including how it works *on* us, subjecting us to *being moved* (physically and affectively) in ways over which we don't always have individual control. In this respect, the text-as-postscript functions as an additional important pivot point. It extends our perspective, as I hope I've suggested, on who (body) or what (text) is possibly remembering a past performance event. But it also extends our perspective – temporally and conceptually – on what remains of that event. As such, the text of this chapter joins the text deployed in Pite's dances, *and* the texts employed to conceive and give shape to those dances (from literary sources to rehearsal studio conversations), in the never fully knowable or explainable matter of how we narrate the experience of movement.

Discussion Questions

1. What is a textscape? What does the essay suggest regarding a textscape's relationship to the history of dance and theatre?
2. How does a textscape influence the audience's reception?

3. Using the description of Pite's work provided by the chapter compare the use of text and movement in *Dark Matters* and *The Tempest Replica*.
4. Are there other contemporary directors or choreographers who are creating a textscape?

Websites

Dark Matters Trailer: https://www.youtube.com/watch?v=VNyLjFiKrfY
The Tempest Replica Trailer: https://www.youtube.com/watch?v=160_fRFWzlU
The You Show Trailer: https://www.youtube.com/watch?v=Z38suCkaISI
Betroffenheit Trailer: https://www.youtube.com/watch?v=57jTy8L4Z-A

Notes

1. An earlier version of this chapter appeared as 'Textual Matters: Making Narrative and Kinesthetic Sense of Crystal Pite's Dance-Theater' in *Dance Research Journal* 46(1), 2014, pp. 61–83.
2. Burt is responding here to the dominant account of Judson Church provided by Sally Banes. Ironically, in *Democracy's Body*, first published in 1983, Banes documents at length the different forms of textual address employed in several of the dances at the first Judson concert in 1962, including the dramatic impact of Yvonne Rainer's penultimate recitation of 'poetic autobiography' in *Ordinary Dance*, and the ways in which this 'heigten[ed] the difficulty of the dancer's action by engaging the memory in simultaneously recalling the text and the complicated movement phrases' (1993: 66, 67). However, in the introduction to the 1987 edition of *Terpsichore in Sneakers*, she associates the 'rekindling of interest in narrative structures', and 'an emphasis on the genre of autobiography', in particular, with a late, 1980s shift – and, clearly to her, betrayal – of the early principles of 'analytic' postmodern dance (Banes, 1987: xxix, xxx).
3. Exemplary in this regard is the work of Jérôme Bel. See Lepecki 2006 45–64; and Dickinson 2014.
4. Here, Schneider is responding to the privileging of live art's ephemerality in much performance studies criticism, with her work serving as a rejoinder especially to the influential theories of Peggy Phelan (1993) and Diana Taylor (2003). Lavery, in his article, notes the overlaps between an earlier formulation of Schneider's argument and his own (2009: 45).

5. Pite uses as her translation of Voltaire's poem the one done by Joseph McCabe (1912), a former English priest who became a committed atheist and rationalist.
6. Perhaps unsurprisingly, Deleuze introduces his concept of the movement-image by referencing the 'action dance' of Fred Astaire and the 'action mime' of Charlie Chaplin; see Deleuze 1986, 6–7.
7. In fact, the company relaunched in the spring of 2014 with a world tour of *The Tempest Replica*. However, not all the original company members returned. And while Pite has committed to remaining in Vancouver to make new work for Kidd Pivot – including, most recently, the award-winning *Betroffenheit* (co-created with Electric Company Theatre, and discussed later in the chapter) – she is candid about the funding challenges she faces as a dance artist in British Columbia; see Smith 2014.
8. In their discussions of mirror neurons, Foster and McConachie both draw from the pioneering research of Vittorio Gallese; see Gallese 2008.
9. This is not the first time Pite, an Anglophone, has used non-English speech in her dance works; at one point in *Lost Action*, Eric Beauchesne addresses the audience in French.
10. On the phatic function in speech, see Malinowski 1923; and Jakobson 1960, 355–6. My thanks to Sima Belmar for reminding me of the phatic possibilities of speech in dance.
11. Following *Betroffenheit*'s London premiere in May 2016, Young was awarded the UK's Critics' Circle National Dance Award for Outstanding Male Performance (Modern).
12. See, for example, her *Ten Duets on a Theme of Rescue*, first performed by Cedar Lake Contemporary Ballet in 2008; and Shaw's remarks (2006: 10), also quoted above, on *Lost Action*.

Works Cited and Resource Material

Agamben, G. (2000) *Means without End: Notes on Politics*. Trans. V. Binetti and C. Casrarino (Minneapolis: University of Minnesota Press).
Ahmed, S. (2004) *The Cultural Politics of Emotion* (New York: Routledge).
Banes, S. ([1983] 1993) *Democracy's Body: Judson Dance Theater, 1962–1964* (Durham, NC: Duke University Press).
———. (1987) *Terpsichore in Sneakers: Post-Modern Dance* (Middletown, CT: Wesleyan University Press).

Barton, B. (2009) Paradox as Process: Intermedial Anxiety and the Betrayals of Intimacy, *Theatre Journal*, 61(4), pp. 575–601.
Bogart, A. (2007) *And Then, You Act: Making Art in an Unpredictable World* (New York: Routledge).
Bogart, A. and T. Landau (2005) *The Viewpoints Book: A Practical Guide to Viewpoints and Composition* (New York: Theatre Communications Group).
Brennan, T. (2004) *The Transmission of Affect* (Ithaca, NY: Cornell University Press).
Burt, R. (2006) *Judson Dance Theatre* (New York: Routledge).
De Certeau, M. (1984) *The Practice of Everyday Life*. Trans. S. Randall (Berkeley: University of California Press).
Deleuze, G. (1986) *Cinema I: The Movement-Image*. Trans. H. Tomlinson and B. Habberjam (Minneapolis: University of Minnesota Press).
Dickinson, P. (2010) *World Stages, Local Audiences: Essays on Performance, Place and Politics* (Manchester: Manchester University Press).
———. (2014) Cédric Andrieux: With Bel, Benjamin, and Brecht in Vancouver, *TDR: The Drama Review*, 58(3), pp. 162–9.
Foster, S. L. (2002) Walking and Other Choreographic Tactics: Danced Inventions of Theatricality and Performativity, *SubStance*, 31(2–3), pp. 125–46.
———. (2011) *Choreographing Empathy: Kinesthesia in Performance* (New York: Routledge).
Forsythe, W. (2003) *Improvisation Technologies* (Karlsruhe, Germany: ZKM).
Gallese, V. (2008) Empathy, Embodied Simulation and the Brain: Commentary on Aragno and Zepf/Hartmann, *Journal of the American Psychoanalytic Association*, 56, pp. 769–81.
Gibson, J. J. ([1966] 1983) *The Senses Considered as Perceptual Systems* (Westport, CN: Greenwood).
Home-Cook, G. (2015) *Theatre and Aural Attention: Stretching Ourselves* (London: Palgrave).
Kidd Pivot (2012) Company, http://kiddpivot.org/company/company, accessed 29 July 2015.
Jakobson, R. (1960) Closing Statement: Linguistics and Poetics, in T. Sebeok (Ed.) *Style in Language* (New York: Wiley) pp. 325–50.
Lavery, C. (2009) Is There a Text in This Performance?, *Performance Research*, 14(91), pp. 37–45.
Lehmann, H. (2006) *Postdramatic Theatre*. Trans. K. Jürs-Munby (New York: Routledge).
Leibniz, G. ([1709] 1952) *Theodicy*. Ed. A. Farrer. Trans. E. M. Huggard (New Haven: Yale University Press).

Lepage, R. and C. Pite (2012) Creative Collaborations: Lepage & Pite in Conversation, Fei and Milton Wong Experimental Theatre, SFU Woodward's, Vancouver: 8 November.

Lepecki, A. (2006) *Exhausting Dance: Performance and the Politics of Movement* (New York: Routledge).

———. (2010) The Body as Archive: Will to Re-Enact and the Afterlives of Dances, *Dance Research Journal*, 42(2), pp. 28–48.

McConachie, B. (2008) *Engaging Audiences: A Cognitive Approach to Spectating in the Theatre* (Basingstoke: Palgrave Macmillan).

Mackrell, J. (2009) Crystal Pite's Kidd Pivot, *The Guardian* 18 September, https://www.theguardian.com/stage/2009/sep/18/crystal-pite-kidd-pivot-review, accessed 2 March 2010.

Malinowski, B. (1923) The Problem of Meaning in Primitive Languages, in C. K. Ogden and I. A. Richards (Eds) *The Meaning of Meaning* (London: Routledge) pp. 146–52.

Mills, L. (2009) When Voice is Image, *Modern Drama*, 52(4), pp. 389–404.

Murphy, M. (2015) Fleshing Out: Physical Theatre, Postmodern Dance, and Som[e]agency, in N. George-Graves (Ed.) *The Oxford Handbook of Dance and Theatre* (New York: Oxford University Press) pp. 125–47.

Murray, S. and J. Keefe (Eds) (2007) *Physical Theatres: A Critical Introduction* (London: Routledge).

Overlie, M. (2006) The Six Viewpoints, in A. Bartow (Ed.) *Training the American Actor* (New York: Theatre Communications Group) pp. 187–222.

Pavis. P. (2003) *Analyzing Performance: Theatre, Dance, and Film*. Trans. D. Williams (Ann Arbor: University of Michigan Press).

Pepper, K. (2012) Stories with Legs, *The Walrus*, http://thewalrus.ca/stories-with-legs/, accessed 4 January 2013.

Phelan, P. (1993) *Unmarked: The Politics of Performance* (New York: Routledge).

Pite, C. (2010) Artist's Talk, *Mixed Repertoire*, Shadbolt Centre for the Arts, Burnaby, British Columbia: 9 October.

———. (2011) Artist's Talk, *The You Show*, The Vancouver East Cultural Centre, Vancouver, British Columbia: 11 May.

———. (2012a) Artist's Talk, *The Tempest Replica*, Vancouver Playhouse, Vancouver, British Columbia: 10 November.

———. (2012b) The Dance Enthusiast Asks: Crystal Pite. Interview with Christine Jowers, *The Dance Enthusiast*, http://www.dance-enthusiast.com/features/view/The-Dance-Enthusiast-Asks-Crystal-Pite-2012-03-17/, accessed 4 July 2018.

Pope, A. ([1733–4] 2009) An Essay on Man, in P. Rogers (Ed.) *The Major Works* (Oxford: Oxford University Press) pp. 270–308.

Schneider, R. (2011) *Performing Remains: Art and War in Times of Theatrical Reenactment* (New York: Routledge).
Shakespeare, W. ([1611] 1997) *The Tempest*, in S. Greenblatt, W. Cohen, S. Gossett, J. E. Howard, et al. (Eds) *The Norton Shakespeare* (New York: Norton) pp. 3047–107.
Shanley, J. P. (2005) *Doubt: A Parable* (New York: Dramatists Play Service).
Shaw, N. (2006) *Lost and Found: Kidd Pivot, Dance Documenta*, No. 2. (Vancouver: Eponymous Productions and Arts Society).
Sklar, D. (2007) Unearthing Kinesthesia: Groping among Cross-cultural Models of the Senses in Performance, in S. Banes and A. Lepecki (Eds) *The Senses in Performance* (New York: Routledge) pp. 38–46.
Smith, J. (2010) Crystal Pite Plays the Puppetmaster in Dark Matters, *The Georgia Straight*, 18 February, http://www.straight.com/article-290358/vancouver/pite-plays-Puppetmaster, accessed 11 September 2011.
_____. (2014) After Break, Pite Is Back—Big Time, *The Georgia Straight*, 26 February, http://www.straight.com/arts/593806/after-break-crystal-pite-back-big-time, accessed 10 July 2015.
Stuart, M. and Damaged Goods (2010) *Are We Here Yet?* J. Peeters (Ed.) (Dijon: Presses du reel).
Taylor, D. (2003) *The Archive and the Repertoire: Performing Cultural Memory in the Americas* (Durham, NC: Duke University Press).
Voltaire ([1755] 1912) Poem on the Lisbon Disaster; Or an Examination of the Axiom 'All is Well, in *Toleration and Other Essays*. Trans. J. McCabe (New York: G.P. Putnam and Sons) pp. 255–63.
_____. ([1756] 2000) Preface to the Poem on the Lisbon Disaster, in D. Wootton (Ed.) *Candide and Related Texts* (Indianapolis: Hackett Publishing) pp. 95–8.
Welton, M. (2007) Seeing Nothing: Now Hear This…, in S. Banes and A. Lepecki (Eds) *The Senses in Performance* (New York: Routledge) pp. 146–55.
_____. (2012) *Feeling Theatre* (Basingstoke: Palgrave Macmillan).
Young, J., C. Pite and D. McIntosh (2016) Shock and Awe: PTSD in Performance. A Free Public Forum Exploring the Themes of Electric Company Theatre and Kidd Pivot's Production of *Betroffenheit*. Moderated by Sarah Crompton. Vancouver Playhouse, Vancouver, British Columbia: 27 February, https://www.youtube.com/watch?v=rfJYmH82XLI, accessed 5 January 2017.

15

Future Narratives
Community, Technology and Globalization

Barbara Sellers-Young and Jade Rosina McCutcheon

Cultural theorist Agustin Fuentes examines the evolution of humans over the centuries as a revelation of the imagination honed by the muscle of creativity. He suggests that the 'art we engage with is also information we generate, use, and revise' (2017: 222) to continually evolve the human story. The chapters in this volume have provided examples of how dance and theatre in the last century have embraced this narrative of creativity. Performances of cultural identity have shared the imaginative space with performances that integrate a variety of popular forms. Directors and choreographers have pushed the boundaries of a stage's potential. Each performance form has provided a different integration of text, body, stage, technology and audience to reveal the role of ritual, the impact of ethnicity and gender, the influence of technology in the creation of a stage environment, the participation of the audience via social media, and the provocative and yet synthesizing role of popular culture. In this final chapter, we discuss the ongoing evolution of narrative in dance and theatre via three influences – community, technology and globalization – that through their constant interaction we theorize will impact the future construction of performance.

Community

In 2011, the James Irvine Foundation carried out extensive research on the position of the performing arts and published a report titled, *Getting in on the Act*. While acknowledging the history of participatory performance in ritual and community celebrations around the world, the report documents a new direction in the contemporary arts community influenced by 'the pervasiveness of social media, the proliferation of digital content and rising expectations for self-guided, on-demand, customized experiences that have all contributed to a cultural environment primed for active arts practice' (2011: 4). Influenced by new cultural affinity communities which intersect between face-to-face and social media, this shift in cultural production is a movement away from 'sit-back-and-be-told culture to a making-and-doing-culture' (4). The report acknowledges this new direction challenges the traditional cultural viewpoint of the arts and artists as a special class separate from the creative potential of individuals. The report suggests that the shift calls for a new 'equilibrium in the arts ecology and a new generation of arts leaders ready to accept, integrate and celebrate all forms of cultural practice' (4).

Principally, the report documents the far-reaching extension of the twentieth-century political engagement in which many visual and performing artists across the globe became committed to creating art that represents the identity and expresses the concerns of a community. In some cases, for example, the New Zealand Māori devised *Maranga Mai*, the performances were at the intersection of ritual and activist styles of performance. These communal artistic processes have come to act as a catalyst to create a dialogic bridge between members of the community – artists and non-artists – and the related social, cultural, political and/or economic issue. In each instance, the goal is to find a means to express in visual and performance forms the issue and thus create a dialogue between a micro-community and the larger community in which it exists.

Getting in on the Act provides three articulations of participation – crowd sourcing, co-creation and audience participation – that impact a performance. Each repositions the role of the audience and incorporates them into the creation of the narrative. Many of these performances take place through the facility of the internet. Crowd sourcing can range from talkback sessions at the end of a performance, artistic theatre and dance contests, and online events that attract audience from around the world. One popular crowd sourcing event that combined individual communities from around the world and the internet is a YouTube video in which people from twenty-three cities and seventeen countries danced to Pharrell Williams' song 'Happy'.[1] Another example is *So You Think You Can Dance*. The production offers projected images of the classical stage body of ballet and modern alongside versions of popular dance forms. The final winner is the result of the votes cast by the viewing television audience in their judgement of which dancer creatively embodies more than one dance form.

Across the globe one of the major trends in theatre is immersive performances in which audience members interact with the actors as they evolve the narrative. This trend is at the intersection of performance styles of the 1960s and 1970s with such groups as the Living Theatre and an extension of social media culture. Sara Krulwich of the *New York Times* writes of the distinct diversity in the styles of immersive theatre. During the performance of *Then She Fell* she was asked to take dictation from an actor playing Lewis Carroll. The *Goldberg Variations* organized by performance artist Marina Abramovic required the audience to 'wear noise-canceling headphones and recline for thirty minutes in silence until the pianist Igor Levit began to play'.[2] London's Punchdrunk's immersive theatre company brought their commentary on *Macbeth*, *Sleep No More*, to the six floors and hundred rooms of New York's McKittrick Hotel. Audience members were asked to put on white ghost masks and meander from room to room in which there were wordless dance and musical tableaux. With names such as *Dream Think Speak* (London, Japan, South Korea, Moscow, Australia, Holland), *Fruit for the Apocalypse* (London), *Speak Easy and Third Rail Projects* (New York), *Bricolage* (Pittsburgh) and *We Players* (San Francisco), immersive theatre companies are establishing an experience that is the interactive equivalent to the environmental unpredictability of those who participate in reality television programmes. We would suggest that in fact the increased interest in immersive theatre is because it is a variation of the narrative structure of reality television and thus both local and exotic. It is local as audiences consume reality television in their living rooms and participate in immersive theatre at local venues. Yet, it is exotic as the participation in the immersive event is outside daily experience.

One example of dance's version of immersive performance is Bal Moderne.[3] Established in 1993 by Michel Reilhac in Paris, the events have occurred in spaces from circus tents, to churches and city centres. People of diverse backgrounds, ages and movement experience come together to learn and perform three short dances created by professional choreographers. The atmosphere is one of playful enthusiasm in which the shared experience of the embodiment of dance and music becomes central. In its format, Bal Moderne revives the community-style dances associated with seasonal celebrations but without a specific cultural or ethnic identity. As such it participates in a process of urbanization and globalization where instead of performing at an event linked to an identity of a historic past, dancers are participating in an event that incorporates any member of the community who wants to dance.

Over the last thirty years dance and theatre companies have responded to this increased desire for participation with such audience engagement events as pre-performance lectures, opportunities for conversations with the artists following the performance, backstage tours, online blogs and opportunities to travel with the artistic staff to tour major arts festivals. Audience interaction has also been part of staged performances from direct to indirect action with the performers onstage. The 2008 week-long performance of the Merce Cunningham Dance Company at the Robert and Margrit Mondavi Center for the Performing Arts at UC Davis provides a set of examples. The initial concert included the Kronos Quartet stationed throughout the audience playing John Cage's *Thirty Pieces for String Quartet* while the dancers performed onstage. The performance of *Split Sides* included VIP members of the audience rolling the dice to determine order of music, dance sequence, costume colour and lighting cues. At the beginning of *eyeSpace* the audience, who had been given iPods as they came into the theatre, were told to set them to shuffle. Each audience member had the choice of listening to the music of the onstage orchestra or the music on their iPod; and they could opt to listen to either at different moments.

Other audience-based experiences are a part of game culture. Jonathan Osborn in Chapter 9 analyses the relationship between the online World of Warcraft, popular music culture and the yearly celebration of online games at BlizzCon[4] to consider the intersections between the imagination and related avatars of the game community, with the popular imagination of the musical stage and how individuals imagine themselves as an extension of this blend. As Osborn notes, 'Unlike the unalterable "genetic" archive of dances programmed into WOW, the players demonstrate, through their performances, a desire to disrupt rigid categories firmly entrenched within the game's matrix and embody an open and fluid poise towards personal form, identity, and agency' (161).

This desire of the participants at BlizzCon is not limited to those who participate in the WOW community. Online gaming has become a huge business in the last two decades. For example in 2016, Sony Computer Entertainment earned 'a gaming revenue of 7.8 billion U.S. dollars, second-only to Tencent's 10.2 billion gaming revenue, and out-earning Microsoft by 1.3 billion and Nintendo by six billion U.S. dollars that year'.[5] The emergence of eSports (competitive video gaming) in 2014 has provided an international forum for gaming players and in 2016 offered a total prize money of over $95 million. The game industry is constantly offering new dance opportunities via online platforms or play stations. Game audiences' expectations of entertainment incorporate the social immersive virtual environment of the digital world.

Created in 1996, Philadelphia's New Paradise Laboratories[6] is Whit MacLaughlin's response to the discovery that the young people he was working with were all on Facebook, constantly texting and playing video games. Their narrative imagination was a complex interweaving of the possibilities of Facebook, Twitter, Instagram, gaming and face-to-face interactions. To facilitate their interests, New Paradise Laboratories created an internet site called Frame to engage an interventionist imagination that 'encourages artistic complexity: it allows a beautiful image to be juxtaposed with a grotesque one. A ridiculous idea to coexist with a profound one'.[7] Thus, this internet site encourages the participant to conceive of the artistic imagination as not linear but revealed in the juxtapositions of moving and still images, music and sound.

There are also numerous examples of co-created dance and theatre pieces in which the values and goals of a community of individuals define the performance. In *Embodied Consciousness: Performance Technologies,*

Jade Rosina McCutcheon in 'The Performance Mirror: Self, Consciousness and Verbatim Theatre' describes the verbatim theatre process in which an actor creates a role based on intensive conversations with a member of the community (2013). 'Verbatim theatre is created literally from the words of interviews with people'; as such, the 'language is all important as it is seen to represent the identity of the person, the truth of their essence and therefore not to be tampered with' (148). Similar interview processes were used by Anna Deavere Smith to evolve the characters for her plays *Fires in the Mirror* (1992) and *Twilight: Los Angeles* (1994). Los Angeles' Cornerstone Theater Company has interviewed members of the African and Latino American as well as faith-based and day labourer communities to create cycles of plays that address the issues faced by each group. In some performances, such as by Oregon's Sanctuary Stage, the members of the community are not only interviewed but also become members of the ensemble. The category of co-creation also includes the interactive style of the Moth described by Judy Halebsky in Chapter 8. It is an example of a community-based event in which people with various levels of expertise in performance share a story of their life. In each case the community audience becomes a crucial ingredient in the presentation's reception. For this reason, the audience is often engaged in a talkback session following the performance.

Julie-Anne Long's discussion in Chapter 11 of *Nothing to Lose* on the topic of body image is a community ensemble piece guided by choreographer Kate Champion. The dancers in this piece contributed to the movement vocabulary and choreographic intent through a series of improvisations. Co-creation is the fundamental approach of many dance and theatre companies in which improvisation is the basis for performance. Contact improvisation as described by Cynthia Novack in *Sharing the Dance* (1990) is an interaction based on moment-to-moment mutual physical and emotional support. As there is no defined choreographic scenario, the narrative of the dance relies on the deep level of cooperation and trust between the dancers who belong to a community of contact improvisation practitioners. Comparable in the theatre community would be the many improvisational comedy theatres such as The Second City in which the performers create the narrative in real time without a reliance on a written script.

As these examples demonstrate, community is being redefined by audience members who anticipate a level of participation in the creation of a performance narrative. In relationship to contemporary dance and theatre, community is not consistently associated with race, ethnic identity or gender. Community may be an affinity group that is interested in a physical activity such as contact improvisation or a participant in a computer game. Community may be revealed through online sharing of performance as the Moth phenomena demonstrates or as stories on social media in which your Facebook or Instagram community relies on digital communication. There is a global community that attends to digital versions of noted theatre and dance companies at the local cinema as well as the technologically savvy affinity group that creates narrative on New Paradise Laboratories' Frame site. A community can evolve from a shared experience of an immersive performance and dissolve into the urban environment following it. Yet, there are communities that are co-created between artists and non-artists that reveal narrative connections of which the projects of Kate Champion, Cornerstone and Sanctuary Theatres provide examples. This is a trend in a redefinition of community that will continue into the future.

Technology

Increasingly, traditional theatre and dance companies have realized they needed to find a way to participate in the revision of the imaginary created by the possibilities of digital technology. In some instances, such as Crystal Pite's Vancouver-based company discussed by Peter Dickinson in Chapter 14, this has been in the inclusion of a narrative relationship between the moving body and the projected image. There are companies such as New Paradise Laboratories in which the diverse possibilities of digital technology to create and share images beyond the boundaries of geography is the central aspect of the narrative. Within the international dance community, there has also been an investigation of a visual language of dance onscreen through yearly festivals such as Los Angeles-based Dance Camera West,[8] which seeks to challenge our conception of dance as a primarily ephemeral form that can only be appreciated in the immediacy of a live performance. Dance and film festivals and this new conception of dance's potential for imagistic narrative have become so popular that there are festivals held around the globe. In general, traditional opera, ballet and theatre have faced this challenge through digital creation of staged performances with such programmes as Shakespeare's Globe on Stage that allow audiences to attend at the local cinema or through sites such as Digital Theatre.[9] Based in the United Kingdom, the Digital Theatre site operates like Netflix and provides an opportunity for a monthly fee to see performances of major British opera, theatre and dance companies.

An alternative to previously described approaches to technology is the approach of The Builders Association. Formed in 1994, the company devises a narrative from an interactive blend of media to create stories in which the technology itself is a character. As Jackson and Weems point out, The Builders Association productions 'adapt and rework textual materials, both fiction and nonfiction stories, to reflect on the impact of new media in contemporary culture' (2015: 3). The narrative through line of their productions is the impact of media on our daily lives. For example, they have examined the role of information media in *Jet Lag*, in which data maintained on each individual is revealed as the person goes through an airport passport control. Other productions have highlighted 'global out sourcing (*Alladeen*), dataveillance (*Super Vision*), and the struggle to remain connected in a digital world (*Continuous City*)' (3).

The Builders Association's productions provide an opportunity to examine how the media impacts our personal narrative. The company's dramatic contemplation of our mediatized world takes place beside the narratives being shared via performances on YouTube, personal stories on Instagram or on blogs, the ongoing evolution of video games in which participants use prompts to create characters and individualized stories. People are also seeking new methods of storytelling via sites such as the New Paradise Laboratories' Frame site. Ultimately, there is a convergence between the daily lives and mass communication that counters previous conceptions of the relationship between text, body, technology, stage and audience. Technology is not limited to the scenic elements of a stage but enables (as in internet games) or is a character (The Builders Association's productions) an ongoing evolution of a narrative in which the audience is not necessarily immediate but part of an internet community. In some instances, the text is a co-creation of members of the community (Frame site) or is shared via the internet outside the cultural boundaries of its geographic community (YouTube) performances. Within the narrative discourses of the media, the body is a fluid imagistic site in which people create unique individual meanings through projected images or through the character of an avatar.

Globalization

Following World War II, there was an explosion of international arts festivals around the globe beginning with the Edinburgh Festival and the Festival d'Avignon in1947, and including festivals in Athens and Epidaurus 1955, Adelaide 1960, Hong Kong 1973, Spoleto Festival, Charleston, 1977, Singapore 1982, Luninato, Toronto, 2006 and New Delhi 2007 to name a few. These festivals integrate the productions of directors and choreographers with international reputations with local artists. Peter Brook, Jerzy Grotowski, Tadashi Suzuki, Anne Bogart, Robert Wilson, Ong Keng Seng, Ariane Mnouchkine, Crystal Pite, Mikhail Baryshnikov, Mark Morris, Laurie Anderson, Akram Khan and many dance and theatre artists perform very specific integrations of text, body and technology on primarily proscenium-style stages with the clear delineation between performance and audience. Yet, the festivals have provided an intercultural experience for artists and audiences as a theatre production from Singapore appears alongside a dance performance from Europe.

At the same time, some festivals such as the Edinburgh Festival have an associated fringe festival that encourages a more experimental and often interactive relationship between audience and performer. Newer festivals such as Toronto's Luminato Festival have integrated elements of both. In 2016, Luminato turned an old industrial building near downtown Toronto into what they referred to as the Hearn Generating Station, a site larger than the coliseum in Rome. The site integrated classical and popular forms to break down the arbitrary barriers that exist between styles of performance and provide an opportunity for participants to create a personal narrative of a Luminato experience. The Luminato publication suggests that new creative possibilities will evolve when, 'We can show everything under one roof, from high to low, pop to serious, underground to established, old to new, left to right'.[10]

This attitude towards the potential of the arts in a global context that increasingly encourages knowledge mobilization and innovation is not limited to Toronto. Economist Richard Florida (2002) has popularized the concept of the creative class, a group of curious and innovative individuals across the spectrum of engineers, scientists and artists 'whose economic function is to create new ideas, new technology and/or creative content' (Florida, 2002: 8). Florida argues that the economy of the future relies on the convergence of the creative ethos of the artist with the pioneering curiosity of the entrepreneur. Or as it is phrased in *Getting in on the Act*:

> This phenomenon is not limited to culture, but part of a larger 'participation economy' in which social connection eclipses consumption. As artists collaborate, sample, remix and repurpose, they obscure the line between creator and observer and toy with fundamental presumptions of originality and authenticity that traditionally define artistic excellence. In recent years, researchers have brought to light the vitality of cultural activity occurring outside of the nonprofit sector in more informal or community-based settings.
>
> (2011: 11)

Stimulated by the growth and ultimately the impact of technology on our economy, there is a desire for towns and cities to include the arts as a component of the innovative environment that encourages the creation of new modes of living in a media-dominated world.

The Future

In his 2017 volume titled *The Future*, Nick Montfort argues the future reveals itself through the intersections of what Richard Florida refers to as the creative class. According to Montfort one cannot predict the future but one can suggest certain trends based on discourse of the present.

With reference to theatre, performance and dance, it is clear that the potential of technology, specifically social media, has opened a new dialogue – between artists and non-artists, communities of difference, across intercultural boundaries – to encourage an inclusion of what in the past would be considered audience but now could be defined as co-creators of the narrative. This is a direction to personalize their artistic voice that we believe will continue as a trend, and performers, dance and theatre companies will, as discussed in this chapter, continue to find ways to adapt to the pressures.

Discussion Questions

1. You have been given an unlimited budget to create a theatre and/or dance production. What would be the subject of your production? Would you be trying to entertain people or to advocate for a particular point of view?
2. How would you incorporate text, body, technology and the stage? Is there a specific style of text or physical technique you would rely on?
3. What memories of the performance would you want the audience to have?

Websites

Bal Moderne: http://www.balmoderne.be/home
Frame Manifesto: http://www.newparadiselaboratories.org/what-is-this/frame-manifesto
Digital Theatre: https://www.digitaltheatre.com/
Dance Camera West: http://www.dancecamerawest.org/

Notes

1. Pharrell Williams' song 'Happy', https://www.youtube.com/watch?v=2MDReKsP3sQ, accessed 15 March 2018.
2. Sara Krulwich, 'Starring Me! A Surreal Dive Into Immersive Theater', https://www.nytimes.com/2016/01/08/theater/starring-me-a-surreal-dive-into-immersive-theater.html, accessed 15 March 2018.

3. Bal Moderne, http://www.balmoderne.be/home, accessed 16 March 2018.
4. BlizzCon, https://blizzcon.com/en-us/, accessed 06 July 2018.
5. Gaming statistics online, https://www.statista.com/topics/1680/gaming/, accessed 28 January 2018.
6. New Paradise Laboratories, http://www.newparadiselaboratories.org/, accessed 10 March 2018.
7. Frame Manifesto, http://www.newparadiselaboratories.org/what-is-this/frame-manifesto, accessed 14 March 2018.
8. Dance Camera West, http://www.dancecamerawest.org/, accessed 18 March 2018.
9. Digital Theatre, https://www.digitaltheatre.com/, accessed 8 March 2018.
10. Luminato Magazine, https://issuu.com/luminato/docs/luminato-mag-for-website-apr22, accessed 17 March 2018.

Works Cited and Resource Material

Brook, P. (1968) *The Empty Space* (London: Touchstone).
Florida, R. (2002) *Rise of the Creative Class* (New York: Basics Books).
Fuentes, A. (2017) *The Creative Spark: How Imagination Made Humans Exceptional* (New York: Random House).
Gilbride, S., A. S. Brown and J. L. Novack-Leonard (2011) *Getting in on the Act* (California: James Irvine Foundation).
Jackson, S. and M. Weems (2015) *The Builders Association: Performance and Media in Contemporary Theater* (Cambridge, MA: MIT Press).
Krulwich, S. (2016) Starring Me! A Surreal Dive Into Immersive Theater, *New York Times*, https://www.nytimes.com/2016/01/08/theater/starring-me-a-surreal-dive-into-immersive-theater.html, accessed 15 March 2018.
McCutcheon, J. R. (2013) The Performance Mirror: Self, Consciousness and Verbatim Theatre, in J. R. McCutcheon and B. Sellers-Young (Eds) *Embodied Consciousness: Technologies of Performance* (Basingstoke: Palgrave Macmillan) pp. 145–58.
Montfort, N. (2017) *The Future* (Cambridge, MA: MIT Press).
Novack, C. J. (1990) *Sharing the Dance: Contact Improvisation and American Culture* (Madison, WI: University of Wisconsin Press).
Radbourne, J., H. Glow and K. Johanson (2013) *The Audience Experience: A Critical Analysis of Audiences in the Performing Arts* (London: Intellect Press).

Index

Page numbers in *italics* indicate illustrations, **bold** refers to tables

A
African dance/theatre   3–4
agit pop theatre   44
Ahmed, Sara   260
Akerman, Chantal   226
Albee, Edward   13
Alexander, Frederick Matthias   4
Archaos   112
Ardjo, Irawati Durban   61
artificial laughter   211
Asma, Stephen   2
Astaire, Fred   98
Auslander, Philip   11
Australian theatre, revolutionary
    artists
  Bangarra Dance Theatre   200–1,
    203n8
  Kai Tai Chan's artistic vision
    187, 188–9
  Kai Tai Chan's *People Like
    Us*   190–4, 200
  Kate Campion's artistic
    vision   187, 194–5
  Kate Champion's *Nothing to
    Lose*   195–200, *197*
  Shaun Parker & Company   200
Azande tribe
  cultural identity and history   23
  women's Islamic aesthetics
    30–1
  Yambio *zar* ritual and
    participants   24–9, *27*

B
Bal Moderne   286
Balanchine, George   100
ballet
  Bausch's non-traditional
    approach   226
  intercultural developments   4–5
  musical theatre productions   95,
    100–1
Ballinger, Rucina   66
ballroom dancing   95–6, 105
Balme, Christopher   44, 46
Banes, Sally   278n2

295

Bangarra Dance Theatre 6, 200–1, 203n8
Barr, Margaret 188, 203n5
Bausch, Pina
  audience engagement 229–31
  Café Müller, childhood encounters 234–5
  dancer/audience contributions 226–7
  gender, sexuality and power themes 7, 227, 231–2, *232*, 236–7
  Kontakthof, gender and identity 228–30, 231
  Kontakthof, gendered behaviour, reactions to 231–3, *232*
  non-traditional ballet 226
Bennett, Michael 103
Berkeley, Busby 99
Betroffenheit (Pite) 269–77, *274*
Bharucha, Rustom 6
Black Crook, The 91–2, *93*, 94
Blankenbuehler, Andy 98–9, 103, 107
Boal, Augusto 4
Boddy, Janice 22–3, 29–30
Bogart, Anne
  Ellen Lauren appraisal 167
  inspirations and creative pieces 177, 270–1
  Room with Ellen Lauren 178–81
  Saratoga International Theatre Institute (SITI) 4, 168–9
Brecht, Bertolt 4
Brennan, Teresa 244
Brook, Peter 5, 13
Builders Association, The 290
Burke, Kenneth 21
burlesque 95
Burns, Catherine 135–6, 145

Burt, Ramsay 243, 278n2
Butler, Judith 227, 228, 236

C

Caballero, Eugenio 118
Cambodian dance drama 53, 54–5
Campbell, Sue 141
Carpentier, Simon 119
Carson, Jo 1
Castle, Irene 95
Castle, Vernon 95
Certeau, Michel de 254, 255
Champagne, Dominique 116–17
Champion, Gower 103
Champion, Kate
  early career 194
  Force Majeure 194
  Nothing to Lose, bodily form revisited 195–7, *197*
  Nothing to Lose, reactionary and emotional 197–200
  real-world issues and audience connection 188, 194–5, 200, 202n3, 288
Chan, Kai Tai
  audience centred vision 187, 188
  One Extra's cultural and artistic identity 188, 188–9, 202n2
  People Like Us, intersecting theatrical narrative 190–4, 200
Chaves, Margarita 81–2
Chekhov, Michael 4, 13
Chorus Line, A (musical) 103–4
Cilento, Wayne 98
Circus Oz 112
Cirque du Soleil
  branding, entrepreneurial narrative of 'experience' 121–4

clowns' functional roles   117
commercial success   111–12
founding narrative   124–5
Guy Laliberté, innovation through experience   111–12, 124, 125–7
'imagi-nation', staged worlds and settings   118–21
'innocent' quester   116
Kà, classic quest tale   114–15, 116, 119–21
Luzia, Mexico's culture explored   117, 118–19
'man/woman of the people' quester   115–16
narrative of the quest   113–15, 127
'new circus' initiatives   112
O, water themed show   116, 119–20
physical narrative of 'character bodies'   113
quester or 'audience avatar' forms   115–17
'traveller' quester   117
classical dance drama, Southeast Asia
all-female troupes, palace/aristocratic genres   54–6
all-male troupes, masculine genres   53–4, 55, 56–7, 64
aristocratic actors and genre traditions   56–7, 64–5
calonarang narrative, modern interpretations   65–7
demonic females, male actor roles   62–3, 65, 68n6
female to male gender confusion   60–1
females as refined males   55, 56
'metrosexual' roles   56, 68n5
refined (*lenyepan*) female roles   58–9, 64–5
semi-refined (*ladak*) female roles   59–62, 64
traditional, contemporary styles and gender   64–5
Climenhaga, Royd   226–7, 229
Cole, Jack   98, 101
community participation
Champion's *Nothing to Lose*   195–7, 288
co-creative projects   288–9
crowd sourcing   285
game culture attractions   153–4, 287–8
immersive theatre   285–6
The Moth events   134–6, 144–5
public involvement trends   284–9
community social drama   21–2
Connolly, Bobby   100
Constantinides, Pamela   22–3, 29–30
Costa, David   92, *93*
Croce, Arlene   234
crowd sourcing   285
cultural identity and ethnicity
Bangarra Dance Theatre   6, 200–1, 203n8
classical dance drama, Southeast Asia   53–67
Maranga Mai, Māori rights play   37–49
mestizaje and indigenous identity   73–85, *80*
personal narrative, shaping of   10
political narratives   9–10
ritual to secular performance   22
zar ritual, social drama enactment   24–32
Cunningham, Merce   12

D

Dance Camera West   289–90
dance in the Broadway musical
   ballet performances   95, 100–1
   ballroom dancing   95–6, 105
   The Black Crook, pioneering
      production   91–2, *93*, 94
   burlesque, vaudeville and
      minstrelsy   94–5, 96
   A Chorus Line   103
   dance directors to
      choreographers   99–101
   director/choreographer's
      innovative
      productions   101–5
   hip-hop   98–9, 107
   jazz dance   98
   Oklahoma! integration   101
   popular culture, influence on and
      by   105–7
   Shuffle Along, tap
      showcase   96–7, *97*
   tap dancing   96–8, *97*
   triple threat performers   103–4
   West Side Story's
      innovations   102, 106
dance theatre
   evolvement of hybrid
      genres   242–3
   Pina Bausch's influence   225–7, 243
   spectator, social form of self-
      reproduction   236, 244–5
   text (speech), value in
      performance   243–6
   see also Bausch, Pina; Pite,
      Crystal
Dark Matter (Pite)   248–55
de Lauretis, Theresa   1, 236

Deleuze, Gilles   259, 279n6
DeMille, Agnes   101
Dickey, Adelaide   95
digital technology
   Cirque du Soleil, interactive
      apps   122–3
   New Paradise Laboratories   287, 289
   performance innovations   288–91
   Tempest Replica, use of projected
      imagery   257–9, 261
   see also World of Warcraft (WOW)
Digital Theatre   290
direct theatre   40
Dirty Cochinas of the AMERICAS
   (Pilar)   78–81, *80*
Djelantik, Bulantrisna   66, 67
Dodds, Sherril   105–6
Dragone, Franco   115
dramaturgy, concept of
Drinkwater, Kelli Jean   195, 198
Duncan, Isadora   12

E

experiential marketing   123–4

F

Feldenkrais, Moshe   4
Finzi Pasca, Daniele   117, 118–19
Fisher, Mark   120
Florida, Richard   292
Fosse, Bob   103, 104, 106
Foster, Susan Leigh   244
Fricker, Karen   113, 114–15, 119, 120
Fuentes, Agustin   283
Funny Sketches of a Formidable Life
   (Théâtre de la Jacquerie)
   collective influences and
      awareness   208–10, *209*

comedic form and embodied
  improvisation   210–13
embodied epistemology   218–19
Grey People, reinvented
  characterization   214–16
Kafka's *The Castle*,
  inspiration   206, 207
socio-economic inequality
  themes   205–8
space and language awareness   217

game culture
  New Paradise Laboratories   287, 289
  World of Warcraft
    (WOW)   149–62, **157**
Garcia, Rene   83
Geertz, Clifford   57
gender and identity
  categorization   227
  classical dance drama, Southeast
    Asia   53–67
  expected behaviour   227–8, 236
  influential imagery   228
  Kontakthof, Pina Bausch's
    exploration   228–33, *232*
  spectator, social form of self-
    reproduction   230–1, 236
Getting in on the Act report   284–5, 292
Gilbert, Helen   49
globalization of the arts   291–2
Glover, Savion   98
Goffman, Erving   21
Gopnik, Adam   144
Graham, Martha   12, 159, 226
Graver, David   113
Green, George Dawes   134, 139

Grosz, Elisabeth   230
Guibert, Jean   121

Hammerstein, Oscar, II   91, 101
Harris, Aroha   43–4
Harvie, Jennifer   118
He Taua   42
Heilpern, John   5
Hijikata, Tatsumi   5
Hill, Constance   98
Hill, Errol   98
hip-hop   98–9, 107
Home-Cook-George   272
Humphrey, Doris   12
Hurley, Erin   118, 119

immersive theatre   285–6
Indonesian dance drama
  all-female genres   54, 55
  all-male genres   53
  calonarang, men as female
    demon   62–3, 64
  calonarang narrative, modern
    interpretations   65–7
  ladak women   60–2
  Panji stories and gender
    confusion   60–1
  sexual divisions in
    performance   56–7
  trance dancer, bodily form and
    performance   64–5
international arts festivals   291–2
Irwin, Robert   114, 116

Jackson, Michael   105–6
James Irvine Foundation   284

jazz dance 98
Johnson, Mark 6–7
Jones, Norman 38–9
Judson Church Theater 243, 278n2

K

Kelly, Gene 98, 106
Kislan, Richard 94, 95, 96–8, 99–100, 101–3
Knowles, Beyoncé 106
Kontakthof (Bausch) 231–3, *232*
Krulwich, Sara 285

L

Laird, Paul 102
Lakoff, George 6–7
Laliberté, Guy 111–12, 124, 125–7
Lamarre, Daniel 123, 124
Langellier, Kristin M. 10
Langer, Jessica 155, 158
Lauren, Ellen
 biography 170–1
 characterization skills 184–5
 Chess Match No.5, play development 181–2
 Chess Match No.5, sensations, experiencing of 182–4, *184*
 physicality and emotional stress 176–7
 Room, intensive work with Anne Bogart 178–81
 Saratoga International Theatre Institute (SITI) 169
 Suzuki Method, training and acting 171–2, 174–6, 185
 Suzuki's *Electra*, creating the role of Clytemnestra 172–6, *175*
 Tadashi Suzuki connections 168–9
 teachers' appraisals 167

Lavers, Katie 117, 118–19
Lavery, Carl 245
Leaños, John Jota 83
Lecoq, Jacques 205–6, 216–17, 218, *see also* Théâtre de la Jacquerie
Lehar, Frank 95
Lehmann, Hans-Thies 244, 250, 252
Lepage, Robert 116, 120–1
Leroux, Louis Patrick 124, 126
Locke, Cybèle 42
Long, Robert 95
Loots, Lliane 196
Lugné-Poe 13
Luminato Festival, Toronto 291–2
Luna (artist) 78–81, *80*

M

MacLaughlin, Whit 287
Mahabharata, gendered performance
 demonic females 62
 female heroines 59
 female with male bravado 60
 refined heroes, bodily form 56, 59
Malafarina, Louis 123
Malaysian dance drama 54
marae theatre 44–7
Maranga Mai, Māori rights play
 actor's embodied performances 43–4
 agit pop style 44
 audience expectations 45–6
 historical and modern protest narratives 39–43, 49–50
 marae theatre attributes 44–7, 49
 meeting house, spiritual significance 47
 origins and performance controversy 37–8, 49
 social and political legacy 47–9

Maunder, Paul   37–8, 49
McGrath, John   44
memory, creation and
    retrieval   141–2, 144–5
Merce Cunningham Company   286
Merleau-Ponty, Maurice   230–1
mestizaje and indigenous identity
    Colombia's conflicted
        identities   81–2
    decolonizing critiques in techno-
        art culture   83–5, *84*
    descendent histories, personal
        impacts   73–5
    integration issues   77–8
    performance and installation
        explorations   78–81, *80*
    racism, personal and societal   76–7
metaphors, integration
    challenges   6–7
Meyerhold, Vsevolod   4
Miller, Marilyn   95, 104
Mills, Liz   271
minstrelsy   95, 96
Miranda, Lin-Manuel   91, 98
'mirror neurons'   264
Mollot, Alain   208, 209–10, 211–14
Montfort, Nick   292
Moth, The
    accessible narrative
        storytelling   133
    agency and empowerment
        144–5
    crafting a narrative   135–6
    founding ideals and
        expansion   134
    Life Flight, narrative construction
        and analysis   138–41
    participation events and personal/
        societal benefits   134–5, 145

Poitier and Brando,
    Mississippi 1964,
        challenging history   142–3
Murphy, Maiya   242

N

narrative in performance
    historical origins and
        developments   2–4
    intercultural exchange   4–7
    narrative definitions   1–2
narrative of live
    performance   225–6
narrative storytelling
    agency and
        empowerment   144–5
    challenging official history   142–3
    'good remembering'
        concept   141–2
    Life Flight, Moth story construction
        and analysis   138–41
    Moth stories and participation
        events   133, 134–6
    Moth stories, student instruction
        and support   136–8, 140–1
Natvig, Richard   22
New Paradise Laboratories   287, 289
New Zealand and Māori rights
    historical protest and modern
        narratives   39–43
    marae theatre   45–7
    Maranga Mai, play origins and
        controversies   37–9, 43–4,
        45–6
    Maranga Mai, social and political
        legacy   47–9
Newson, Lloyd   194–5, 203n7
Nicholas Brothers   97–8, 106
Novack, Cynthia   288

O

Oklahoma! (musical)   101
O'Mahony, John   227
One Extra *see* Chan, Kai Tai
Ong, Keng Seng   5, 6
oral performance   3
Osumare, Halifu   107
Otara Waitangi Action Committee   37–8

P

Page, Stephen   6, 200–1, 203n8
Panji stories   60–1
Parker, Shaun   200
Pavis, Patrice   245
Perlmutter, Donna   234–5
Phelan, Peggy   225–6
Pilar, Praba
   descendent histories, impact on life   73–5
   indigenous integration issues   77–8
   mestiza identity, father's racism challenged   75–7
   mestizaje and Colombia's indigenous identity   81–2
   mestizaje, performance and installation explorations   78–81, *80*
   techno-art projects, decolonizing practice   83–5, *84*
Pite, Crystal
   Betroffenheit, narrative into performance   269–77, *274*
   dance and choreography career   246–7
   dance theatre and narrative   243–4, 246, 248
   Dark Matter, textual inspirations and dance   248–55
   Kidd Pivot, formation and artistic vision   247–8
   pivot, definition of   241
   Tempest Replica, Shakespeare reimagined   255–63, *263*
   The You Show, audience engagement   264–9
Pollock, Griselda   228
popular culture
   Broadway musicals, influence on and by   93–107, *97*
   Cirque du Soleil, entertainment experience   113–27
   imagery and new technology   11
   The Moth, participatory storytelling   133–45
   reflection of societal change   11
   World of Warcraft (WOW)'s game culture   149–62, **157**
protest narratives   39–43

Q

quest narratives
   Cirque du Soleil performances   113–15
   failure a possibility   116–17

R

Ramayana, gendered performance
   demonic females   62
   female heroines   55, 58–9
   female with male bravado   60
   refined heroes, bodily form   56, 58
Rasch, Albertina   100
Reed, Kimberley   138–41
Rettberg, Scott   158
Rivera, Chita   104
Robbins, Jerome   101–3, 105–6
Robinson, Bill 'Bojangles'   97–8, 104

Rodgers, Richard   91, 100, 101
Rojas, Emilio   78

S

Saratoga International Theatre Institute (SITI)
   Anne Bogart pieces   177–8
   Chess Match No.5, development process   181–4, *184*
   founding and development   168–9
   Room with Ellen Lauren   178–81
   Suzuki and Viewpoint training   169–70
Sawitri, Cok   66–7
Schacter, David   141
Schechner, Richard   21, 22, 40
Schmitt, Bernd Herbert   123
Schneider, Rebecca   246, 278n4
Seibert, Brian   97
Servos, Norbert   234, 235
Shae, Jacqueline   155, 163n3
Shakespeare, William   5, 260
Shaw, Nancy   254
Shay, Anthony   9
Sheets-Johnstone, Maxine   218
Shuffle Along (musical)   96–7, *97*
Silberman, Marc   4
Sklar, Deidre   245
Smith, Anna Deavere   288
Sobchack, Vivian   230–1
social drama enactment, South Sudan
   Saida's personal scenario   24
   women's societal pressures   22–3, 30–1
   Yambio *zar*, performances and representations   24–9, *27*, 31–2
   Yambio *zar*, social/cultural variations   29–30

Yambio's ethnicity and history   23
zar curer   24
zar, opportunity for female communality   31–2
zar ritual, form and aims   22
Spring, Anita   32
St. Denis, Ruth   5–6, 12
Stanislavski, Konstantin   4, 5, 13
Stempel, Larry   91
Stroman, Susan   104
Stuart, Meg   243
Suarti, Desak Nyoman   65–6
Suzuki Company of Toga (SCOT)   168
Suzuki, Tadashi
   Ellen Lauren as Clytemnestra in *Electra*   172–6, *175*
   Ellen Lauren's sustained connections   167, 168–9, 185
   Shakespeare texts   5
   Suzuki Method of Actor Training   4, 169–70

T

Tait, Peta   113–15
tap dancing   96–8, *97*
Taylor-Corbett, Lynne   104
Taylor, Diana   160, 163n7
techno-art culture
   decolonizing critiques and practices   83–5, *84*
   mestizaje and indigenous identity explored   78–81, *80*
   Praba Pilar's decolonized identities and their influences   73–8
Tempest Replica (Pite)   255–63, *263*
textscape   244
Thai dance drama   53, 54–5

Tharp, Twyla   104
Théâtre de la Jacquerie
    comedic form and embodied
        improvisation   210–13
    creative premise   208–9
    embodied epistemology   218–19
    *Funny Sketches of a Formidable
        Life*, collective
        creation   208–18, *209*
    identity through
        performance   219–20
    imagery and character
        reinvention   214–16
    space and language
        awareness   217
Tirikātene-Sullivan, Whetū   38
trance performance and women's
    cooperation   29, 32
triple threat performers   103–4
Tuck, Eve   85
Turner, Victor   21–2, 31
Tuwhare, Hone   40, 47

U

Urban Shaman Contemporary
    Aboriginal Arts
    Gallery   78, 83

V

Vandewart, Lindsay   122
vaudeville   95, 96
Verbatim Theatre   288
Verdon, Gwen   104, 106
Viewpoints, actor training   169–70
Vinayakram, Mahesh   119
Voltaire   248–50

W

Walker, Ranginui   38, 40
Wayburn, Ned   100
Weir, Lucy   229

Welton, Martin   244, 250, 269
West Side Story (musical)   102, 106
Wigman, Mary   5, 226
Wilson, Ame   115
World of Warcraft (WOW), narrating
    and negotiating identity
    corporate ideology   158–9
    dance and cultural traits, character
        in cohesion   155–7, **157**
    dance quest and character-building
        challenges   149–53, 159
    dance, real-world alternative
        agendas   159–62
    player and research attractions
        153–4, 163n2, 287
    stereotyping and racism
        critiques   157–8

Y

Yang, K. Wayne   83
You show, The (Pite)   264–9
Young, Jonathon   270–7, *274*, 279n11

Z

Zambrano, Marta   81–2
zar ritual, social drama enactment
    form and aims   22
    opportunity for female
        communality   31–2
    Saida's personal scenario   24
    women's societal pressures   22–3,
        30–1
    Yambio *zar*, performances and
        representations   24–9, *27*,
        31–2
    Yambio *zar*, social/cultural
        variations   29–30
    Yambio's ethnicity and history   23
zar curer   24
Zellner, Bob   142–3
Zenenga, Praise   4

www.ingramcontent.com/pod-product-compliance
Lightning Source LLC
Chambersburg PA
CBHW070749020526
44115CB00032B/1582